MANAGING MARTIANS

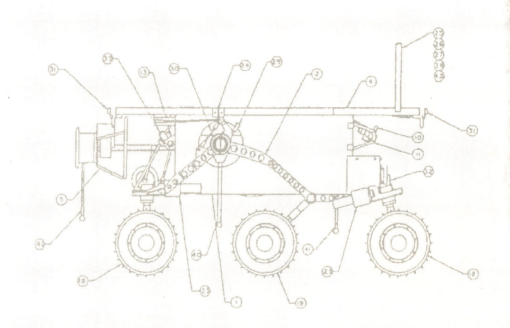

MANAGING MARTIANS

Donna Shirley

WITH DANELLE MORTON

BROADWAY BOOKS
New York

To the

Martians

BROADWAY

MANAGING MARTIANS. Copyright © 1998 by Donna Shirley.
All rights reserved. Printed in the United States of America.
No part of this book may be reproduced or transmitted in any
form or by any means, electronic or mechanical, including
photocopying, recording, or by any information storage
and retrieval system, without written permission from the
publisher. For information, address Broadway Books, a
division of Bantam Doubleday Dell Publishing Group, Inc.,
1540 Broadway, New York, NY 10036.

Broadway Books titles may be purchased for business or
promotional use or for special sales. For information, please
write to: Special Markets Department, Bantam Doubleday Dell
Publishing Group, Inc., 1540 Broadway, New York, NY 10036.

BROADWAY BOOKS and its logo, a letter B bisected on the
diagonal, are trademarks of Broadway Books, a division of
Bantam Doubleday Dell Publishing Group, Inc.

Library of Congress Cataloging-in-Publication Data
Shirley, Donna.
Managing Martians / Donna Shirley, with Danelle Morton.
— 1st ed.
p.   cm.
ISBN 0-7679-0240-8
1. Shirley, Donna.   2. Women aerospace engineers—United
States—Biography.   3. Mars Pathfinder Project (U.S.)
4. Space flight to Mars.   5. Mars (Planet)—Exploration.
I. Morton, Danelle.   II. Title.
TL789.85.S52A3   1998
629.1'092—dc21
[B]   98-6431
                                                          CIP

The photographs on insert pages 2 through 8 were provided by
the Jet Propulsion Laboratory of the California Institute of
Technology, under a contract with the National Aeronautics
and Space Administration. All rights reserved. All others are
part of the author's personal collection.

FIRST EDITION

Designed by Deborah Kerner

98 99 00 01 02 10 9 8 7 6 5 4 3 2 1

Acknowledgments

I am grateful to the many people who helped with this book, in particular my daughter, Laura, for doing without her mother for large chunks of time over the last three months, and the staff of the Jet Propulsion Laboratory, especially my boss, Norm Haynes, for his willingness to indulge this side activity.

I gratefully acknowledge the many people who were interviewed and who corrected drafts of the book, including: Ron Banes, Tony Bejczy, Don Bickler, John Casani, Glenn Cunningham, Rajiv Desai, Bill Dias, Howard Eisen, Dave Evans, Matt Golombek, Eran Gat, Lonne Lane, Bill Layman, Jake Matijevic, John McNamee, Henry Moore, Jack Morrison, Dave Miller, Brian Muirhead, Mike O'Neal, Tom Rivellini, Tim Scofield,

Tony Spear, Henry Stone, Scot Stride, Lin van Nieuwstadt, and Brian Wilcox. Any errors or omissions are my own.

Thanks, also, to my agent, Julie Castiglia, and to the Broadway Books team: Charlie Conrad, Trigg Robinson, Ted Sammons, and Jennifer Swihart.

And finally a debt of eternal gratitude to the generations of engineers, scientists, technicians, secretaries, administrators, and managers who have taken humanity into space and kept us there.

—D.S., La Cañada, CA
March 1998

Contents

He was on Mars. He had reached what to ancient man had been a moving red light among the stars, what to the men of only a century ago had been a mysterious and utterly unattainable world—and what was now the frontier of the human race. . . . But he knew he was still a stranger; he had really seen less than a thousand millionth of the whole surface of Mars. Beyond . . . the crimson hills, over the edge of the . . . plain—all the rest of this world was a mystery.

ARTHUR C. CLARKE, *The Sands of Mars*

MANAGING
MARTIANS

Six Wheels
on Soil

efore dawn on July 4, 1997, I woke with my mind over a
hundred million miles away. My waking thoughts were
all of Pathfinder, the United States' first attempt to
land on Mars in twenty years, as it hurtled through the
silence of space just hours away from its encounter with the red
planet. The 100-foot-high Delta 2 rocket that had boosted the
spacecraft from Cape Canaveral, Florida, seven months earlier
was finally about to deliver something very precious to me, and I
can't say I wasn't anxious.

Cabled down firmly inside this streaking bullet was Sojourner Truth, the world's first robotic planetary rover. I headed
the team that had designed and built this revolutionary six-
wheeled scientific laboratory, a 25-pound robot about the size of

a microwave oven that could do what humans could only dream of: explore the surface of Mars. I'd spent nearly ten years of my life preparing the two of us for this moment.

I could picture her cradled in the heart of the lander like the tiniest Russian nesting doll. She crouched with her belly to the floor inside a lander that was packed in a cushion of deflated airbags. Once off the lander, she would motor over the surface of Mars taking pictures and poking at the rocks like a tourist. She was a sturdy little gal. We'd whirled her in a centrifuge at a force 66 times that of gravity, twice as much pressure as we expected her to endure in flight, and she'd come out perfectly. If Pathfinder landed the way it was supposed to, I was sure she'd be fine.

I knew the Pathfinder's innovative landing mechanism almost as intimately as I knew the rover. Retro-rockets would slow the craft to a stop just before it smacked into the Martian surface. Moments before it hit the ground, huge airbags would pop. If everything worked—if all the radios communicated, the signals and sequences were sent and received, every one of the explosive bolts fired promptly and the airbags popped firm exactly on cue—it would plump up and bounce across the ground like a giant superball until it came to a rest. It was an inspired and thoroughly tested design, but one that had never before been used to land on a planet.

Surely this scheme had a better chance of keeping the Sojourner intact than anything previously devised. The teams that designed the lander and the rover had spent hours concocting every imaginable disaster scenario and building in ways to overcome those. We were combating long odds, if history was to be believed. Throughout thirty-seven years of exploration, Earthlings hadn't been terribly successful landing on Mars.

Two Russian Phobos spacecraft were lost on their way to

Mars in 1988. While the United States' two Viking missions landed safely in 1976, our Mars Observer failed to reach orbit in 1993. The Russians' Mars 6 and 7 got to Mars in 1971, but couldn't deliver their landing craft. Mars 6 crashed into the surface and Mars 7 missed the planet completely. As recently as November 1996, the Russian Mars 96 mission plunged ignominiously into the Pacific, never getting anywhere near its target. What if something like that happened to my rover? The data assured me that Pathfinder was approaching Mars just fine, but almost anything could happen during the punishing six-minute descent to the surface. Crash and burn was a definite possibility, I knew. Crash and burn.

Of course she wasn't really *my* rover. I had headed the team of thirty talented engineers and technicians that had spent four years designing and building the rover. A separate 300-member team, led by project manager Tony Spear, had spent the same amount of time building the Pathfinder lander. All of us could rightfully think of this mission as our own. No matter what any of us were doing at that moment on Earth, we could picture Pathfinder and Sojourner about to begin their descent and we knew our hopes could be dashed against the forbidding landscape.

I hadn't slept at all well that night. I've always been a fitful sleeper anyway, tossing and turning in the wee hours anticipating the day to come as my mind races with ideas and plans. In the early morning hours before Pathfinder entered the Martian atmosphere, dreams yanked me just to the edge of consciousness time and again. These weren't the idyllic dreams of me flying solo over the surface of Mars, such as I'd had since I was a small child in Oklahoma. The dream that eventually convinced me I might as well get out of bed was more of a farce.

In this dream, I saw the Pathfinder team standing around a field when suddenly our spacecraft fell from the sky before us. It had landed on Earth! We watched it bound to a stop but the airbags didn't deflate. My teammates seemed merely befuddled by this disaster. I hopped around eagerly, wondering how they could be so detached. I wanted to open it up, see how Sojourner had survived the descent. Everyone else said we had to let the lander open by itself. I guess I should see this dream as an encouraging omen, I decided as I got out of bed. If Sojourner could endure the descent through the Earth's dense atmosphere—even in my dreams—then the wispy carbon dioxide atmosphere of Mars would feel as gentle as a tropical breeze.

I found no comfort in my morning ritual, no solace from my habitual cup of tea. I barely tasted my orange as I methodically swallowed it. Sitting at home was just making me restless. I felt like a child the night before Christmas anticipating a desperately-wished-for present. I put on my favorite suit—Mars red—and decided it was best not to wake my daughter, Laura, who was home from college for the summer. She planned to catch up with me around 10 A.M., the moment the Pathfinder was scheduled to enter the Martian atmosphere. She could use the sleep for the eventful day ahead, I thought. I drove the six miles from my house in La Canada to the Jet Propulsion Laboratory (JPL), in California, arriving at 6:30 A.M., an hour before I was supposed to report for work.

Though I'd driven the two blocks of Oak Grove Drive nearly every day for the thirty years I'd worked at JPL, I'd never seen it as packed with journalists as it was that day. Local, national, and international television trucks lined the street. Von Karman Auditorium, near the entrance to the JPL campus, bustled with print and radio reporters already hard at work on this story.

Photographers snapped pictures of the full-scale models of the Pathfinder we'd displayed on the JPL mall and in the auditorium. Video crews jockeyed for position around the models and on the risers at the back of the auditorium. Competition for a good spot was so heated that JPL had taped off separate areas for each crew to prevent squabbles. I knew the Fourth of July was a slow news day, but I'd never expected the interest to be as high as this. Something about Pathfinder and Sojourner had really captured the public's imagination.

The generation that had grown up watching *Star Trek* and *Star Wars* really hadn't seen a planetary landing in its lifetime. For this generation, the Pathfinder mission was akin to Neil Armstrong's moon landing on July 20, 1969. We knew we already had a built-in international audience of the millions of people who had tracked the mission's progress on the Internet Web site we'd constructed for Pathfinder before it took off on December 4, 1996. Popular culture fostered an interest in space, but the real world rarely delivered the goods. Today—on Independence Day no less—the real world was delivering. More than felicitous timing drew people's attention to Pathfinder, though. Much of the fuss was because the target was Mars.

Of all the planets, Mars has been the one most prominent in human imagination. Mars's fiery red color was the first thing that caught our collective eye, becoming a focal point for our own anger and passion. Four thousand years ago the Egyptians called it Har de'cher, the Red One. The Babylonians saw it as Negal, the Star of Death. The Greeks named it Ares, the war god. The Romans called the same god Mars.

Mars's retrograde motion—the fact that it appears to stop in its east to west orbit, reverse direction, stop again, and then resume east to west travel as the Earth and Mars pass each other in space—led ancient astronomers to distrust the motives of the red planet. Both the Greeks and the Romans attributed negative traits to Mars: passionate lust, disorder, and murderous intentions—except when they were engaged in war themselves, in which case these same traits were considered desirable. The Roman Empire lauded Mars as the god of their aggressive military culture.

Fact and fantasy about Mars have always been closely linked. Cycles of fantasy drive the curiosity about Mars, which generates exploration. When telescopes allowed us to know the length of a Martian day—only a few minutes longer than our own—they gave us tantalizing glimpses of a dynamic, changing surface. Fiction played the themes of love and death, good and evil against that knowledge. Until quite recently there was a pretty thin line between knowledge and speculation.

Tycho Brahe, a Danish astronomer who lived in the second half of the sixteenth century, observed the stars with his naked eye and compiled a vast amount of information about the motions of the planets. Unlike Copernicus, Brahe believed that Earth was at the center of the solar system. In 1604 Johannes Kepler used Brahe's observations to conclude that the sun was central, and the orbits of the planets were ellipses, not circles. Mars was so prominent in the sky, its extremely elliptical orbit could be detected without a telescope. From these observations Kepler developed his three basic laws of planetary motion, laws that are still used today to determine at what time and in what direction to launch a spacecraft to encounter its target planet.

In 1609 Galileo Galilei built his first telescope and began to study the planets and stars, including an intense study of Mars in 1610. Although his telescope only magnified twenty times, Galileo believed he saw phases of Mars, like those of the moon.

As telescopes improved, they were able to establish that Mars had features.

Christian Huygens, a Dutch astronomer, first sketched Mars's most recognizable feature—the wind-swept plain of Syrtis Major—in 1659. At about the same time, Giovanni Cassini, for whom the Cassini mission to Saturn is named, made his detailed sketches of the markings of Mars. Today, Huygens is the name of the probe the Cassini spacecraft will drop into the atmosphere of Titan, Saturn's largest moon.

The most influential early observer of Mars was Giovanni Schiaparelli, who referred to the linear features of Mars as *canali*, or channels. Between 1877 and 1888 he compiled his observations in a map replete with *canali*. Earlier astronomers had noted these streaks and linear features, but Schiaparelli's use of the term *canali* set the stage for most of the fiction about Mars written before the first spacecraft flew by. The person mainly responsible for the transformation of *canali* into *canals* was the turn-of-the-century American astronomer Percival Lowell.

Lowell, the well-educated scion of a rich East Coast family, was the Carl Sagan of his time. He was an excellent communicator of science to the public although he had no formal training in astronomy. He was wealthy enough to build his own observatory under the clear skies of Flagstaff, Arizona, and intelligent enough to formulate a consistent and plausible theory about conditions on Mars. Between 1895 and 1908 he published three books: *Mars*, *Mars and Its Canals*, and *Mars as an Abode of Life*. He believed Mars supported not only life but a race of intelligent, nonhuman beings.

After all, he saw polar ice caps like those on Earth which he postulated were the source of water for the planet. He also theorized that the Martian atmosphere was similar to Earth's but only 10 percent as dense. Lowell thought Mars's features were too linear to be merely natural phenomena. He believed he saw straight lines running thousands of miles across the surface. To his mind these were actually canals the Martians built to irrigate their crops with meltwater from the polar ice caps. The waves of darkening—the changes in color of the features he observed on Mars over time—were Lowell's evidence of vegetation growth and harvest.

Lowell had his critics in the scientific community but not in the popular imagination. H. G. Wells's Martians in his 1895 book *The War of the Worlds* were tentacled beings. Trying to escape their dying planet, the Martians arrived dramatically on Earth in cylinder-shaped spaceships which plunged to the ground like meteors. They used teleoperated robots for transport and fired a "heat ray" (the equivalent of the laser beam) to destroy Earthlings.

Wells's portrayal of Earthlings as innocents and victims of creatures more powerful and terrible than we tapped into popular fear. The proof of this came on Halloween night in 1938 when Orson Welles created a national panic by broadcasting a dramatic version of *War of the Worlds* over the radio. Despite the announcement that the broadcast was just a radio play, many in the public believed every word. I doubt the audience would have been as gullible if the program had depicted an invasion from Saturn.

Decades of Edgar Rice Burroughs's Martian tales supported the idea of life on Mars, too. The Martians Burroughs described in his first book, *Princess of Mars* (1912), were much more humanoid than Wells's. In fact his hero, John Carter, actually mated with a Martian female who, despite the fact that she laid eggs and never suckled her young, had large breasts. The great science fiction writers—Robert Heinlein, Arthur C. Clarke, Ray Bradbury—created Mars to suit their fancy. Martians were kangaroolike creatures in Clarke's *The Sands of Mars* and golden-eyed humanoids living on the banks of the canals in Bradbury's *The Martian Chronicles*. Perhaps the most heavenly version of Mars was promulgated by Christian apologist C. S. Lewis, whose early 1960s trilogy of space novels described Mars as a place of innocence and wisdom ruled by incorporeal creatures of great intelligence and spooky mental powers. The spate of Mars science fiction and fantasy books came to a halt when Mariner 4 flew close to the red planet in 1965.

Mariner 4 raced past the planet at several thousand miles an hour snapping just a few pictures with its crude camera. Those few images were enough to kill off Lowell's Martians. Mars was bleaker than anyone had thought.

The small part of Mars imaged by Mariner 4 looked as heavily cratered as the moon. The atmosphere was thinner than even Lowell had imagined. Mars was a red ball against the blackness of space with an atmosphere so thin it created no gaseous boundary as you see surrounding Earth. Subsequent fly-bys detailed the rugged layered area around Mars's south pole in 1969. In 1971, the first Mars orbiter, Mariner 9, waited out a huge dust storm for several months before it was able to send pictures of the spots it had detected through the haze.

As the atmosphere cleared, these spots proved to be the tops of gigantic volcanoes standing on a huge bulge in the planet's crust, a geologic form later dubbed Tharsis. The volcanoes were the size of some of our larger states and were three times as high as Earth's highest mountains. The great Martian volcano Olympus Mons at 90,000 feet high is the largest known mountain in the solar system. Olympus Mons is so huge the Martian crust sags under its weight, creating a dry moat around it. Just south of the Martian equator runs Valles Marineris, a canyon as long as the United States is wide with walls 5 miles deep in places. In contrast our Grand Canyon is just 231 miles long. Channels and canyons mark the Martian surface, all signs that water may have once existed there.

Where there once was water, there once could have been life, scientists believe. Not the kind of life imagined by science fiction writers, but some form humans definitely want to investigate as a way of understanding our own planet. Mars seems to be the closest analog to our own conditions. If life once existed there, what happened on Mars to obliterate it? Could something similar happen on Earth? The information gleaned from our initial explorations of Mars has increased our interest in finding out about its history and what form life might have taken. We have ten missions to Mars planned in the next decade. As leader of the Mars Exploration Program I saw this first Pathfinder landing as the most crucial: all succeeding missions would be based on innovations we were testing with Pathfinder.

I thought Pathfinder was a really cool spacecraft: small, light, cheap, and inspired in concept. Our robot Sojourner Truth was named after a real heroine, too, not just a heroic concept such as Intrepid or Challenger. Its namesake, nineteenth-century American evangelist Sojourner Truth, had traveled around the South preaching the evils of slavery. Our Sojourner would travel around Mars, bringing back the truth about the red planet. If everything worked on Pathfinder, we'd have piles of new data for analysis.

My goal in getting to JPL early was to sneak a visit with the team of engineers who were monitoring the Pathfinder's progress. Following some small launch-related glitches, Pathfinder's journey from Earth had been so uneventful as to be boring. I was eager for a sign that events were continuing to be without surprises.

The minute the JPL public information officer saw me, however, relief swept over her face. She steered me over to a journalist who needed an explanation about some aspect of the mission and directly thereafter I tore myself away for a press briefing.

Onstage the mission operations manager described what would happen that morning. At 10 A.M. Pathfinder would shed its cruise stage, the solar cell–covered disc that had provided power and communications for the seven-month trip to Mars. About thirty minutes later, the remainder of the spacecraft would plunge into the Martian atmosphere. A combination of a high drag heat shield, parachutes, rockets, and airbags would allow the spacecraft to hit Mars without creating yet another crater in the pockmarked surface.

This was the riskiest part of the mission. The lander, a three-foot-high, pyramid-shaped structure now nestled inside the heat shield, would hit the ground enclosed in giant, energy-absorbing airbags. After bouncing and tumbling for several minutes, the airbags would deflate and the lander would open like a flower, revealing the rover attached to one of its petals. If all went well, we should expect to see our first pictures from the lander that afternoon.

I'd sacrificed the camaraderie of monitoring the landing with my Pathfinder colleagues in mission control to serve as the mission's representative to the media. Someone, we all agreed, had to handle the press so the operations team could do their jobs without interruption. We couldn't exactly have reporters crowding in the control room looking over everyone's shoulders. My boss and I had volunteered to perform this duty, although standing in front of cameras explaining what was supposed to be happening wasn't really what I wanted to be doing. Every bone in my body ached to be with my team.

At 10:06 A.M., the moment when I knew the Pathfinder was starting its dive to the surface of Mars, I was standing in JPL's sweltering main plaza in front of CNN's cameras and behind the trashcan I was using as an impromptu display table. I'd piled the top of the can with Pathfinder models to illustrate the various stages of landing. As I maneuvered my models explaining the landing sequence to a CNN reporter, I sensed my colleagues in the mission control area would soon be receiving radio signals that told them when each action commenced. Pathfinder was designed to send occasional feeble signals to let us know everything was proceeding as planned. Signals from Mars took ten minutes to make their way to Earth. All six minutes of the drop would be over before we even knew if it had worked. There was nothing we could do to control it.

I squinted at a tiny, sun-swamped television monitor on top of another trashcan, trying to see what the flight control team was up to. In the glare, I could only catch glimpses of the team as they paced nervously or sat riveted to their monitors. I felt completely cut off each time I saw them clustered around the computer terminals, hanging on every transmission from space. If I were standing in the flight control room with my colleagues, I thought, I wouldn't be any calmer but at least I'd be in the company of my team.

Up on Mars, Pathfinder started its drop. As Martian gravity sucked it toward the surface at 17,000 miles an hour, Pathfinder threw away the cruise stage that had provided power for seven months during its 119-million-mile trip. From Pathfinder's perspective Mars was a red crescent, lit from the right side. But the spacecraft had no exterior cameras to monitor its descent. As it hurtled toward the dark side of the crescent, it couldn't see Mars's massive volcanoes or enormous canyons in the darkness of 3 A.M. Martian time.

Of course no sound came through from Mars millions of miles away, but the whole team knew that in the next two minutes Mars would have its own Fourth of July fireworks display.

Pathfinder set off yellow and orange sparks in the icy darkness as its heat shield flaked away to prevent the spacecraft from incinerating in the friction of the atmosphere as it slowed to a mere 800 miles an hour. Explosive bolts popped like firecrackers, ejecting the huge parachute which billowed above the lander, braking it to 120 miles per hour. More explosive bolts cut the heat shield away and the spacecraft jerked free of it once and for all. The backshell popped the lander loose and it slid down a 30-meter cable swaying back and forth below the parachute and the backshell. Three solid rocket motors on the backshell fired, bringing what was left of the mechanism to a halt about 50 feet above the ground.

Four huge, multilobed airbags made of Vectran,™ a bulletproof vest material, inflated around the lander in a second, protecting it like members of a SWAT team. Explosive bolts cut the Vectran™ cable that connected the backshell to the lander. The rockets carried the parachute and backshell away, allowing the lander to drop to the ground at 40 miles an hour encased in its 15-feet-tall pillow of airbags.

The airbags hit the surface and the lander bounced almost 50 feet back up, about the same distance it had just fallen. For several minutes it tumbled across the brick red crumble that is the surface of Mars. Finally it came to rest just where we wanted it to: at the mouth of Ares Vallis or Mars Valley. Millions of years ago, Mars geologists believe, a gigantic flood created this valley—really a 3-mile-deep canyon—as it ripped rocks out of the ancient highlands of Mars and toppled them onto the plain where Pathfinder had landed.

From my vantage point overlooking the trashcans, I glimpsed movement on the video monitor. In the control room the flight engineer was swinging back and forth in his chair as he called out to his crew.

"Parachute deployed," he shouted, as his colleagues stood up expectantly. "Heat shield released. Rockets have fired."

Then silence. Horrible, nail-biting silence. I pictured Sojourner clinging to her petal within the lander, flipping and bouncing in her carefully constructed nest. I always compared her to the yolk cradled at the center of an egg. Was her carton going to hold her in place just right?

"We have a signal!" the flight engineer yelled.

The team exploded in cheers and hugs and impromptu jigs. Even though I was in full view of the CNN audience, broadcasting live, I did my own modest victory dance. Pathfinder hadn't crashed or burned! It was on the surface of Mars—and alive. My Christmas package had arrived. I restrained myself from hugging the nearest available person—the CNN reporter.

"Did I just see you wipe away a tear?" he asked with astonishment. "It's unusual to see an engineer of your caliber crying."

"Tony's crying too," I said, pointing to the monitor. On the screen, Pathfinder project manager Tony Spear's face was crumpled with emotion as he cried tears of joy and relief.

———

Tony and I had had a real up and down relationship over the last twenty years. Way back in the early 1970s we'd worked on the Mariner 10 project, which flew by Venus and Mercury in 1974. We'd come face-to-face in 1992 when I became the leader of the team that was to build the Mars rover, and I started my campaign to get the rover to hitch a ride on Pathfinder's trip to Mars.

No one at JPL gave our rover project much of a chance, least of all Tony. We had a budget of $25 million at a time when billion dollar projects were the norm. Our challenge was to make a tiny robot that could function in the 150-degree-below-zero temperatures and the radiation that sleets through Mars's atmosphere. Tony's assignment was to build a spacecraft that could land safely on Mars at a fraction of the cost of a regular mission. To Tony, initially, the rover was a parasite and my team and I were an annoyance.

Tony believed it was hard enough to design and construct a mission to Mars for under $200 million when the Viking missions had cost over $3 billion in 1997 dollars. He didn't want the rover taking up space, consuming power, and requiring its own communications hardware partly because, like most everybody else at JPL, he didn't believe the rover would really work.

The rover was too dinky for most of the experienced engineers to take seriously. All studies and preliminary designs for a rover back from the 1960s to about 1991 envisioned one the size of a pickup truck able to roam hundreds of kilometers sampling the Martian soil. Compared to that design, my little rover was seen at best as a toy and at worst as a joke.

Plus he didn't have much respect for my team. Many of us, myself included, had never delivered flight hardware, the touch-stone of competence at JPL. If you've never sent a piece of hardware up into space, then no one believes you could ever do that job. It was a classic Catch-22 that had dogged my professional progress for years.

I was the part of the rover team that most annoyed Tony. I just wouldn't go away no matter how hard he tried to get rid of me. He and I battled over this project for two straight years. There was a time when I thought of him as my enemy, the person who most stood in the way of getting the rover on Mars. For a time he thought of me as the enemy too: the person whose inexperience and stubbornness might sink his project.

But the rover had earned her way onto Pathfinder, providing public excitement and a way to deploy instruments. Now in this time of triumph, Tony and I were sharing strong emotions again. This time it was joy. Neither of us was the type to hold a grudge. At this moment I saw him as the man who had helped me realize my childhood dream of going to Mars.

Growing up in the small southern Oklahoma town of Wynnewood, I never searched the skies above my head to find the red planet. The Mars I envisioned was more real and detailed than any mere bright dot in the sky. At age twelve and searching for my own place in the world, I'd read Arthur C. Clarke's *The Sands of Mars*, a book that pointed me toward the sky.

I was a smart, mouthy tomboy in a 2,500-person town where the ideal of womanhood carried with it a lot of chiffon and mascara. Instead of pictures of music or screen idols adorning my bedroom walls, my ceiling was hung with the model airplanes I'd assembled. I didn't smell of White Shoulders perfume. I smelled of airplane glue.

Since a tender age I'd fantasized about being a pilot. At two I stared up at the clouds billowing in the Oklahoma skies. At six

I dreamed of being a bush pilot. At ten I decided to be an aeronautical engineer and build airplanes. As an adult I understand how much of that fantasy was wrapped around an urge to escape my boring environment. The world of space travel Clarke described was a lot more attractive to me than the one I was living in. No question in my twelve-year-old mind, my future would transpire in the sky.

Clarke's Mars was a technocracy where scientists ruled domed living spaces with a cool, logical eye. It was a place where intelligence was not only appreciated but treasured. New discoveries were made every day. There was adventure inherent in just living on a frontier. And there were women on Clarke's Mars. Although I wasn't sure if women would really explore space in my lifetime—certainly no woman in Wynnewood expressed a desire to—I was going to try.

More than forty years later, a woman still couldn't get to Mars, but men couldn't either. Despite four decades of space research and exploration, we still don't know enough about human survival in space or the conditions on Mars to be certain humans could be safe and useful there. Wernher von Braun had dreamed of sending humans to Mars way back in the 1950s, but the national will and budget failed.

The Apollo missions to the moon cost the equivalent of more than a hundred billion in today's dollars. Until politicians decide to commit that kind of money to space exploration by humans again, spacecraft and robots will have to do our exploring for us. Even if my feet weren't going to make their mark on Martian soil, Sojourner's tracks would be the next best thing.

But there was no time for musing on the past. After the CNN show and a few more interviews, I was scheduled to be on National Public Radio while we waited for the next message from the lander. All signs told us the landing had gone well. The first signal from the surface had told us the lander was healthy and that it had stopped bouncing and rolling.

We had had the best luck possible. There was only a one-in-four chance that the lander pyramid would end right-side-up with its special thumb-size antenna able to transmit the news to Earth, which at 3 A.M. Mars time was very low on the Martian horizon, but rising. With Pathfinder's radio transmitting with less power than a refrigerator lightbulb, the antenna radiated its signal in all directions. Only a tiny part of those radio waves could find their way from Mars into the football-field-size "ear" of the Deep Space Network antenna in Spain. This widely dispersed signal also had to fight its way through the airbags that still encased the lander. With all these obstacles, we hadn't really expected to hear the "I made it" signal for two hours or more, but we had gotten the signal within only a few minutes.

The right-side-up position was good news for the rover team, which depended on a level lander to get Sojourner out and about. Now for the next signal we had to wait for the airbags to deflate, the petals to open, and the Earth to rise more. That probably wouldn't be for another couple of hours so I could take a bit of a breather.

An hour after the landing, I was on National Public Radio's *Friday Science Forum*. NPR was staging a one-hour call-in show about our mission to Mars on the lush, green grass on the JPL mall (thank goodness in the shade). The guests were three scientists—the mission's weatherman and representatives of the camera team and the rover team—and me representing the engineers. As the anchor asked each of us in turn to describe our job and what it meant to manage a mission to explore Mars, we heard announcements from flight control faintly in our headphones. The Mars weatherman was describing in his dry British accent the kind of data he expected to receive about the Martian climate when I interrupted: "Did they say we got an opening signal?" I turned to the NPR anchor. "Anything you get from mission control, we want to hear!"

"We have a signal that the petals are open," came the flight engineer's voice through the headsets.

"My God, we really made it!" I exclaimed, oblivious to being on the air. "That's spectacular."

The signal, received much earlier than we had hoped, was faint but true.

"And I'm out of a job," gleefully announced the flight engineer, who had been in charge of the entry and landing, to a rush of cheers behind him. Now it was up to the surface operations team.

As the sun rose above the surface of Mars, the cameras on the lander tracked its progress. The lander's computer knew where the sun was in relation to the Earth, so it could direct the lander to point its main antenna toward home and download the data it had gathered from the landing. The weatherman was ecstatic. He had a working weather station on Mars. Of more immediate interest to the rover team and the public were its photographs. They would give us the first view of how both the lander and the rover had survived the journey, as well as the first up close images of Mars's surface since the Viking missions twenty years before.

While I waited for the next signal to tell us that the airbags had deflated, there were more media interviews. My daughter and her boyfriend came by and brought me a sandwich to munch while I was being interviewed by the *Los Angeles Times*. Laura told me that she had "lost it" herself when she saw me crying on CNN. She was almost as nervous about Sojourner as I was. For years she had shared me with her "sister" the rover as I worked long hours to get Sojourner ready to go.

As I sat on a bench in the shade with the reporter, people stopped to listen and sometimes throw in a comment or two of their own. The atmosphere was celebratory and even those who had opposed our unconventional mission were gracious enough to come by for a word or two of congratulation.

"Hey, Jim!" I shouted at Jim Martin, who had headed the Pathfinder's final review board. "You never thought we could do it!"

Jim, a 6-foot-6 giant with a gray crewcut, was the project manager of Viking. As the manager of the last successful Mars mission, he'd chaired the review board that tracked Pathfinder's design and construction. With Viking, Jim had supervised a huge budget and spent seven years working on the two orbiters and two landers. He was very skeptical our crazy low-budget landing scheme could work, and even after Tony Spear had accepted the rover, Jim had been disapproving of our little vehicle. Passing his review had been a tremendous challenge.

"I made you work," he called back with a broad grin.

Then I spotted some of the rover engineers headed to Von Karman Auditorium for interviews.

"All right, you guys," I teased, "it had better work."

"Leave the driving to us," one of them shot back.

A nervous-looking Lin Sukamto, the lead engineer for the rover's radio, came up to me.

"I feel so sick," she whispered. I gave her a hug.

"Well, I've been nervous for years," I told her and the reporter.

I was back with CNN at about 1:30 P.M. when the first picture from the lander camera showed up on the monitor. No Martians—only dirt and rocks, but dirt and rocks never seen by humans before. In the monitors I could see the team in mission control whooping and applauding.

"Look!" cried someone. "A hill!"

"That's where the rover's going," said Tony.

"You wanted a good landing site," gloated Matt Golombek, the project scientist. "I deliver!"

Matt, a forty-two-year-old with an infectious laugh and unflappable enthusiasm, was one of the best Mars geologists in the world. He'd argued with NASA for two years about this landing site. His was finally chosen over eighteen other candidates. It was indeed spectacular. The photographs showed rocks all around, some stacked like books on a shelf.

The catastrophic flood that had tumbled these rocks to Ares Vallis dwarfed any such event on Earth, scientists theorized, except perhaps the flood that formed the Mediterranean Sea. The rocks left by such a flood should be different from the rocks splashed from meteor craters that surrounded Viking. And sure enough, the first black-and-white photographs showed a rich jumble of rocks, dominated by twin peaks on the horizon. Many rocks appeared within an easy rover stroll of the lander. The scientific possibilities were tantalizing and the team wanted to get the Sojourner roving as soon as possible. But there was a glitch.

The first color picture showed the rover squatting on the petal of the lander with the red Martian soil and red-gray rocks in the background. But it also showed puffy lumps of airbag material blocking one of the rover's exit paths, a potentially dangerous situation. The ramps, which were coiled like party noisemakers in front of and behind the rover, couldn't unroll.

Without the ramp, the rover couldn't get off the lander's petal. Even if the ramp managed to unfurl, airbag material on top of it could destabilize the rover as she headed down. Until the ramps were safely out, Sojourner wasn't going anywhere.

A problem, but not an insurmountable one. The lander had been designed to handle all kinds of hazards. For instance, if the petals opened tilted against big boulders, the motors on the lander's four petals were strong enough to flex straight out like a gymnast doing an iron cross and raise the lander level, suspending it flat above the ground to allow the rover to motor off.

The team decided the best way to handle this problem was to raise the petal to free up the airbags so they could be pulled in. Fortunately the Pathfinder "gremlin," a twenty-seven-year-old engineer named David Gruel, had simulated this very situation in his assigned job of mission sabotage.

Dave's job was to creep at night into the "sandbox," where a mock lander and rover simulated the system on the surface of Mars. There in the sandy, rock-strewn room, whose walls were covered with images from the Viking landers, stood fully functional models of the lander and the rover. Well, two rovers actually. There was a model almost identical to Sojourner, and another with just wheels and chassis. This stripped-down version was only three-eighths the weight of the one identical to Sojourner. This "Sojourner lite" could simulate the weight of the real rover on Mars, whose gravity is only three-eighths as strong as Earth's.

Dave delighted in creating diabolical terrain for the lander and rover team to overcome with just the information it received from the lander's cameras. The sandbox had blinds, which Dave closed each night before he rummaged around in the faux Martian landscape. Most of the time he stuck to realistic situations, such as when he built a big berm of sand or constructed a wall of rocks around the rover. He was also partial to pranks. The time he hid a potted plant in the sandbox, the rover team happily sent it over to see what strange creature had materialized on Mars.

The team already had a solution to the problem the rover was now facing on Mars, because Dave had once bedeviled them by plopping a lot of loose airbag material on the rover petal. To be absolutely certain their procedure would work, the team retired to the sandbox for a little practice.

The lander model was already opened with airbags tucked under the petals as they appeared to be on Mars. The team draped a piece of airbag over one of the petals and sent a signal to the computer to raise it. Once the petal was up, a motor pulled on cables sewn to points inside the airbags until they were tucked close to the lander. The lander model then lowered the petal without obstruction.

The process worked perfectly, so commands were quickly sent to the real lander on Mars to do the same thing. Initially the airbags had been retracted forty-two revolutions of the winch; the team instructed the motor to turn it five more. When photos showed the airbag neatly tucked away, the team immediately sent commands to fire explosive bolts and release the rover's ramps. A few minutes later, the camera sent back a picture showing the ramps deployed. Success! But there were still problems.

The weak gravity of Mars had not pulled the front ramp down to the ground. It was sticking straight out like the tongue of a naughty child. If the rover drove onto it, the end would probably buckle and touch the soil. But the rover was programmed to stop at a sudden jolt. We might end up with the rover halfway down the ramp and refusing to go farther.

The ramp behind Sojourner dropped properly to the surface. The rover would have to back down that ramp, and all the apparatus for avoiding hazards was mounted on the front of Sojourner. She would be backing up "blind" and there was still a little bit of airbag touching this back ramp, which might be an obstacle for the rover.

Back to the sandbox. The rover team quickly tested running the rover over airbag material. Would the spiked wheels get tangled in the material? Probably not, but by the time the tests were done in the sandbox, another problem cropped up. The rover and lander were having trouble communicating with each other. Both lander and rover teams scrambled to figure out what was wrong, but before they could diagnose the problem, Earth had set and communication with Mars was lost for the day. The rover would have to wait another sol (a Martian day) to deploy.

"Murphy (of Murphy's law that if something can go wrong, it will) seems to have saved up all the Pathfinder's problems for the rover," I grumbled to a reporter.

Press briefings and interviews went on until midnight. At least between interviews and press conferences I had finally gotten to go up to the mission control area and congratulate the team. I was flooded with emotion and hugged everyone in sight. The lander team was still elated. The navigators had directed the lander to almost the exact spot we had chosen. In fact, there was a dollar-a-guess pool to bet where the landing would actually occur. The pot had been won by a young scientist who was on the lander camera team. He was waiting for the rover to move so he could make "rover movies" with the lander camera. We called him the first movie producer on Mars.

The scientists were ecstatic, licking their chops in anticipation of the images and weather data to come. The rover team were still waiting. I joined them in feeling the pride of our accomplishment but I felt a twinge of regret I was not involved with them in solving this crisis. Working with that team had been as close to a family experience as anything I'd had in my professional life. Problem solving with that bunch was exhilarating, a creative situation where no idea was too far-fetched, each member could feel safe making a contribution, and all gloried in a well-thought-through solution. I longed to make my own contribution to help them solve this problem but also knew they'd do just fine on their own.

The rover team had caucused and decided to back the rover down the fully deployed ramp, since they didn't plan for the rover to use her hazard avoidance capability anyway. They wanted her on the ground, not timidly halting in mid-ramp. Their commands were ready to be sent to the lander for relay to the rover early the next morning (Mars time). There were various theories about how to get the rover and the lander to communicate better. The simplest was just to turn both of them off and try again, much like rebooting a balky computer.

Since this particular morning on Mars was during the afternoon on Earth (a Mars sol is forty minutes longer than an Earth day), all of this would have to wait until the next day. I stumbled home at last, too revved up to sleep much. My schedule from the public information office for the next day said "Sleep Late," but I couldn't. I spent part of the morning on the Internet, surfing the electronic versions of the various national newspapers and delighting in accounts of Pathfinder's success.

I raced back to JPL that afternoon to catch sunrise and Earthrise on Mars. As soon as Earth popped over the horizon we found rover-lander communications had been restored by the "reboot," so the rover was free to ramble. Explosive cable cutters severed the bonds that held Sojourner to the lander's petal. She drove her front and back wheels in opposite directions, boosting her to a standing position at her full height of a foot. We next commanded Sojourner to back down the ramp and come to rest near a lumpy rock that the head of the lander camera team had christened Barnacle Bill.

Standing once again in front of a CNN camera, I could not have been more anxious waiting to see if Sojourner's journey could begin.

Pictures from the lander started coming back to Earth. The first Martian movie of the rover was alarming to watch. The young scientist had set up a series of lander camera pictures to catch the rover moving down the ramp, but the first picture showed only the empty ramp.

"I don't see her," I cried out in anguish.

Had Sojourner refused the command? Had the cable cutters failed to fire? Was she still clamped down to the petal?

The next image showed the ramp flexing and the next (at last!) revealed Sojourner making her way down the ramp. Two more pictures and she was on the ground.

"Six wheels on soil!" declared the voice of the rover controller, signaling that Sojourner was off the lander and moving over the surface of Mars on her own. Second only to my newborn daughter, Sojourner Truth on Mars was the most beautiful thing I'd ever seen.

That afternoon the lander camera team unfurled a 360-degree panorama of the scene around the lander. Even before the camera rose to its full height of just over 5 feet, the photographs offered magnificent views. There were rocks in the foreground perched on dusty, sandy-looking soil. More rocks littered the scene all the way to the horizon. In the distance were the edge of a crater and the small mountains the scientists had dubbed Twin Peaks. A hush fell over the room as the audience drank in the Martian landscape.

"These are our eyes, " the camera team leader said, his sonorous voice rising to this poetic occasion. "We are all on Mars."

I became news myself as reporters scrambled for an angle that would give a little human drama to the story. I represented a number of "firsts": first woman to manage flight hardware at JPL, first team leader of the first Mars rover, first team leader of any planetary rover, and the first woman to manage a space flight program. I was jokingly referred to by one science fiction buff as Deja Thoris, the queen of Mars.

By the end of the second day I didn't feel much like a queen. I felt like an obsessively talking head. I seemed to be in front of the cameras most of the day answering the same questions again and again. I was standing in front of another camera as Earth's night began to fall when a stream of people came by headed for Von Karman Auditorium. They were the Pathfinder team, fifty or sixty strong.

"Where are you guys going?" I interrupted the interview to ask.

"To the press conference," said the lead engineer for Sojourner's "brain" and "eyes."

"Sorry, folks," I said to the TV crew and, like a rat following the Pied Piper, I fell in behind the team.

We streamed into the auditorium, past the stage, and gathered in front of a full-scale model of the lander and rover with a painted backdrop of Mars behind us. Cheers, high fives, and clapping went on for minutes with even the jaded press corps standing and applauding. Some of the team grabbed the panorama and held it in front of us as the cameras snapped and flashed. I felt tears rushing into my eyes again as I shook hands with Tony Spear and as many of the team as I could reach. At last I was standing with my comrades virtually on the surface of Mars.

1
In Flight

o check 'er out, Donna," said Charlie Davis, my muscular blond flight instructor. Eagerly, I trotted out to the little wood-and-fabric airplane that I thought was the most wonderful machine in the world. I was sixteen and panting to take my first solo flight.

"Checking 'er out" was part of the preflight ritual. I flipped the prop to make sure it turned smoothly, checked the oil, and drained out any water that might have accumulated below the gas in the tanks inside the wings. I checked the tires to make sure they were properly inflated and examined the plane fabric for holes. Once I was satisfied everything was fine, I got in.

To enter, I opened a big, flimsy door in the plane's side and crawled up into the front seat, throwing my left leg around the stick to center it between my legs and putting my feet on the rudder petals. I pushed on the rudders to make sure they were free and nimble and moved the stick fore and aft to check the elevators and side to side to make sure the ailerons would flex on command. Charlie stood in front of the plane ready to flip the prop as soon as I switched on the magnetos. Swinging the propellor acted like turning the starting handle on an old car; it made the engine turn over so the magnetos could start supplying sparks to the fuel in the cylinders. Once the engine was running smoothly, Charlie ran to the side of the plane and crawled in behind me, with me struggling to hold the door open against the slipstream. The door slammed and we strapped in and taxied to the end of the runway, turning to face into the wind.

Takeoffs and landings are the riskiest parts of flying because they occur on the hard, hard ground. In a light plane like the Champ, the pilot accomplishes them mainly by learning the feel of the aircraft. In taking off, this means knowing just when the plane has enough speed for the wind to lift the plane off the ground. In order to let you solo, the flight instructor needs to believe you've mastered that feel.

Charlie had me perform a monotonous drill: take off and climb, beyond the end of the runway turn left and keep climbing to 800 feet, level off and turn left again flying back along the runway, then start descending, turn left and approach the runway into the wind, sinking and sinking until I was back nearly at ground level just above the end of the runway. To land you have to slow the plane down almost to a stall, ideally just as the wheels kiss the runway gently. Then, because it was a long runway relative to the Champ's takeoff distance, I'd push the throttle in to the max and take off again. We spent a lot of time doing these "touch and go's"—taking off, landing, and then doing it again. Each circuit took about ten minutes and Charlie had me do it for nearly an hour, bored to tears by the repetition of the drill.

"Okay," he yelled over the din of the engine after I bumped down for the sixth or seventh time. "I think you're good enough to take it around."

Was I hearing him right? I thought as I taxied back to the hangar. Charlie wriggled out of the backseat and I was alone in the airplane for the first time.

I didn't have the sense of freedom and mastery I'd dreamed about since childhood. I was scared to death. For the twenty-one hours I'd spent with Charlie in back of me, he'd been yelling instructions at me the whole time I flew: "A little more left rudder! A little more right! Keep the wings level!" Sometimes I'd found his instructions annoying because I was confident I knew how to solve my problems in the air. I didn't realize until my solo how emboldened I was by the fact that Charlie had his own complete set of controls in the backseat, able to bail me out of a jam in an instant.

The wind was blowing pretty strongly that day, making for a bumpy flight. I certainly wasn't graceful about my first solo. Flying free is a balancing act and to enjoy it you need to feel graceful. In my little light plane the wind blew me sideways as I tried to repeat the drill. Suddenly that predictable pattern didn't seem as monotonous as it had a few minutes before.

Coming down was the really tricky part. The plane wobbled around and the ground seemed to be coming up incredibly fast. Is it time to pull up yet? I was thinking. No, I'm still a little too high. So I put the nose down and ducked up and down like a porpoise leaping through the air until I finally hit the ground. Kerplunk!

I taxied to the hangar where Charlie congratulated me even though it wasn't a particularly graceful landing. Elegance was a completely overrated trait, I decided. The joy was in the freedom I'd just tasted. I couldn't wait to get back to Wynnewood to tell my family of my triumph.

I'd grown up confined by the expectations and entitlements that came with being the product of a merger of the two most prominent families in this 2,500-person town. On my father's side the Shirleys were the town's landed gentry, owning thousands of acres of prime farmland that had been passed down from our Chickasaw ancestors. The Shirleys weren't farmers anymore, however. My father's relatives lived quite comfortably on the income they received from leasing the land to sharecroppers. Grandmother's second husband, whom we called Grandpa, owned a cotton gin, which was the town's second biggest business behind the Kerr-McGee refinery.

My mother's family wasn't wealthy, but her father, the Reverend Dr. Charles Brooks, was a renowned Methodist minister. He was as famous for his carefully reasoned Sunday sermons and biblical scholarship as he was for the money he raised at boisterous revivals. Grandaddy served on the commission that chose standards for the Oklahoma schools when the territory became a state in 1907. Newspapers statewide covered my parents' marriage in 1936 in lengthy articles that detailed the engagement, nuptials, and honeymoon.

My father set up a medical practice in Pauls Valley, Oklahoma, seven miles north of Wynnewood, where I was born in 1941. When I was three years old he enlisted in the Navy, serv-

ing as a ship's doctor in the Pacific and in the occupation of
Japan for a year after the war ended. Shortly after he enlisted my
mother and I moved to southern California to be nearby when
he got shore leave. I thrived at a private kindergarten and then
at the Robin's Nest school where I was reading at the third-
grade level before I finished first grade. I was six when I started
second grade. As soon as my father's tour of duty was over my
folks bought a big house on a few acres of fruit tree–covered
land in San Jose, California, and my father joined a medical
practice, planning to specialize in heart disease.

My family's independence ended abruptly when my father
was summoned back to Wynnewood by his mother to care for
her bad heart. Wynnewood was too small a town for a specialist
so he became a general practitioner. Upon our return he threw
himself into his work, putting in long hours at the hospital and
coming home exhausted and preoccupied with the fate of all
the lives in his care. Most nights he was home by 6 P.M. for
supper but often the phone would ring at 2 or 3 A.M. to summon
him to deliver a baby or deal with an emergency. He was called
so often he started sleeping in his underwear because pajamas
were too bulky underneath his trousers. In many ways he be-
longed more to the town than he did to my sister and mother
and me, and he was immensely popular and revered.

My father's uncle and his wife, known to us as Auntie and
Unkie, had a sycamore tree in their front yard that was my
favorite place to read when I was a little girl. Its broad, strong
branches were steady and close together, creating a natural lad-
der to my perch. About 20 feet off the ground, two branches
formed a lopsided Y nestled in a thicket of pale green leaves.
Wedged in that pocket, my left leg relaxed flat on the level
branch before me, my right foot steadied my weight on the

branch angled toward the sky. Gusts sweeping down from the Great Plains to the rolling southern Oklahoma hills where Wynnewood lay rustled the leaves all around me. The breezes played against my skin, cooling me in the stultifying Oklahoma summer as I hid among the foliage. I was only six years old but already I wanted to experience freedom and adventure. The fastest way to do that was to enter the world of fictional characters like Toby Tyler.

I'll bet I read *Toby Tyler or Ten Weeks in the Circus* at least ten times that year my family returned to Wynnewood, because Toby was living the kind of life I longed for: he'd run away from home to join the circus. I admired his courage in fleeing a world that didn't understand him.

My entry into the second grade at Wynnewood Elementary School had been a rude shock. Instead of the lush grass of the schoolyard in San Jose, the dirt surrounding the school was covered in scraggly growth so trampled by the kids it lay lifeless under our feet. There was only one elementary school for white kids in Wynnewood, and one class for each grade. The teachers taught to the middle of the class, not to the top, leaving a lot of time for my mind and mouth to wander. School, which had been the whole focus of my life in my years in California, became an exercise in enduring boredom. But then so was most of my young life in Oklahoma.

My mother, as a preacher's daughter, was supposed to be perfect: always well behaved, cheerful, and helpful, always at church on Sunday, and never in any trouble. She brought these standards to the rearing of my younger sister, Margo, and me. The combination of being preacher's kids and Shirleys meant that there were many expectations surrounding us. In addition to always behaving correctly, we were supposed to be pretty, well-dressed, and popular, and to make good grades.

That was a heavy burden for a socially awkward six-year-old walking into a classroom where everyone had formed their friendships in kindergarten. I had a difficult time making friends with the girls anyway because I wasn't interested in dolls, dress up games, or pretending to be a princess. Once you got the clothes on there really wasn't much to do except wait for a man to come rescue you or marry you. I much preferred to play cowboy or detective but few of the boys were willing to play those kinds of games with a girl.

As the carefully dressed daughter of the town doctor, I was doubly suspect. In the winter when the icy Oklahoma wind whipped through the town my sister and I walked to school with blue and quivering legs. I begged my mother to let me wear pants to school but she wouldn't allow it. Only the lower-class parents, such as the sharecroppers whose children frequently came barefoot to school, let their girls wear pants or overalls. As an unrepentant tomboy, I found this distinction unjust.

Perhaps this is one of the reasons I became the school's champion of the underdog, an advocate for anyone whom I believed was treated unfairly. I wasn't afraid to use my fists to back up my sentiment. In fact one of my earliest memories of life in Wynnewood is of me fighting Bertie Jones in the third grade.

Bertie was one of the barefoot boys, older and tougher than me, with a shaggy thatch of blond hair atop his head like a twentieth-century Tom Sawyer. One winter day at recess Bertie was picking on a smaller boy, which infuriated me. I leaped at him, oblivious to the fact that I was wearing a heavy, muskrat-brown, fake fur coat that my mother thought was the pinnacle of childhood haute couture.

We set to it in front of a jeering audience of our peers. Bertie kept shoving me down. Each time I started to get up, he'd shove me down again. By the time the teachers separated us, I'd mashed the scrawny yard weeds deep into the fake fur fibers of my coat. Our teacher hauled the two of us into the classroom, banishing me to the cloakroom to pick the bits of dead grass out of the fur.

While I labored in the cloakroom, I could hear her lecturing Bertie in front of the class. "Little gentlemen must not fight with little ladies," she said. Gentlemen? Ladies? Was she talking about the same school I was attending? She certainly couldn't be talking about Bertie Jones and me. I could barely suppress my giggles when she brought me out from the cloakroom to instruct: "Little ladies must not fight with little gentlemen."

When the world around you seems unreal, the world of fiction becomes oddly realistic. For one thing, it's a world of your own choosing, unlike the circumscribed world of Wynnewood that stretched below me as I sat in my perch in the sycamore tree.

Auntie and Unkie owned the entire block below my tree. They lent my parents an elderly white frame house on the corner opposing their own comfortable brown one. The other two corners of the block were occupied by plots of crops, my mother's collie kennel runs, and a corral for her old American saddlebred mare. Catty-cornered across the street from my house stood my paternal grandmother and grandpa's sandy yellow brick home. Next door to them lived my father's older, tubercular brother and his wife. Their son, who was four years older than me, lived with Grandmother and Grandpa.

Sunday was often the worst day of the week for me because it was formal family doings from dawn till dusk. The day always began with my mother forcing us into our Sunday dresses for our appearance at my grandfather's church. After Sunday school, we sat through my grandfather's sermons. We all took great pride in his sermons, but being young, I struggled mightily to listen knowing that if I squirmed I'd bring disapproval from my mother.

Directly after church there was Sunday lunch, usually with my father's family and a stifling affair when it took place at my grandmother's house.

First the whole family would gather in the formal parlor, an uncomfortably furnished place used only for holiday and Sunday meals. The adults would sit around stiffly making desultory conversation. My sister, my cousin, and I were expected to be decorous, but we would rather have been outside, messing up our Sunday clothes by playing in Grandmother's beautiful flower garden or romping in our yard with the animals.

In addition to my mother's beautiful purebred collies, we always had cats. As children we were frequently given animals for holidays. We never got too attached to the chicks we always received for Easter. Once they were out of infancy, they usually grew up to be roosters. My grandparents would just get rid of them and we wouldn't miss them. We did get awfully attached to two ducklings we got one year. We named them Ducky and Lucky and they grew to be fat, friendly old quackers that dogged our heels whenever we let them out of their wire pens.

At Grandmother's house, just as we kids were getting to the

verge of mayhem, Sunday dinner would be served. Every week we politely complimented the same dishes: stewed chicken and dumplings and pale, overcooked vegetables served on the best china. The chickens were homegrown. Auntie and Unkie kept egg layers and some of my fearsomest moments were when I had to go gather the eggs, flailed at by the wings and beaks of fat hens who seemed almost as big as I was. I'd never felt sorry for one of these hens when it became Sunday lunch. Many a time I'd seen Bea, my Auntie's stout and strong servant, wring the neck of a fat old hen with her bare hands on the morning of this meal by whirling the chicken around by the head until the body came loose, flopping freakishly around the yard.

One afternoon the Sunday meal tasted odd to Margo and me. We asked Grandmother why the meat hidden under the dumplings and gravy tasted so different.

"It's duck," she said calmly.

My sister and I looked at each other in puzzlement and then in horror.

"Ducky and Lucky!" my sister and I screamed. We fled the table and raced across the street to the empty pen, weeping in an unsuccessful search for our dear departed ducks. We sat in the yard a shattered pair, shaken by the image of Bea's viselike grip around the necks of Ducky and Lucky.

Sunday lunches at Auntie and Unkie's were much more fun even though the cast of characters was often the same. First of all, the menu was different: ham and red-eye gravy, mashed potatoes and home-grown corn, cabbage, or green beans. More than that, Auntie and Unkie were warm and welcoming people who, though they never had any children, dearly loved spending time with kids. This atmosphere of love and acceptance permeated the household and the Sunday meals.

My father had spent a good part of his childhood at Auntie
and Unkie's house and my sister and I continued that tradition.
Their house was a fabulous place to me as a small child. The
big, shady front porch had a swing where I would sit and talk to
Auntie for hours. I was closer to Auntie than to any other relative. She taught me to cook and sew, and told me stories of her
life and the history of my family. In the large, airy kitchen my
sister and I could always count on getting bread and honey or
fresh-baked cakes and pies. On nights when I would sleep over I
had my own room instead of having to share one with my sister.
I sank into a soft down mattress on the large wooden bed without a care in the world.

Auntie and I used to sit in the sewing room and read the
popular magazines of the 1950s. Favorites were *Collier's* and the
Saturday Evening Post. Collier's was the first place I encountered
the idea that humans might one day explore the moon and
Mars. I was about ten when I saw the brightly illustrated stories
of rockets blasting out of Earth's orbit in an article written by
space pioneer Wernher von Braun. My childhood mind was already miles above Wynnewood, propelled by the fantasies of
flight I'd had since I was six. My fascination with space travel
made me want to fly even higher. After reading these stories, I
didn't search the Oklahoma skies looking for the planets I
dreamed of exploring; I fantasized about piloting the ship that
would take me there.

I always looked forward to Sunday lunches at my mother's
parents' house, which was a couple of blocks from our house,
next to the grade school. They were relaxed and informal and
afterward I could listen to the radio with Grandaddy. We rooted
ardently for the Oklahoma Sooners football team. Later in the
afternoon we thrilled to the adventures of the Green Hornet,

the Lone Ranger, and the Shadow. It was even more exciting when some of my five maternal uncles came up from Texas with their families and played football on the lawn with my cousins and me.

Attached to Grandaddy and Grandmama's house was a small apartment my grandparents rented out to a single mother and her son. He was the only boy I knew who didn't mind playing boy's games with a girl. We had complicated cowboy adventures where we stashed our horses in a cave and had to get to them without alerting the bad guys. Our heroes were movie cowboys whose exploits we marveled at every Saturday in the serials that played at the Sun and Deal movie theaters, ten cents a show.

I had a swooning crush on Roy Rogers because he was so handsome and brave and, of course, because he was a cowboy. This hopeless love affair ended abruptly one Saturday afternoon when I saw him actually kiss a girl on screen. Sissy stuff! I wasn't jealous of the girl and I certainly didn't want to take her place. I wanted to be Roy's buddy. After all, girls didn't get to ride and shoot. Dale had to wear a little skirt and sit around waiting for Roy to come home. What was the fun in that? I wanted to be doing exciting, adventurous things, not girlie things. The only role models I had were men.

This wasn't a sexual identity confusion; this was love of action and heroics. Until I discovered Wonder Woman and Mary Marvel comics, there were no women heroes for me to emulate. Mary Marvel and her companions, Captain Marvel and Captain Marvel, Jr., could say "Shazam!" and change from ordinary people into superheroes. I spent many hours saying "Shazam!" but nothing ever happened.

When I turned eight, my grandpa indulged my cowboy fantasies by getting me a horse named Banner. Banner had been a candidate for the glue factory and was skinny and unhealthy when Grandpa rescued him. With care and feeding, he became a fat, smooth-gaited pony for me.

Shortly after we acquired Banner, my mother entered me in an Oklahoma City horse show. As a young lady my mother, Ada Brooks, had earned a degree in physical education from the Oklahoma College for Women in Chickasha. While she was proud of earning a degree, she wasn't that thrilled about earning it from a girls' school. Her father had somehow managed to scrape up the money to send four of her five brothers to Southern Methodist University, but his pockets were not as full when it came to my mother's education. This was a source of great bitterness for my mother and may in part explain why she was so ambitious for my sister and me.

At college my mother's specialty was riding. Before she married my father she taught riding at Monticello, an exclusive girls' school. I know my mother wanted to pass on to her daughters her own love of horses. She rode English style on her American saddlebred but we learned to ride western style like most Oklahoma kids.

Before the big horse show my mother put Banner and me through our paces day after day. To win the competition, the child had to demonstrate how well he or she could control the horse through different gaits: walk, trot, and canter. My mother bought me a flashy western riding outfit for the event and I felt fine sitting on a high-pommeled western saddle as I rode around our yard at home, Banner responding obediently to the reins.

As we entered the ring on the day of the competition I had a horrible sinking feeling. All the other little girls around me were decked out in English riding habits and used English-style flat saddles on their horses. I felt so out of place, but I knew better than to argue with my mother. She assured me that my different style of dress would just help me stand out from the crowd.

Banner and I entered the ring and trotted smartly, my confidence growing as he graciously obeyed my lead. Then suddenly a brass band struck up a tune in the stands. Banner was terrified. He reared and snorted and began to race madly around the ring. I clung helplessly to the saddle horn, unable to hold him back.

A man leapt from the stands and jumped in front of Banner, grabbing him by the bridle to force him to a stop. I was embarrassed and ashamed that my horse had run away but all I could think about was how humiliated my mother would be because I was disqualified.

The man led Banner and me out of the ring. I spent the rest of the event staring disconsolately through the fence at the other kids in their prim English riding habits on their well-bred ponies. Banner had calmed down by this time. I was thinking maybe they would give me a prize just for trying. Of course they didn't and my mother offered no sympathy. She never quite forgave me for embarrassing her. Trying was not good enough. With my mother, only successes counted.

As an adult I have a different perspective on my mother's rigid perfectionism. I know she was very bitter when we moved back to Oklahoma and had to face the fact that she was going to spend the rest of her life in Wynnewood. She wanted to be out in the world, on her own with my father and her girls making a new life in California. Once we got back to Wynnewood, my father was under his mother's influence. He threw himself into his work, leaving my mother to her own devices. My mother was a vibrant, intelligent woman who would have been much better off if she could have let off some of that energy by having a job.

In the fifties, wives of respectable men didn't work. It was considered unseemly for a woman of my mother's social position to earn a salary. I understand now how frustrated she must have been, but as a child it was very hard to endure the way she took those frustrations out on my sister and me. She channeled all her considerable energy into making perfect children out of a much less than perfect Margo and me. When we wouldn't, or couldn't, do exactly as she expected, she'd make us fetch the fly swatter to demonstrate just how disappointed she was with us and the world.

If my room wasn't clean or if the chores weren't done to her specifications, that might set off a beating. There were plenty of chores to do. My sister and I were responsible for keeping the house clean and doing the dishes and the ironing. We were also required to tend the horses and feed, clean up after, and groom the fifteen purebred collies my mother raised in Shirhaven Kennels.

I don't want to leave the impression that my childhood was unrelievedly bleak or that my parents' child-rearing skills were limited to abandonment and abuse. I loved the time my mother and I spent with the dogs both grooming them and showing them at the many weekend dog shows in which my mother and I competed. The dogs were a source of mutual pride for my mother and me, a sunny spot in our frequently tempestuous relationship. My mother praised my skill in handling the dogs and the awards I won in the junior division of the shows. Also I loved the dogs—big, soft bundles of fur who were affectionate and always happy to see me. Around them I felt the kind of unconditional love that evaded me at home.

In addition to showing horses and dogs, I also had to support my mother's interest in swimming. My mother was a camp counselor and later she ran our county's swim program in the summers. She also formed a Girl Scout troop just so my sister and I could have the scouting experience. By the age of ten I was going to Scout camp on my own and helping my mother by teaching the smallest children the rudiments of swimming.

The lessons took place at a pool in Pauls Valley or at a dammed up stream in the Arbuckle Mountains called Cedarvale. Although Cedarvale was a beautiful setting—a deep pool about a quarter mile long overhung with trees and featuring a great rope swing—it was a scene of terror for me.

When I reached the age of twelve, my mother enrolled me in life saving at Cedarvale under her instruction. I was the only junior life saver; the rest of the class were senior life savers aged fifteen to eighteen. I was at least three years younger and consequently a weaker swimmer. But, as I was her daughter, she believed these were minor obstacles that I, with my superior genetic makeup, would easily overcome.

Besides the holds and carries devised to save a drowning person, the life saving course had strength and endurance requirements. Part of the training simulated recovering a body. We had to pick a 10-pound sack off the bottom of the pool, a fairly easy task in the clear water of the Pauls Valley swimming pool. Cedarvale was murky and 20 feet deep. The bottom was covered by large stones that looked a lot like a bag of sand in the cloudy water. Often I'd fail to grab it in three or four tries. Each time I came up without it, my mother's face contorted with frustration. If I gave up and an older kid was sent down to retrieve the bag, I stood by the side of the pool humiliated as my mother berated me in front of my classmates. For years I had nightmares of drowning at Cedarvale.

During the distance swimming requirement my drowning nightmare very nearly came true. We were all to swim four whole lengths of Cedarvale to fulfill the mile swim requirement. My mother yelled "Go!" and we leaped into the water together but soon I trailed behind. By the second lap I was still swimming out when the rest of the group was swimming back.

Churning along with their heads down, several of them ran over me. I inhaled water and started to drown. When I surfaced, flailing, I screamed for help. A few of the others swam out and towed me to the wooden dock at the end of the pool. As I lay on my back gasping for air, my mother stood over me belittling me for yelling for help.

My mother sounds like an ogre in these stories, which would be a surprise to many in Wynnewood who admired her for her well-run dog kennel, her successful children, and her many charitable works. The best thing I can say about the hard physical labor and rough athletic circumstances my mother forced me into is that she made me fearless. In my adult life, I've called upon that strength countless times whether it be in skiing, or sailing, or mountain climbing. She provided me with a strange form of inner strength, too. In many professional situations, I've been the only woman in a roomful of hostile male engineers and I've been able to maintain my poise. In many ways surviving my childhood gave me the confidence, misplaced or not, that I can endure and even triumph over anything.

One aspect of my life my mother could not control was my popularity or lack thereof. My atrophied social life was a sore trial to my mother. Having to be the best didn't stop with swimming and Girl Scouts and straight A's. I also had to be beautiful and sought after by boys. I was neither of those things. My six-inch growth spurt at age thirteen was not accompanied by a spurt in social development. I was still a tomboy well into my senior year in high school, and, because I was almost two years younger than most of my classmates, I was physically behind even then.

My bones were still growing, so my front teeth stuck out and my jaw was more prominent than my cheekbones. The optometrist discovered I was nearsighted in one eye and farsighted in the other, so I wore glasses—the geeky kind with colored plastic rims. My taste in clothes was abominable, even during the era of poodle skirts and penny loafers when abominable clothes were the norm. I have a picture of me wearing two different plaids at the same time. Atop this bold fashion statement, I wore my hair short, which emphasized the awkward shape of my face. Suffice to say, I was not love's young dream. Neither was I high on Wynnewood's social pecking order.

So when at thirteen I was asked out on a date, my mother was ecstatic. This boy had, as far as I could tell, no redeeming features. To my mother, however, because he was white and male he was therefore acceptable. She wouldn't let me refuse. He arrived for the date wearing a T-shirt with cigarettes rolled up in the sleeve and driving a mufflerless Chevy.

We went to a drive-in movie and he immediately wanted to neck. I insisted that he buy me popcorn, which I ate one well-chewed kernel at a time, and then a Coke which I sipped at approximately the same speed. On the way home he demanded I slide over and sit next to him. When I refused, he slid over to my side of the car, put his arm around me, and drove with his left foot and hand. When we arrived home I stomped into the house indignantly.

"How was your date, dear?" my mother asked.

"He kissed me!" I spat.

My mother didn't see this as a problem. I refused to go on any more dates until the junior prom two years in the future. I was different from my peers in other ways, too. In high school the state administered I.Q. tests and I scored 30 points higher than anyone else. It was something to be proud of, but it only reinforced the obvious fact that I had no real peers.

This wasn't for lack of effort on my part. I'd joined the band when I was ten and was soon promoted to the high school band because my instrument of choice was oboe. The oboe was an exotic instrument in Wynnewood. The school's instrument budget was allocated for the more mainstream brass, drums, and clarinets that could also be used by the marching band. Only the children of the relatively rich, such as myself, could play oboe or bassoon because their parents could afford to purchase the instruments for them.

What the band offered was something I was longing for: comradeship. I wanted to be with a group of people working toward a shared goal. Of course then I had no idea why I was so attracted to the band. Only years later when I worked on team projects at JPL did I understand this was what I was craving in Wynnewood.

Marching bands don't use oboes during football season so I was assigned to play the snare drum. The drum was suspended at mid-thigh by a strap over the right shoulder and rested on a curved metal fitting on the left leg. I was so much younger and smaller than the high school students, I couldn't carry the full-size drum. On me it swayed and banged around my shins. My mother bought me a special small snare drum but even then it was too difficult for me to keep up with the comparatively long strides of the rest of the band members. The band director decided I could participate by playing the cymbals.

Every August our band marched in the Oklahoma State Fair parade, a five-mile march from downtown Oklahoma City over the broiling asphalt to the fairgrounds. The band had only one uniform: wool maroon jackets with gray trousers and stiff plastic maroon-and-white headgear. These uniforms were perfect for inflicting the maximum misery at the peak of the boiling hot Oklahoma summer. Misery or no, I was very excited about marching with my bandmates and making the big cymbals crash in the parade, especially the great smash I got to make near the end of our school song, "Loyal and True."

As the band was mustering on a side street the morning of the parade, the band director cast a critical eye on me, my childish body swimming in the smallest band uniform the school had. My pants were turned up nearly to the knee just so I could walk. An honest assessment of my little body in this wool uniform alarmed the director. He decided I was too small to survive the march. So someone else played the cymbals and I sat forlornly in the bus that drove in front of the band, my nose pressed against the rear window watching my bandmates sweat proudly as they played.

Eventually I did get to march in the band and in my senior year was elected band vice president. I was also senior class vice president (girls *never* ran for president) and I edited the yearbook. Despite these obvious signs of esteem from my classmates, I still felt lonely. Well into high school my escape was still books.

Although none of the boys I knew in Wynnewood held any attraction for me, I had an enormous crush on Jimmy, the teenager portrayed in Arthur C. Clarke's science fiction novel, *The Sands of Mars*. Jimmy had taken time off from college to take the seven-month journey to Mars as a flight apprentice. He was smart, modest, and competent in a world where intelligence was the key to status, not looks or possessions. When I thought of going to Mars, it was more than Jimmy I craved. Clarke described a world that was my ideal of community and comradeship. I wanted to be with the Jimmys of the real world. I wanted to work with the people who built the machines that would fly to Mars. What really captured my imagination was not the astronomy aspect of science fiction but my own romanticism of flight.

From earliest memory, I loved airplanes. I read books about them and built crude models even as a small child. When I was six, a girlfriend and I made a life plan: she would become a nurse and I would be a bush pilot flying her into the darkest outback to save people's lives.

When I was ten, my family went to my uncle's medical school graduation. I saw listed on the program a group of people who were receiving degrees in aeronautical engineering. "What's that?" I asked. My mother said, "Those are people who build airplanes." My heart leaped. "That's what I want to be," I cried. I had instantly decided on my career goal.

To this day, the best birthday present I've ever received was the flying lessons my father bought me for my fifteenth birthday. In many ways my father didn't know what to do with his daughters once they were out of the toddler stage. The one thing he could support, and did so avidly, was a sustained interest. I consider myself fortunate my father was generous enough to pay for me to learn to fly.

The summer of my sixteenth year I'd earned my driver's license. My dad, a car buff, bought me a black Renault Dauphine, similar to a Volkswagen bug. I drove myself to the Pauls Valley airport to continue my flying lessons after my successful solo. The airport was a dinky operation: just a galvanized steel hangar with a big noisy sliding door and a scruffy little office next to a quarter mile runway. To a gawky, sky-struck girl it was the most thrilling place on Earth. The fact that it was so scruffy made it all the more real to me.

In the office pilots lounged on the ragged Naugahyde sofa, their feet propped on the filthy coffee table as they took long drags on their cigarettes. On the wall of the office hung yellowed aviation charts of the area. The ruler of this turf was Charlie Davis, the swashbuckling blond body builder who taught me to fly. Besides running the airport and giving flying lessons, Charlie made extra money with flying odd jobs. My flying was not yet as daring as his, but I had some adventures of my own.

The Champ was powered by a mere 65 horsepower engine. With two large wheels mounted near the front of the fuselage and a small swiveling tail wheel, pilots called it a "tail dragger." The pilot sat tilted back. I had to peer around the engine to see where I was going. The instrumentation, such as it was, consisted of an air speed gauge and a needle ball. The needle sat straight up in the ball suspended in liquid. If you banked your turns right, the needle would remain straight showing that you'd balanced the speed and the direction of the plane perfectly.

There was a tug of war between Charlie and me over just how often he'd let me solo. After I'd successfully taken the plane up and brought it down on my own, Charlie needed to be able to trust my skills as a navigator. He took me on a number of cross-country trips, some as far away as the Texas panhandle, so I could get a sense of how to find my way back home using the Champ's rudimentary instruments and a compass. Oklahoma was divided into mile-square plots during the great land rush of 1889. One only needed to get a visual fix on the section lines that ran straight as a die east/west or north/south for as far as the eye could see to plot a course. The adventure inherent in flying to Texas was that that state had no section lines, so the pilot had to navigate.

Finally in February 1958 Charlie let me solo cross country to Norman, Oklahoma, where I was to go to college, and back. For my second solo cross country in May, the sky was solidly overcast by a bank of puffy clouds. I took off and headed out on my 50-mile solo to Chickasha. I mostly kept my head down—poring over the map, watching the compass, looking for landmarks, and plotting my angle to the section lines, but every now and then I looked up at the clouds overhead. Suddenly a hole opened up in the overcast. Bright sun poured through and I could see a brilliant patch of blue sky. Like a moth to a flame, I spiraled up and through the hole, bursting out over a breathtaking view of the sun silvering the billowing tops of the clouds as far as I could see.

There wasn't a single trace of ground anywhere in sight: no hills or farms nor the rooftops of Wynnewood, just a magnificent horizon-to-horizon expanse of glory. It was the kind of freedom I'd always craved.

I followed my compass heading, oblivious that the wind might be blowing me off course, and timed my flight. At the moment when it was the right time for me to be over Chickasha, I noticed a hole below me through which I could see a patch of ground. I spiraled down and surprisingly found myself directly over an airport. I landed. Sure enough it was Chickasha. The laconic guy in the hangar signed my log book without many questions. I gulped a cup of coffee and quickly headed back to Pauls Valley.

It was a windless day and my hole in the clouds was still right above the Chickasha airport. I soared back up above the clouds and headed for Pauls Valley, glorying again in the magnificent view as I putt-putted along. Sure enough there was another gap in the clouds right over the Pauls Valley airport. I spiraled down, lined up on the runway, and made a good landing.

Beaming with pride, I showed Charlie my signed log book and described the magnificence of the flight above the clouds. The fury on Charlie's face was a cold slap to my independence.

"You did what?" he bellowed. "You idiot!" he bellowed again. "What the hell did you think you were doing?"

"What do you mean?" I said. "It was great."

"You can't fly straight up through clouds like that. Not in that thing," Charlie continued.

"What are you talking about? I found a hole and I went through it and then I came back," I said, unable to comprehend what was making him so mad.

"What if the clouds moved? Did you ever think of that? What if those holes had closed up while you were up there?" he demanded. "How would you have let down through the clouds with no instruments?"

He was right. I had been lucky. I had no idea if I'd come out in the right place or even upside down. If there had been no gap in the clouds I would have had to come down through them, flying in a total fog with no reference points and no instruments. I could have broken out of the clouds upside down with no time to recover before crashing.

"I'm sorry, Charlie," I quavered. "I just didn't think."

"Well," he grumbled, "next time think a little more."

I should have learned my lesson but my craving for adventure led me into other stupid escapades.

Rita Newell, my best friend from school, had always begged

me to take her flying. We knew that neither Charlie nor our parents would look kindly on me taking Rita for a ride. I couldn't legally have a passenger until I had my private pilot's license, for which I had to put in a lot more flight time. Late in the summer, weeks before we were to go off to our separate colleges, Rita and I decided to do it anyway. One afternoon when Rita knew her parents would be away from home, I dropped by in the Champ to take her for a spin.

The plowed field next to her house was short and bordered on two sides by telephone wires. In order to get to Rita I had to do the kind of aeronautic maneuver that only a stunt pilot or a foolish kid would attempt.

I flew in low, just over the telephone lines, and dropped swiftly down holding the stick left and the rudder right to get to the ground as fast as possible. Just before hitting the ground, I straightened out and pulled the nose up for a landing. The fence at the other end of the Newells' field was coming up fast and I had to whirl the plane around quickly to avoid crashing into it.

Rita was waiting. As soon as I turned the plane around she ran out and wriggled into the passenger seat. We taxied back to the upwind end of the field. I turned into the wind, which fortunately was blowing briskly and would make for a short take-off. I held the brakes down and pushed the throttle all the way open until the engine was running full speed. When I released the brakes the plane bumped over the ruts in the field, fighting to get enough speed to take off in that short distance. At first each bump just bounced us and then thumped us back onto the ground, but finally we were going fast enough to lift off just before we hit the fence. We actually skimmed *under* the telephone lines on our way up into the sky.

Once up, we were giddy. We buzzed close over Wynnewood squealing as we waved our wings at the tiny figures on the streets below. We passed by the sycamore tree in front of Auntie and Unkie's house, the one I never climbed anymore. Then we flew over the school we would never attend again and back over the fields to the Newells'. We only had a few minutes in the air because I had to be back at the airport within an hour.

This time I was nervous about landing in the abbreviated distance. Gritting my teeth, I repeated the landing maneuver— slipping over the telephone wires, bouncing over the ruts of the field and making a sharp left to avoid the fence. Rita jumped out and waved me on as I repeated my takeoff. Without the extra weight I flew over the phone lines and headed back to the airport smiling at my caper. I knew that more adventures lay ahead. College was only a few weeks away.

2
Temporarily Tethered

I clutched three precious things in my hand as I threaded my way through the throng of students on the University of Oklahoma campus a few days before the beginning of my freshman year: a map of the campus, my admission packet from the College of Engineering, and a card announcing that my adviser, J. C. Brady, awaited me in room 114 of Felgar Hall. I hurried along the sidewalk, the heat of Oklahoma's early September sun alternating with shade from the trees, past the brick buildings the color of Oklahoma clay. I was overwhelmed. The University of Oklahoma was five times as big as Wynnewood.

All around me students were greeting friends they hadn't seen all summer and running up the steps and across the lawn. I was surrounded by thousands of young people who shared my energy and curiosity. I'd already been pledged by a good sorority, Gamma Phi Beta, where they had chosen me not just for my good grades but because I liked to fly. I was still wrapping my mind around the idea that I'd landed in a place where being a woman pilot was an asset instead of an oddity. Another woman pilot in Gamma Phi Beta, named Gene Nora Stumbough, had lobbied hard for the sorority to pledge me. My step lightened as I closed in on Felgar Hall determined to be an aeronautical engineer despite what anyone said.

At Wynnewood High we'd all taken skill and interest tests to help us decide what we should do with our lives. This seemed like a huge waste of time to me because I knew, and had known since age ten, I was going to build airplanes. When I got my test results back I had to look twice to confirm they were really mine. I'd scored in the nineties in my verbal abilities but only average in math and way below normal in spatial perception. In the section on interests, I'd rated those related to engineering skills of highest interest to me. The career counselor assured me solemnly that given my skills I could be a journalist or a librarian, or even a nuclear physicist, but never an engineer.

The suggestion that I become a librarian and spend all my days indoors cataloguing other people's adventures was madness to me. No barrier, not even lack of aptitude, could get in the way of me learning how to build airplanes.

I entered Felgar Hall and opened the door to J. C. Brady's office with a huge smile of anticipation on my face.

"I'm Donna Shirley," I said brightly.

"What are you doing here?" Brady asked blankly.

"I'm here to enroll in aeronautical engineering," I said.

"Girls can't be engineers," Brady snorted.

I stood awkwardly in the silence that followed as we looked steadily at each other waiting for someone to blink.

"Yes I can. I've been accepted into the College of Engineering," I sputtered. "I want you to help me decide what I should take first."

I was too dumbstruck to take a seat while Brady rummaged through the stack of student folders on his desk trying to find mine. He scanned my grades, took a look at me and then another at my entrance exam scores while I kicked myself for expecting something besides this kind of treatment. At the annual district interscholastic meet at Oklahoma State Teachers College in my senior year in high school, I'd represented Wynnewood in mechanical drawing. There I got my first indication of how most of the male world would view a female engineer.

I'd felt the evaluator's eyes following me to my seat as I took my place in the competition room on a spring Saturday earlier that year. He smiled smugly as he strode over to my desk with a large folded sheet of drawing paper in his hands.

"So we have a young lady competing for the mechanical drawing medal this year. I'm sure the gentlemen won't object if I give our fair guest a little head start," he said to the room, as he quickly flipped the paper open to give me half a second of a peek at the illustration we were supposed to produce.

I blushed crimson and stared at the top of my desk. For the first time in memory, I was speechless as the boys around me roared in laughter. No one in Wynnewood ever made that kind of fun of me in class. One of the advantages of being raised in a small town is that once the community has figured out what makes you tick, it pretty much leaves you alone. When I talked my way out of the home economics requirement in high school so I could take mechanical drawing instead, I was accepted in that class without much comment by my fellow students, all of whom were boys. Here, I was furious that an adult would humiliate me like that and also at the rudeness of the boys. Embarrassment redoubled my determination.

On each of our drawing desks was a box containing the objects we were to draw. When the evaluator said "go" and switched on the stopwatch, we opened the boxes and took out a simple mechanism. We had an hour to draw this mechanism from different perspectives and to ink the drawing. I bore down on my work trying hard not to be distracted by the glances and sniggers of my competitors. Every few minutes the evaluator cruised by my desk to needle me.

"You're doing just great there, little lady," he'd say as he passed. There was something about the way he emphasized "just great" that made it sound like he was complimenting a child on an incompetent first attempt. I kept my eyes focused on my drawing.

With five minutes to go, my drawing did look great. My lines were strong and true and in the correct proportion. I inked it in, satisfied that the thickness of the lines was consistent. I've really got a chance to win this, I thought. Then, as I reached over to tighten the cap on my bottle of India ink, my hand slipped and I knocked the bottle over, spilling ink all over my drawing.

The pleasure my instructor took in disaster further humiliated me.

"Aw," he said when I turned in my work. "Too bad."

Instead of proving him wrong, I had reinforced his feeling that girls couldn't handle this kind of work. I was crushed and disappointed in myself. When I became an engineer, I'd set the world of guys like that upside down, I swore to myself then.

And now I was in college facing another one of these bigots.

"So you want to be an engineer?" Brady said sarcastically. "You need to be in calculus. Your test scores show you can handle advanced chemistry. You have to take English and Intro to Engineering. Other than that, just sign up for anything you want."

"Flying," I said.

The woman at the enrollment desk was skeptical.

"Nineteen semester hours. That's a lot for a first term," she said, as she signed off on my schedule. "Most freshmen take fifteen."

That was most freshmen, not me. Maybe I hadn't been the most popular girl in Wynnewood, but I knew I was the smartest. After all I was valedictorian, graduating first in my class of forty-nine students from Wynnewood High. This college class load couldn't possibly be too much.

The arrogance of youth! The image of myself that I'd nurtured back home—that I was more than just better than the rest, I was invincible—came crashing down around my feet my freshman year.

The Intro to Engineering course was to introduce young engineers to the different disciplines in one time-consuming course. We learned to survey and use a slide rule, to mix concrete and to measure the strength of different kinds of materials by breaking them apart. Flying, with the drive to the airport and ground school, was wonderful, but it took a lot of time.

My self-image as a smart kid was so ingrained that it took me a while to realize how poorly I was doing. I was flunking two courses. I'd aced high school chemistry, but it had been taught with a 1929 textbook and no lab. My solid streak of good grades in algebra and trigonometry still hadn't provided much preparation for college calculus. At mid-terms I couldn't avoid it any longer. There was a melodramatic moment when I found myself staring out my fourth-floor dorm window contemplating how a swift plummet to the sidewalk could release me from my torture and misery. I didn't want to have to face my parents with the news that college was too much for my brain. Flunking out of school was my worst fear. I'd never be able to show my face at home again.

Eight weeks into the school year, my parents received red cards, notifications from the college that I was flunking calculus and chemistry. They drove the sixty miles from Wynnewood to Norman, Oklahoma, to demonstrate their concern. I think they were frightened, almost as frightened as I was. None of us could believe this was happening to me. To their credit, they didn't berate me for laziness. They asked if I needed a tutor to help me through this. "No," I said, "what I need to do is study."

All of high school had been so simple for me that I had no idea how to study. I'd done a lot of physically difficult things, competing against people older and stronger than I, but I'd never faced a mental challenge I couldn't handle. Instead of stepping up to a rightful place in the company of my peers, I was out of my depth.

At Christmas break I studied all day, every day. I ended the semester with B grades and a humbler opinion of myself. I realized that if I really wanted to be an engineer I'd have to work so hard I couldn't have a social life. As I'd not had a social life before, this didn't seem like much of a sacrifice. At barely seventeen I was still gawky and socially inept and couldn't imagine that I'd be the object of anyone's affections.

At the sorority I was lumped among the "closet cases," which meant I'd been pledged to help the sorority fulfill its academic standards, not for my looks. I wasn't required to attend events where beauty was the main point. As pledges, closet cases like me were set up with the most hideous blind dates imaginable. I remember one where my date amused us by chilling his thumb with an ice cube until it was numb enough that he could stub out his cigarette on it. How utterly charming, I thought. I concentrated on just getting through these wretched evenings.

Female engineering students were enough of a rarity that the school newspaper ran a precious article commenting on the six of us: "There are certain girls on campus who always refuse a very generous portion of male attention and are unhampered by the competition of other females," the article said. "Who are these lucky souls? They are the half dozen or so girls majoring in engineering."

The breathless tone of that article reflects the tenor of the times. The writer doesn't express outrage that women would dare to invade a male atmosphere or that they don't have the skills to handle it, he just doesn't take them seriously. The sneering implication is that the motive for a woman to major in engineering is to increase her chances of meeting a man. When the reporter asked me why I was majoring in aeronautical engineering I didn't say I wanted to meet handsome pilots. I was quoted: "I like airplanes."

Besides my flying classes, I joined the Airknockers, the college's daredevil flying club. We flew Aeronca Champs just like the ones I'd flown in Pauls Valley. I loved the weekends when we'd all jump in our planes and fly off together to some distant college for an intramural competition.

Gene Nora Stumbough was one of the top competitors and I worshiped her for it. She was my own Amelia Earhart. In a picture I have of the club from 1958, I'm right next to Gene

Nora, wedged up just as close as I can possibly get. I followed her around like a puppy dog my freshman year. She introduced me to the 99's, an international women's flying club comprised largely of salty old gals who had ferried all kinds of aircraft during World War II. They, in turn, introduced me to the Pink Lady, a feminine-looking but potent alcoholic snow cone. With Gene Nora and the 99's I finally had some powerful female role models.

My primary flight instructor at OU was Pete Howard, a World War II pilot who was the head of the flying school and qualified to test pilots for licenses. Pete, like Charlie back home, was a great pilot, but they had completely opposite personalities. Charlie was an irrepressible daredevil. Pete was cautious and thorough and thought Charlie took too many risks. He complained about Charlie buzzing low and waving his wings at Pete's friends when they played golf on the Pauls Valley course. I liked them both immensely. I was especially proud when I got my private pilot's license after a tough check-in ride with Pete.

It turned out Pete had every reason to be suspicious of Charlie. One weekend when I was home from college, Charlie asked me if I wanted to scout the powerlines with him. I'd always wondered what it would be like to fly that close to the ground so I jumped in the backseat of the Champ and we took off.

The powerlines dipped in and out of the hills around Wynnewood and the most efficient way to check them was to fly over. We were looking for woodpecker holes in the poles. We flew right next to the powerlines, so close that Charlie had to tilt his wings up to avoid smashing into trees. We were speeding along at 60 miles an hour 20 feet above the ground, dipping and twisting with the curves of the hills and the tops of the trees. At first it was exhilarating but pretty soon after that it was nauseating. I was glad I didn't end up having to use the airsickness bag by the end of that very long hour with Charlie. I knew I could never tell Pete about the flight, but I was aching to tell Johnnie.

My freshman year I studied frequently with a handsome fellow engineering student and budding pilot named Johnnie. He was 6 foot 2 inches, lanky and dark and more importantly the first man I'd ever met to whom I didn't have to explain things. He was even smarter than I. He wanted to be a petroleum engineer and he was in Air Force ROTC so he could eventually become a pilot. His father was an oil driller and he couldn't afford the extra fees my father paid so I could fly. He was working his way through school, which I found very noble. He loved to hear about my exploits with the Airknockers but he expressed no interest in me outside of being a study buddy. Considering how hard everything else was for me, I figured it was just as well we seemed doomed to friendship.

Even after my successful recovery from the near-disaster of my first semester, engineering was a grind. The math got harder and my problems with spatial perception made learning circuit diagrams in electrical engineering really tough. In some classes I really had to focus my attention to avoid injury. In welding I had to learn not to flinch despite the hot sparks of metal that burned holes in my jeans. If my hand shook, I'd ruin the weld. If I took my eye off the lathe or drill press in machine shop, I could take off a finger. I was keeping my grades up, but it was a struggle.

After I found out I could take summer classes, I never went home for summer again. The summer after my sophomore year I got my multiengine rating, which is a certificate to fly a plane with more than one engine, at the University of Illinois at Urbana-Champaign.

We called the plane the Bamboo Bomber. It was a big, old wood-and-fabric prop plane built as a World War II trainer. With one big radial engine on each wing, it looked like a miniature DC 3. Piloting that kind of plane was physically challenging. There was no hydraulic help with the steering. I had to grip so hard my hands would be imprinted with ridges from the steering wheel tape when I finished my flights.

The mechanics at the university's aviation mechanics school were always working on the Bomber but it never seemed completely flight ready. We'd start it up and oil would spray all over the wings. We reasoned that if we waited for it to be in perfect working order, none of the students would get their certifications that summer. Our rule was if there was only one thing wrong with it we'd take her out. But if there were two things wrong with it, plane and student were grounded. We were required to wear parachutes but we were too cool for that. We used them as seat cushions when we flew.

At the end of the summer when the FAA inspector came out to qualify me for my multi-engine rating, the look on his face when he saw the Bamboo Bomber showed me how daring I'd been to fly that old crate. It was pretty clear he didn't even want to get in the thing. He clambered into the right seat and strapped his parachute on nervously.

"I don't have to wear mine, do I?" I asked.

"No, but I'm not waiting for you," he shot back.

So we took off. There were specific maneuvers I had to demonstrate to get my rating. He asked me to pull up into a stall. I reached out and pulled the throttles back. By the time the engines were at half power, he barked: "That's enough."

We never did get into a stall and we only made one landing before he told me to taxi back to the hangar, and feverishly signed off that I'd passed my check ride. He couldn't wait to get out of that plane.

By the time sophomore year began, the sorority was starting to have its effect on me. I'd learned to wear makeup, picked up fashion cues from my sisters, and stopped wearing my hair in a frizzy perm. I wasn't beautiful, but I wasn't too bad. When my proportions suddenly snapped into place that fall, so did my social life. Johnnie, it turned out, had been intimidated by me! Sophomore year he pledged a fraternity to become my social equal and immediately asked me out. After I brought him to the first sorority dance of the year, my incredulous sorority sisters brought me out of the closet. I was truly swept off my feet by Johnnie, smitten in the way I'd only seen in movies.

Johnnie pursued me in the time-honored stages of romantic attachment in Greek life. First he gave me his "drop" with his fraternity letters to wear on a necklace, then his fraternity pin. The semester in my junior year that we got engaged my grades dropped from a 3.5 out of 4.0 to a 1.2.

Suddenly none of my academic and professional goals mattered to me. This was not the same Donna who had begun college full of high ideals and purpose. Having a peer group, something I'd longed for all my life, turned out to be more than I could handle. I was burned out by the heavy workload engineering classes demanded of me and distracted by being popular for the first time in my life. I completely lost sight of my dream. I just wanted to graduate and get married.

None of this was lost on my hyperaware mother who was eager to advance my future on all fronts. One spring day in my junior year she called me at the sorority and breathlessly suggested I enter the Miss Wynnewood pageant because there simply weren't enough girls running to make it a real contest.

Of all the fantastic dreams I'd had for my future, being a beauty queen hadn't made the list. My mother was so excited by the possibility of having an actual beauty queen in the family it was hard to deny her the pleasure.

The flurry of activity during the run up to the competition was extremely satisfying for my mother, and not terribly annoying for me. We met in Oklahoma City to buy me a ball gown for the competition. One couldn't purchase the kind of grand confection required to receive the honor of bearing the title Miss Wynnewood in the modest stores of Pauls Valley or Wynnewood. I ended up with a fluffy wedding-cake skirt with tiers and tiers of white chiffon and a tightly fitted bodice with bare shoulders. We also bought a white, one-piece bathing suit and leg makeup to give my stems the proper presentation in those pre–panty hose years.

At lunch my mother was all atwitter about what my talent would be. She lobbied for me playing an oboe solo, but I hadn't played the oboe in three years and I never was that great at it anyway. I thought my only real talent was flying. This was how we hit upon the idea of me writing and reciting a poem about flight.

On the fateful day of the competition Johnnie and several of my sorority sisters drove down to Wynnewood to support me, ready to rib me if I lost. As they were driving down to Wynnewood for the spectacle, I was trapped in a dressing room with my mother painstakingly rubbing makeup on my legs and monitoring my every move lest I smudge the tint onto my white bathing suit.

At the talent competition I delivered a stirring poem that began:

When the prototype of man first stood erect,
He could tip his head and look at the sky.
Not so the animals, noses to the earth,
Their destiny was not to fly.

I looked at my mother from the podium, and seeing her eyes alight with such pride and anticipation was almost too much to bear.

One of my competitors was Rita Newell, the buddy who'd soared with me over Wynnewood before college began. She won Miss Congeniality and I got the big bouquet. I would have been just as happy if Rita had won, but I knew my mother wouldn't be a gracious loser. When I was crowned Miss Wynnewood, it was a proud moment for my relatives.

I'd have liked it if my career as a beauty queen ended at that pinnacle. The requirement for Miss Wynnewood, however, was to go on to compete for Miss Oklahoma. Being the realistic person that I am, I knew I didn't have a chance. Not so my mother, nose in chiffon. Her destiny was to try and try.

She tried desperately to convince me to lose 20 pounds before the Miss Oklahoma contest. Seeing as I'm nearly 5 foot 8 inches and was at that time 130 pounds, I found the notion of being any thinner a bit extreme. I placated her by promising I'd lose weight for the Miss America pageant.

So a few months later I found myself with forty-seven other young women prancing around Oklahoma City with ribbons proclaiming our hometowns stretched across our chests. We had lunch with the judges, and dinner with the businessmen, and photo sessions until I was nearly blinded by the residual glare of the flashbulbs.

As Miss Wynnewood, I was forty-eighth of forty-eight con-testants in the alphabetically ordered list. By the time the judges got to me, it was pretty difficult to come up with some-thing new to say about whatever topic they were quizzing con-testants on. My sure-fail tactic was to say something extremely intellectual. It was no surprise to me when I didn't even make it out of the first round.

My mother took this loss very hard but she didn't blame me. She was especially upset because the woman who won wasn't any better looking than me. Her talent, such as it was, was the deciding factor in the competition. She performed the Lord's Prayer in Indian sign language. The judges believed she would be a spectacular ambassador for our state at the national pag-eant with this uniquely Oklahoma skill. Unfortunately, the Miss America judges were not impressed.

Being a beauty queen didn't help my grades—they were in ruins and an engineering degree seemed unattainable. The fast-est and least painful way to get out of school was to change my major to something less demanding. I'd always made A's in English so I decided to switch my major from aeronautical engi-neering to journalism. Johnnie had decided he wanted to be a doctor. Our plan was for me to put him through med school by being a writer. Unfortunately, the publishing industry was not cooperative. The magazine stories I submitted as part of my classwork garnered a steady stream of rejection slips.

I'm proud to say I didn't completely lose sight of who I was in this mad dash to the altar. Before the second semester of my junior year ended, I realized I didn't want to marry Johnnie. In fact I didn't want to marry anyone.

Johnnie's favorite fantasy for the future was of the two of us as senior citizens sitting on the porch of the house in which we'd raised our children waiting for our grandchildren to come by for a visit. In the glow of falling in love, I'd never realized how little interest this fantasy held for me. Even if I wasn't going to be designing airplanes, I still wanted more adventure than spending my whole life waiting for my retirement.

I was the object of incredulity from my sorority sisters and disapproval from my parents when I broke off my engagement. My parents, and particularly my mother, thought I'd gone nuts changing my major and breaking my engagement in the space of a few months. For the first time in my life I didn't care what they thought. My stint as Miss Wynnewood was my final act in trying to please my mom. I think my parents were simply relieved when I graduated. I'd not fulfilled my potential, but at least I'd managed to get out of college with my diploma. I'd also collected several pilot's licenses: Single Engine Land and Sea, Multi-engine Land, Commercial, and Flight Instructor. I'd even soloed in a sailplane and taught a couple of students to fly.

I still had a strong interest in engineering. When aerospace company recruiters came to the campus, I asked if they had any jobs in technical writing. Only one, the recruiter from McDonnell Aircraft, responded with any enthusiasm. He even took me out to dinner to discuss career prospects. I was puzzled by this until he invited me up to his hotel room. I declined, but, to my surprise, was later offered a job as a specification writer. In January of 1963 I loaded all my worldly goods into my Corvair and headed out for my single gal adventure in St. Louis.

I arrived in the dead of winter. I'd had this idea I'd rent a cheap furnished apartment but arrived to find that kind of thing didn't exist in St. Louis at the time. I ended up renting an expensive (for me) apartment and borrowing $2,000 from my father just to get myself set up. I nearly starved before I got my first paycheck after three weeks.

McDonnell Aircraft was a huge facility adjacent to Lindbergh Field in an industrial park in the suburbs around St. Louis. Junior employees parked the farthest distance from the main plant. One of my first investments was a huge brown corduroy coat lined in fake fur, the reverse of the garment I'd worn to battle Bertie Jones. The thing must have weighed 20 pounds but I needed every ounce of it as protection against the frigid St. Louis winter.

I'd arrive each day in darkness at the farthest reach of parking lot and scuttle like a little gnome in my huge coat, hat, mittens, and boots through a half mile of slush to my desk. By the time I left, night had fallen. I'd tramp back out again in my heavy wrappings. When the days grew longer in the torrid, humid summer, I was wringing wet with sweat by the time I reached my place at work.

Once inside, you entered 1984. Each floor of the three buildings accommodated five thousand workers in row after row of desks stretched out in parallel lines. Each identical desk had a phone and a male employee in a white short-sleeved shirt, dark slacks, and a skinny tie.

The specification department, where I reported to work, was an especially dreary place. The job of writing descriptions for every part of every machine the company built was very important and incredibly tedious. Badly written specifications cost the company a lot of money. If the descriptions of components for the aircraft were not precise, the subcontractor could deliver a part that was useless and still have a case for blaming McDonnell for the mistake.

My coworkers were mostly bitter, middle-aged men whose undistinguished engineering careers had led the company to dump them at this dead end. Any decent engineer would be designing the aircraft components, not writing the specifications for them. But these men weren't very good engineers. They weren't very good writers either, and they weren't very happy about any of it.

Enter bright-eyed Donna eager to make her mark on the world. No wonder they hated me instantly.

My skills were actually perfect for this job. My engineering training helped me understand the designs and materials the engineers wanted described. Also I was the only person in the department with any training as a writer. I quickly vaulted over my colleagues in my boss's eyes based simply on the clarity of my writing.

After a couple of months, my boss called me into his office to offer me increased responsibilities. Basically he wanted me to teach the engineers how write. I was thrilled to be given such an important assignment so soon after I'd arrived in the department. I was determined to do a thorough job.

My desk was a hive of industry when I became the group's new editor. I'd read my colleagues' work and send it back to them with comments and suggestions on cleaning up the grammar and the word choice. I noted when a sentence was illogical and offered a clearer alternative so my colleagues could learn from their mistakes. I wasn't always Miss Bright and Cheerful. If I saw the same kind of mistake over and over again in a writer's work, I could be blunt about my displeasure.

About two weeks into this project, my boss summoned me into his office.

"They say either you go or they do," he said.

I was stunned and furious. I'd worked very hard. I thought I was doing such a good job.

"Look, you're absolutely right in everything you're telling them," he said. "You just need to tell it to them differently. You can't rub their noses in their mistakes."

"I just wanted them to learn."

"These guys don't want to learn. They just want to get by and go home. You've got to figure out a way to get them to fix their worst mistakes," he said. "It doesn't have to be perfect."

"It doesn't have to be perfect?" I was astonished.

"It only has to be good enough so we don't lose money. You and I can't write all these specs by ourselves," he said. "We need those guys. Figure out how to get them to fix their biggest problems and figure out how to make them like it."

Thinking about it now, I realize how irritating I must have been to them. Here I was, this twenty-one-year-old pipsqueak just out of college telling them how to do their job. The fact that I was female surely made it even worse. How was I ever going to make them enjoy this? I thought as I made my way back to my desk.

One thing every man likes is a pretty girl apologizing to him. It was so galling to say I was sorry for something I really wasn't sorry for. But there I was batting my eyelashes and seeking forgiveness from men I didn't respect.

"I'm sorry." Bat. Bat. "I'm pretty green at this." Bat. Bat. Bat. "I guess I was way out of line. If you wouldn't just mind please fixing this one little sentence. If it's not too much trouble." Bat. Bat. Bat.

We ended up with specs that weren't perfect, but they weren't a disaster either.

At the six-month mark, I'd paid off enough of my debts to

afford human food again. Months of peanut butter sandwiches were making me gag. To celebrate I bought a juicy steak and a bottle of Lancer's Rose, the absolute pinnacle of fine wine in St. Louis. Sadly I didn't know anyone well enough to invite to share this moment. As I carried my precious cargo up the front walk, the bag broke and my bottle shattered, leaving a sad stream of fuzzy pink wine on the walkway. At least the steak tasted good.

On my next assignment I was with a group of writers who appeared to have very little to do. Even though there wasn't enough work to keep us all busy during the week, we were required to put in overtime on the weekends.

It didn't take much asking around to uncover the answer to this puzzle. The boss, Joe, was an accomplished empire builder. All those weekend overtime hours were to prove his case for more employees. As far as Joe was concerned, the more people he controlled, the more power he wielded.

Almost every day Joe dropped by my desk, enveloping me in a toxic plume of cigar smoke as he leaned close to me for a chat. I was repulsed by the stubby cigar that was a permanent fixture in his chinless mouth. Then he started asking me to join him after work for a drink. I kept putting him off—not only was he obnoxious, he was married—but he persisted. Finally, I figured out how to put a stop to this harassment for good.

I met him at a local watering hole and sat with him at the bar, looking deeply into his eyes.

"Joe," I said tenderly. "I know we're very attracted to each other but it's something we've got to fight."

Joe looked shocked.

"Why?"

"We've got to think of our careers," I said, grabbing his doughy hand with urgency and sincerity. "If we were ever to get involved and someone found out, we'd lose our security clearances and our jobs. You understand, don't you?"

Joe sat up a little straighter on his bar stool and removed the cigar from his mouth for emphasis.

"You're right!" he said, squaring his shoulders with new resolve. "We have to think of our careers."

I was starting to hate my job. Spec writers were treated like second-class citizens by the engineers designing the projects. The engineers who were spec writers considered those without engineering degrees to be even lower down the pecking order. The office atmosphere was a lot less than stimulating. It was petty and even a bit creepy.

The other woman in my department seemed to spend all her time sleeping at her desk. I asked why they still kept her around when she was obviously producing nothing. Someone explained she'd once saved the company a lot of money.

During the Korean War, the Navy had asked McDonnell to put some specific engines on the Banshee jet fighter. McDonnell told the Navy that the engines were underpowered. If they were placed on the Banshee, the plane wouldn't fly. The Navy wrote back and told McDonnell to put the engines on the jet anyway. Well, after they were built they *wouldn't* fly, just as McDonnell predicted. The Navy had to send the jets down the Mississippi River on barges to have them refurbished. When the Navy blamed McDonnell for the error and refused to pay for the work, no one could find a copy of that letter from the Navy. This woman, who was a total packrat, produced a copy, saving the company and thereby guaranteeing her job for life.

Hearing that story was something of a turning point for me. To think that you could have one moment of clerical glory and spend the rest of your professional life sleeping at your desk was scary. It was a reminder to me that at one point in my life I'd had very big plans. That, coupled with my repulsion at the corporate and personal shenanigans transpiring around me, demonstrated to me that those dreams never really died. It didn't take long to revive them and put my life back on track.

I was certain I could do as well as some of the engineers I was working with. In fact, in writing the specifications for the F-111 fighter aircraft, I picked up a couple of engineering errors and attempted to point them out to the designer. But without an engineering degree no one would take me seriously. I reapplied to the University of Oklahoma and was accepted again in the aerospace engineering department. I took a leave of absence from McDonnell in 1964 to complete my engineering degree.

This time I was more mature and had fewer distractions, although I still had a major block about circuit diagrams. I eked out a D in Advanced Electrical Engineering by promising the professor I'd never touch anything electrical as long as I lived if he'd just let me pass. I graduated in the spring of 1965 with the bachelor's in Aerospace/Mechanical Engineering I should have earned two years earlier. My self-esteem soared as my dream came back into focus. I returned to St. Louis ready to finally use my skills.

But when I got back to McDonnell I was still in the spec department, working for a buddy of my old cigar-smoking boss, Joe. I applied for a transfer to the aerodynamics department but my boss refused to let me go. I stormed into his office to protest.

"You're my best spec writer," he said. "You can quit but I won't transfer you."

Then I'll quit, I thought, and started interviewing other companies.

A few weeks later a memo came around from the senior vice

president of McDonnell. "It has come to my attention," he wrote, "that employees are being prevented from transferring. This will cease." I put the memo and my transfer request side by side on my boss's desk. He glared at me and made vague threats, but signed my transfer.

At last I was an aerodynamicist! After a few months working on an airplane proposal, I got transferred to helping develop the proposal for a NASA mission to Mars that would land in 1971. This was a big project with two orbiters and two landers and was supervised by the Jet Propulsion Laboratory in California.

My part of the proposal was to study possible shapes for the entry vehicle and analyze the incoming trajectories. I was spacestruck again, just as I had been as a teenager. When I came to work each morning, sitting down at my desk was a pleasure. I could envision my shape hitting the entry corridor just right, cutting through the Martian atmosphere, and landing safely on the surface of Mars. I happily put in long hours calculating every angle and parameter. To me, there was no better job in the world than to come into work every day and mentally leave the Earth as you devised the safest vehicle and best route for your trip into space.

As the proposal was nearing completion, a panic seized me. What if McDonnell didn't get the contract to build this? Then I'd be back designing airplanes. JPL would manage the Mars mission contract no matter which aerospace contractor got the nod from NASA. And, lo and behold, I saw an advertisement for a job as an aerodynamist at JPL in the *St. Louis Post-Dispatch.*

JPL told me to come for an interview with the supervisor of the aerodynamics group. Then, three days before my job interview, there was an airline strike. JPL wired me not to come because they couldn't guarantee a flight for me. Just a minor glitch as far as I was concerned. I went to the St. Louis airport and took a standby flight to Los Angeles. The plane landed on a sparkling southern California summer day. JPL had originally reserved a room for me at the Huntington Hotel, a grand old place full of beautifully restored antiques and rich Oriental rugs in an elegant old Pasadena neighborhood, and the hotel honored the reservation. The aerodynamics group supervisor was awfully surprised when I called him from my hotel room, but he agreed to see me.

JPL made a dramatic first impression on me. My eye was so used to the flat expanses of the Midwest. Here was a bustling space science laboratory like a sprawling college campus set up against the mountains. I wanted this job even before I went for the interview.

Clearly 1966 was a boom period in aerospace. I'd received several job offers before I arrived at JPL. Every other company representative who had interviewed me for a job glanced briefly at my résumé and started trying to sell me on the company. In contrast, this supervisor grilled me about everything I claimed I could do. The interview was like taking your orals in graduate school. I told him I'd been working on a Martian entry vehicle shape.

"It says here you can run six degrees of freedom computer program," he said. "How do you do that? How much of the equations did you write?"

When I got out of the interview I was starstruck for real. What a place, I thought. I wonder if they'd let me work there.

It turned out that the JPL supervisor's boss, impressed with my chutzpah in flying out during the airline strike, persuaded the supervisor to hire me. They made an offer (the lowest one I got) and I jumped at it. I crammed all my worldly goods into my minute, green Austin Healy Sprite and drove across the desert to Los Angeles in the middle of an incredible August heat wave. The Sprite had a thin firewall between the engine and my feet. Even though I'd added extra insulation, I blazed across the desert with my feet making their own burning descent into JPL's atmosphere. I didn't care how hot it was. I was on my way to Mars. Little did I realize it would take me thirty-one years to get there.

3

Learning to Love Robots

I hung a long pole with a little model at the end over the stream of air that blasted up from the bottom of the vertical wind tunnel. When the model was spinning fast enough, I yanked a cord to cut loose my Martian entry vehicle, the same shape that had gotten me back into engineering three years before. The little model spun and rocked back and forth, levitated by the blast of air. It was 1967 and my colleagues and I had flown from JPL to NASA's Langley Research Center near Hampton, Virginia, with our one-tenth scale models of the blunt sphere-cone shapes we thought had the best chance of surviving a descent through the Martian atmosphere.

The shape, best compared to a Chinese peasant hat with a round top, would fall from space with the top of the hat first, the Mars lander nestled inside it. The part facing the wind had to be as blunt as possible to create maximum friction and therefore maximum drag. On the other hand, if the shape was too blunt, it would be unstable. Were it to wobble and perhaps even tumble, it couldn't protect the lander. How rounded should the convex bottom be? If we sharpened the shoulder to create more drag as it fell through the atmosphere, the edges might melt as heat built up from the friction. I'd worked on shapes ranging from the Chinese peasant hat to a dunce cap at McDonnell, and at JPL we'd been playing with them for a year, one of the best years of my life thus far.

The sixties were a time of enormous growth for the space program and hence for JPL. The lab was hiring young engineers by the dozens to work on Mariners 6 and 7, which would pass Mars in 1969, and to gear up for the 1971 Mars landing. Most of the new employees were moving to California right out of college, creating an energetic and highly social population. When I arrived at JPL in 1966 I was the only female with an engineering degree there out of about 2,000 engineers, although there were women mathematicians and at least one scientist. The article about women engineers in the University of Oklahoma student paper had come true. JPL was a great place to meet men. As a spec writer and junior engineer in St. Louis I'd been unable to afford my flying hobby, and flying in the smoggy, crowded airspace over Los Angeles held little appeal. JPL's skiing club and sailing crowd offered me two other aerodynamic pastimes. I was having such a good time I didn't even mind the math.

The fact that working on these Martian entry shapes was completely untrodden ground compensated for the fact I spent my whole day crunching numbers. I was running the six degrees of freedom equations simulating how the shape would rotate on three axes as it was buffeted by the Martian atmosphere. The problem was we could only guess at what that atmosphere would be.

We knew it was incredibly thin. When Mariner 4 went behind the planet in July 1965, its radio signal cut off abruptly instead of the gradual fade it would do if the signal had to fight its way through a thicker atmosphere, such as that surrounding Earth. The guess was that it was somewhere between 1 and 10 percent as thick as Earth's. Most scientists had discarded Lowell's idea that the changing patterns on Mars's surface signified a Martian harvest, although a few clung to the idea that the "waves of darkening" might be some form of vegetation. A 1963 spectrometer reading from the telescope at Mt. Wilson on an exceptionally clear night when Mars was close to Earth showed virtually no water vapor but plenty of carbon dioxide. Plants "breathe" carbon dioxide, but plant life as we knew it could never survive in those arid conditions. Another popular theory about Mars's seasonal patterns was that the planet suffered severe dust storms that could last for weeks. That said, would the winds of the weak Martian atmosphere be as strong as those on Earth? Or could they be even stronger?

It seems almost laughable to think back on the conditions we worked under in designing this shape. These were the days before small, fast computers on everyone's desktop. When I first got to JPL, some people (all women) were actually called computers. They solved the trajectory analysis and aerodynamic calculations by brute force, punching in lengthy equations in a room full of noisy mechanical calculators. Within a year of when I was hired, the lab bought a room-size computer on which we could reserve time.

We fed our equations into the computer on trays of

punched cards. Woe betide you if you tripped on the way to the computer building, as I once did, panicking as I tried to get the cards back in sequence before our run time was to begin.

We did rough estimates as to what to expect from our computer runs on slide rules, as there were no electronic calculators. Keypunch operators frequently made mistakes punching in the long strings of symbols and numbers. One error in the sequence would invalidate the entire run. Two days later, we'd get back stacks of computer paper and discover the error only after combing through page after page of data. Then we'd need to schedule the run again. Many times we decided it was safer just to key in the data ourselves. Today a single designer can model an entire mission in one sitting at a modern workstation.

Even with all the calculations in the world, wind tunnel tests were still necessary. My entry vehicle shape caught the stream of air, bobbing and weaving back and forth as the wind tunnel operator played with the velocity while we recorded the whole thing on a 16 millimeter movie camera. Later we'd analyze this film frame by frame to compare the results to our theories. Our competitors from Langley, who were working on an entry body shape of their own, stood beside us at the plate glass window, just as interested as we were in what our models would do.

Langley called their design a tension shell. With the way its sides cut sharply in from the shoulders to join a rounded tip, it looked more like a nipple. It had more drag than our sphere-cone, but if it wobbled only a couple of degrees it would tumble out of control. Our cone could swing over a range of ten or twenty degrees without becoming unstable. Thirty years later when Pathfinder flew to Mars, its lander was encased in the same blunt sphere-cone shape I'd worked on from 1966 through 1968.

My colleagues and I had narrowed down the parameters of the entry vehicle shape and calculated a range of entry conditions that we thought would make for a successful landing, and we were planning a full-scale program to design and test the vehicle. Suddenly Congress cut the funding, saying the project was too expensive and ambitious. This was my first brush with the political vicissitudes of the space business. There are about a hundred projects envisioned for every one that actually makes it into space. This political skirmish had an immediate impact on me. I was out of a job.

I had just finished my master's degree in Aerospace Engineering at night school at the University of Southern California. I had naively thought when I came to JPL, which is part of the California Institute of Technology, that I'd be able to go to school at Caltech. Wrong. Not only did Caltech not admit women, it didn't accept part-time students. Now, shiny new degree or not, I was JPL's junior aerodynamicist and thus the most expendable.

One of my friends tipped me off to an aerodynamics job with a small private company in a nearby town. I spent six months working on airplane wing shapes in a company run out of the owner's house. When I discovered he was using this wacky idea that he had me working on—attaching simulated feathers to the tips of airplane wings—to bilk the government, I quit on the spot. It was just unimaginable to me that anyone could do such bad work, lie, and cheat and still face himself in the mirror every day. To me the point of all of this was to advance knowledge. The boss had actually tried to get me to fudge my aerodynamic analysis results to support the theory he was selling to the government. I wanted to get back into the space business in the worst way. I was still sailing and skiing with my JPL buddies, so I started calling them for job tips. Within a week I landed a job in the JPL trajectory analysis section.

I'd never done trajectory analysis, but it seemed reasonable to assume I could enjoy plotting a path between the planets. Each object the spacecraft will pass has its own gravitational field. The gravitational pull an object has is proportional to its size and distance from the spacecraft. Planets aren't perfect spheres; they tend to be squashed a bit at the poles and fat around the equator. Sometimes they're lumpy and this means the gravitational field around a planet isn't smooth. Trajectory analysts have to factor in which part of the planet the spacecraft passes to determine how much gravitational pull it will encounter. To make an accurate trajectory, the analyst also calculates the number of photons, tiny energy particles from the sun, that will hit the spacecraft. In space even a particle that small exerts a force.

While some might see trajectory work as an intriguing three-dimensional math challenge, I unfortunately found it unbelievably tedious. I wanted to understand a whole system, not just one piece. Also, I wasn't working on a real mission as most of my friends were. I was studying missions for the far future. My office mate and I ended up switching jobs and I spent two years designing an automated drug identification system to combat the nation's newly exploding drug problem.

In February and March of 1969, JPL launched Mariners 6 and 7. Just ten days after man first walked on the moon, Mariner 6 started sending pictures back of Mars's equator and seven days later Mariner 7 photographed the southern polar cap. Spectrometer readings of the polar cap found only dry ice— frozen carbon dioxide. It detected none of the nitrogen and

1944, Daddy and me at Grandmother's house—ready to send him off to the Pacific.

Miss Wynnewood of 1961.

The Airknockers, the University of Oklahoma Flying Club, 1958: Pete Howard, our instructor, is on the left. Gene Nora Stumbough and I are seated at the right.

Al Hibbs, the Senior Voice of Mariner 10, and me, the Junior Voice, at JPL in 1974.

The Little Blue Rover takes a stroll in the Arroyo Seco next to JPL.

Robby looms over Rocky 3 and members of Dave Miller's Robotic Intelligence Group, 1992.

Rocky 3 entertains kids at the Planetary Society's Rover Expo in Washington, D.C., 1992.

Rocky 4.3, decked out in computer and cables, places the Alpha Proton X-Ray Spectrometer on a rock in the sandbox at JPL, 1993.

THE ROVER TEAM, July 1992, on the mall at JPL. Rocky 4 is in the front center. Lin Sukamto is at the far left. Bill Dias is fifth from the left. Ron Banes is seventh from left, and Tom Rivellini is in front of Ron, in the dark shirt. A bearded Brian Wilcox is in the middle of the back row, peering over the shoulder of the short fellow in the suit. Don Bickler is looking over the other shoulder and I'm just in front of Don. Henry Stone is to my left and then come Bill Layman, Jake Matijevic, and Howard Eisen.

THE ROVER TEAM, 1995. Front row, from left: Brian Cooper, the rover driver, Jake Matijevic, Lin Sukamto. Two technicians are behind Marie Curie, the spare rover. Next to them are Andy Mishkin, the backup rover driver, and Scot Stride, the radio technician. In the back row, left to right: A mobility consultant, Hank Moore (with cap), Tam Nguyen, and four mobility and power people. Ron Banes is in the very back peering over Howard Eisen's shoulder (Howard has his arms crossed). Next to Howard is Ken Jewett who designed the featherweight rocker bogies. Henry Stone is in front of Ken Jewett and behind Andy Mishkin. Standing on the far right are Jack Morrison, the programmer of Sojourner's brain, and Allan Sirota, the rover system integration engineer.

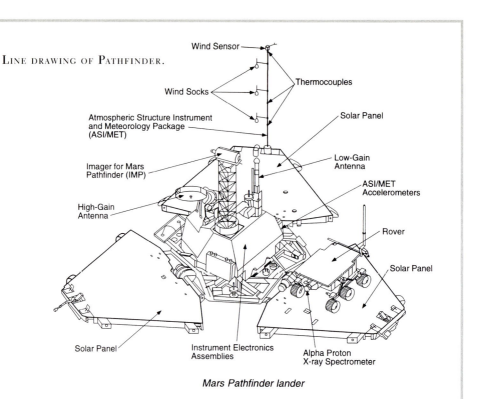

Wind Sensor

Thermocouples

Wind Socks

Atmospheric Structure Instrument
and Meteorology Package
(ASI/MET)

Solar Panel

Imager for Mars
Pathfinder (IMP)

Low-Gain
Antenna

ASI/MET
Accelerometers

High-Gain
Antenna

Rover

Solar Panel

Solar Panel

Instrument Electronics
Assemblies

Alpha Proton
X-ray Spectrometer

Mars Pathfinder lander

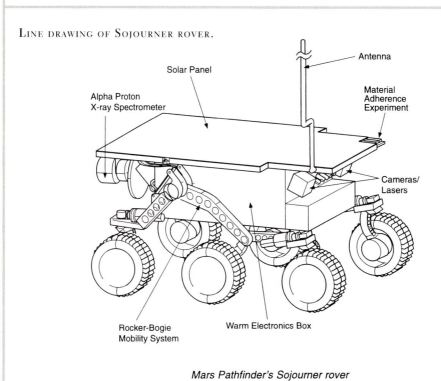

Antenna

Solar Panel

Material
Adherence
Experiment

Alpha Proton
X-ray Spectrometer

Cameras/
Lasers

Rocker-Bogie
Mobility System

Warm Electronics Box

Mars Pathfinder's Sojourner rover

Part of the Mobility team in "bunny suits" assemble Sojourner in the clean room at JPL, 1996. Howard Eisen is on the right.

Closing the petals on Pathfinder in 1996 at Cape Canaveral, closely supervised by a crowd of bunny-suited engineers and technicians. Last glimpse of the rover before landing.

Running the rover for a space fan. Dan Goldin, NASA's administrator, makes a point to Vice President Al Gore at JPL in 1996. Ed Stone, the Director of JPL is to my right.

Preparing to launch Mars Global Surveyor from Cape Canaveral, Florida, November 1996. Glenn Cunningham, the MGS Project Manager is at the far left. Norm Haynes, my boss as Director of Mars Exploration, is at the back right. Finding me is like looking for Waldo. I'm about eleventh in from the left, peeking between two guys in white shirts.

July 4, 1997. First color picture from Pathfinder. Sojourner squats on the lander's petal with the twin peaks in the background.

July 5, 1997. All six wheels on soil next to Barnacle Bill.

July 8, 1997. Sojourner samples Yogi.

A rover's eye view of the lander on Mars.

ammonia gases that are vital to life as we understand it, nor any water. Ultraviolet sensors onboard both of the Mariners recorded intense levels of radiation from the sun, making it pretty hard to sustain the position that life, even plant life, existed on Mars.

While the news about conditions on the surface of Mars was discouraging for those who'd hoped for some form of life there, the encouraging part was that our spacecraft were proving they could go the distance. None of the seven missions the Soviets had sent to Mars by then had succeeded. The United States was three for four. The big Mars landing project was dead, but NASA contracted with JPL to send a Mariner to Venus and Mercury in 1973. The drug identification system, part of JPL's civil systems program, had proved to be unfeasible with 1970 technology and I wanted to get back in space. Through my social contacts I was hired as the Mariner Venus-Mercury 1973 mission analyst.

Mission analysts are the utility infielders of space mission development. The mission analyst looks around and sees what part of the mission needs fixing and fixes it. In fact when I walked into my boss's office and asked what my duties were, he said: "It is customary to define your own job."

I put myself in charge of picking the launch date for Mariner Venus-Mercury, or MVM73 for short. Every mission has a launch period, a length of time when the orbital dance of the planets lines them up so that they are reachable from Earth with affordable rockets. The normal process is to set the launch date as early as possible in that period so that if there are any weather delays or mechanical difficulties, the mission can still be launched before the period closes. Our period was the four weeks between mid-October and mid-November. Each launch date affected the trajectory, which, in turn, changed when the spacecraft would arrive at Venus or how much of Mercury would be visible during the subsequent swing-by. That meant different launch dates were better or worse for some of the experiments. In order to recommend a specific day, I had to understand what the scientists wanted from this mission so everyone could get at least some of what they wanted.

JPL had gambled that we could fly MVM73 for a very low cost—$98 million—and could afford only one spacecraft. So the scientists had to wring the most from this single opportunity. There were seven principal investigators on the mission. Some of them were just about the prickliest and most stubborn people imaginable and had interests directly in conflict with each other. Just before I was hired on they'd battled over which side of Mercury to fly by. Trajectory analysis showed that, as the spacecraft approached, Mercury would be half lit with the sun coming from the left. The camera people of course wanted to fly on the sunlit side so they could photograph. The particles and fields people wanted to fly on the dark side so they could test for the presence of an ionosphere and magnetic field. They had already decided to fly on the dark side of the planet and use two very long telephoto lenses to photograph approach and departure. But there were still plenty of issues to be fought out.

The years between 1970 and 1973 helped me perfect my communications skills. One of my jobs became explaining the science to the engineers who were building the spacecraft and designing the trajectories, and describing the limitations of the spacecraft to the scientists with the goal of satisfying all of them. In searching for a way to communicate the impact of one launch day versus another, I realized the only language both sides understood was mathematics. A friend suggested I devise equations to communicate the importance of the different dates. In some ways these equations, which I called value functions, were just nonsense equations but they got across the points I was trying to make.

I'd ask a scientist to rate where a particular scientific objective ranked for his instrument. For instance, how important did he believe it was to take pictures of the Earth and the moon after launch to calibrate the camera for looking at Venus and Mercury? Was seeing them as important as seeing a larger portion of Mercury in sunlight on the fly-by? I'd give these "goodness" parameters a numeric value and work out an equation that represented launch date versus goodness on a scale of zero to one.

This was a slow process and it took almost two years before each science team had a value function that it agreed on. When we had agreed upon a number, I added up all the equations to get a total science value for each launch date. Amazingly, there was a single day—November 3, 1973—which was best for all seven experiments. The next two days were almost as good, so we had a little cushion for glitches. Recommending November 3 was recommending risk. The project manager would have to agree to throw away two weeks of our four-week period. If any weather or mechanical problems prevented us from launching on November 3, 4, or 5, we could slip into the later part of the launch period, which was not good for science. I was proud when the project manager chose my launch date. For a long time the only thing I had on my wall that signified a real accomplishment at JPL was the letter that said we were launching on November 3.

After that I was promoted to MVM project engineer and I found myself supervising people who were working on something it was almost impossible for me to understand. Mariner 10 was the first mission to try out the idea of gravity assist, which had been developed in the 1960s. The theory was that if you flew by a planet—say Venus—at just the right distance and angle, the planet's gravity would pull the spacecraft in and swing it around so the spacecraft's trajectory would change. The gravity of the planet would act like a stationary ice skater clutching the hand of a skater whizzing by, swinging her around and releasing her in a new direction. The change in trajectory, if it was accomplished just right, would propel the spacecraft onward without it having to carry as much fuel as it would need if the flight path were directly from Earth to Mercury.

Hitting that spot was like trying to thread a needle from 50 million miles away. The trajectory analysts calculated that each one-mile miss in hitting the invisible target translated into a thousand-mile error in reaching Mercury. I could grasp the concepts but since I was still doing my own mission analysis work I didn't have time to understand the math in detail. I had to trust the navigators. Similarly, I had to trust the other people on the Mission Design Section's MVM team of which I was the leader. The trajectory analysts, and the people who designed the software to point the instruments, and the people who wrote the software to send commands to the spacecraft were all experts and really could only review each other's work in detail.

When you are managing really brilliant, creative people, at some point you find it's impossible to command or control them because you can't understand what they are doing. Once they've gone beyond your ability to understand them, you have a choice to make as a manager. You can limit them and the project by your intelligence, which I think is the wrong way to do it. Or you can trust and use your management skills to keep them focused on the goal.

A lot of bad managers get threatened when their "subordinates" know more than they do. They either hire people who are inferior to them so they can always feel in control or they bottleneck people who know something they don't so they can maintain control. The whole project suffers from the manager's insecurities.

I knew I couldn't validate the gravity assist team's math, but the three members of the team could check each other's. It was one of the most useful lessons I ever learned as a manager: knowing when to step back.

There was a lot of tension in the air on the humid November night in Florida when MVM was awaiting its launch. I had been at Cape Canaveral for several days because I was working with the range safety officer, the person who monitors the rocket as it leaves Earth's atmosphere. His finger is on the button that can blow up the rocket if there is a danger that it will fail and crash into an inhabited area. My job was to make sure he knew exactly when to get nervous. We didn't want him to press the button unless he absolutely had to.

Two years before, Mariner 8 had failed when launched from an Atlas/Centaur rocket identical to the one engulfed in vapor on the floodlit launchpad. Fortunately Mariner 9 had stood at the ready and was launched successfully two weeks later to send us our most spectacular and surprising photos of Mars thus far. The canyons and volcanoes that emerged after the global dust storm cleared showed a world that almost certainly at one point in its mysterious history had water and might even have some form of microbes surviving still. MVM, if the gravity assist trajectory worked, would give us insight into the geological history of Mercury and Venus as well. With only one spacecraft, we had only one chance. Nothing could go wrong with this launch.

In the launch control area I had a console next to the project manager's so I could advise him on what to do if we were unable to launch that night. My mouth was dry and my heart was pounding during the slow countdown. The launch team, and the flight team back in Pasadena whom we could see on the monitors, stared intently at their consoles as the moment of launch approached, making sure that the numbers were within the right ranges. Finally, the launch commentator intoned, "ten, nine, eight, . . ."

Suddenly, everybody in the Cape launch control room bolted from their consoles and ran outside to see the rocket actually take off. I stayed frozen, staring at the screen that showed the rocket and its precious payload gleaming in the arc lights. "Three, two, one, *zero*. And we have liftoff." I still didn't move. Somehow, I was convinced that if I took my eyes off the image of the rocket, it would fail. I sat there, willing it into space.

It must have worked because the Atlas/Centaur roared off the launchpad in a ball of flame and headed off flawlessly. As soon as the spacecraft was on the right trajectory to Venus, had freed itself from the launch vehicle shroud and started communicating with Earth, the mission name was changed from MVM73 to Mariner 10. We were official.

As soon as we were official, I added another duty. I joined Al Hibbs—who had served JPL for years as its "voice" on radio and television science shows—as the junior voice of Mariner 10, describing its frightful space odyssey for the media. My main job after launch was being part of the team that controlled the spacecraft. As it turned out the flawless launch was to be the only trouble-free moment in this calamitous mission. It seemed as if we were always just patching Mariner 10 together long enough to get it on to the next phase and the next crisis. It was ultimately a very successful mission; the spacecraft just broke all the time.

The star tracker, which was supposed to keep the star Canopus in view at all times to navigate correctly, kept seeing strange, bright particles. When the star tracker followed the bright particles the spacecraft was thrown off its orientation. It would get confused, shut everything down and call for help. The particles turned out to be the heat-reflective paint flaking off the high gain antenna and they continued to plague us through most of the mission.

The gyroscopes that were supposed to stabilize the spacecraft and tell us where we were weren't working either. We figured out how to do maneuvers without turning the spacecraft, because every time we turned the spacecraft we risked a failure of the gyroscopes. By January, before MVM even reached Venus, its first target, it was operating on backup power and had accidentally jettisoned most of the attitude control gas used to balance the angle, or attitude, of the spacecraft when it drifts off course. But the engineers refused to give up on their mission to hit a very narrow sliver of the space near Venus and swing on to Mercury.

The guidance and control team carefully examined what was still working on the spacecraft. The two solar arrays that provided power for the spacecraft stuck out from the sides like Dutch windmill vanes. They were designed to rotate into a position so they could catch the maximum solar energy while near the Earth. They could also tilt away from the sun as the spacecraft got closer to it on its way to Venus and Mercury. The guidance team figured out how to "solar sail" by using the force of the photons tapping on the solar arrays to balance and steer the spacecraft.

By differentially rotating the arrays, the solar sailors used these minuscule bits of energy to turn the spacecraft like a windmill. Calibrating the photon wind as Mariner 10 passed different celestial bodies required a lot of advance planning. The spacecraft had to be constantly monitored to make sure it didn't turn too fast or the attitude control gas jets would fire, wasting the little bit that was left. The spacecraft was controlled most of the time by programs in the onboard computer. These control programs told the spacecraft step by step what to do: "Point the scan platform here, point the high gain antenna there, turn on instrument X," all at exact times matched to where the spacecraft was in its trajectory. The onboard computer was very primitive. It only had 512 *words* of memory. Today even a computer with 512,000 words of memory is passé. Every single command had to count and the control team negotiations about these commands were heated. When things went wrong we'd have to replan and reprogram and retest everything.

Everyone was working long hours. The guidance and control team spent much of the mission sleeping on tables in the control room. There were no days off and the days were often as long as twenty hours. Like troops in a war the operations teams grew very close. In addition to arguing and making fun of each other we occasionally partied as only the young can. One memorable morning my group ended a long session making breakfast at my house after several drinks at a local bar. It took me days to get all the egg off my kitchen ceiling.

The members of my group had a habit of writing down silly

statements that people made and posting them on the walls of the meeting room. Periodically these statements were compiled into a book, called the Mission Fules Document (a takeoff on the official Mission Rules Document). As we passed Venus in February of 1974, for instance, a cartoon appeared on the wall showing the spacecraft panting, "So much for the *secondary* objective." A solar sailor contributed: "I wish there were a day called 'Grunday' between Sunday and Monday so we could have a day off."

As we approached Mercury things got ever more frantic. Solar sailing was working, but the attitude control gas was perilously limited. The gyroscopes were still questionable but we were dependent on them to fly on the dark side of Mercury where the sun sensor wouldn't work. The high gain antenna had failed mysteriously before Venus. The detailed pictures of Mercury the spacecraft was designed to transmit needed that powerful signal. There wasn't enough memory onboard the spacecraft to store the images, so they had to be sent back in real time. The investment in the camera's telephoto lenses, and in a lot of sophisticated equipment added to the big Deep Space Network antenna in the California desert, would be wasted if the high gain antenna didn't work. As the junior voice I dreaded announcing over the NASA radio that we had only a few pictures from Mercury. Miraculously, probably due to the higher temperatures as we neared the sun, the antenna healed itself. The imaging team breathed huge sighs of relief as pictures of Mercury came streaming in.

The mission was completely successful. Mariner 10 looped around Venus, threading the needle precisely despite the navigational challenges. It went on to encounter Mercury on March 30,

1974, and then return to Mercury not once but twice in the next year.

In all it returned nearly 3,500 pictures of Venus and 2,400 of Mercury before it was turned off on March 24, 1975, a year and a half after it was launched. Ultraviolet pictures of Venus revealed a swirling pattern of clouds rotating rapidly (once every four Earth days) around the planet. The clouds move in the direction opposite to the planet's slow rotation—one Venus day is 243 Earth-days long.

Mercury, as expected, looks like the moon: heavily cratered with large, flat circular basins showing evidence of the early bombardment of the inner solar system by meteors. Mercury has no atmosphere, also as expected, but the big surprise was the magnetic field. No one had expected a tiny planet like Mercury to still have a liquid core, which is the main mechanism to produce a magnetic field. But, nevertheless, Mariner 10 found a small one. Probably the rocks have particles aligned with the former field and "remember" when Mercury in its youth had an active core.

We also made discoveries about how to do difficult projects with teams of creative people. We built close-knit, hardworking, and productive teams of scientists and engineers, of quasigovernment employees and contractors, of programmers of primitive computers inventing a new trade and managers inventing new contracting and cost-control concepts. To this day those of us who went through Mariner 10 operations share a special bond forged of hardship and humor.

The constraints were incredible. At $98 million Mariner 10 was the lowest-cost planetary mission ever attempted at the time. We had to launch on time or miss the opportunity altogether to get our cosmic pinball boost from Venus to Mercury. We had to operate with the people we had—making up for what we lacked in numbers with cleverness, enthusiasm, and dogged determination not to let the spacecraft die.

Before Mariner 10 completed its third swing-by of Mercury, my career took a detour, as did the careers of many of us working on space missions at the lab. During the 1970s oil crisis, I led a group of engineers, economists, and policy analysts writing plans to develop alternative energy. We were bitterly disappointed to see them ignored when Ronald Reagan took over the White House and declared the energy crisis over. In some ways I was glad of the regular hours after the intensity of Mariner 10. I'd fallen in love and married another JPL engineer. My daughter, Laura, came along in February of 1977. I took off six weeks after her birth and then worked half-time for another nine months. After Laura was weaned and we'd found good day care, I went back to work full-time. But there was a problem: I couldn't seem to get a reasonable assignment. My boss made a few queries and found out that many managers at JPL now assumed I was "fulfilled as a mother" and didn't want a "real job." A couple of meetings with them straightened that out, but the episode made me start thinking about my future. I realized I'd again lost my direction. My real passion was still space.

In October 1979, I got a job leading a small mission design study to orbit Saturn and drop probes into the atmosphere of both Saturn and its large and mysterious moon Titan. From there I moved to a study on how to make military space satellites more autonomous through better computer fault protection.

For fifteen months I managed the ninety or so engineers

doing all of JPL's trajectory analysis and mission design, but I didn't like line management. I wanted to work on projects. When I heard that my voice partner, Al Hibbs, was running a study generating ideas for a space station, I begged Al to let me help him out part-time on the station study. Within a couple of months I was the full-time leader and back in space.

The idea of a space station was near and dear to the hearts of many engineers who, much like myself, had sparked their youthful imaginations on Wernher von Braun's orbiting launch platform. I too had examined *Collier's* magazine's detailed drawings on the porch swing at Auntie and Unkie's house, imagining myself walking through its corridors. The astronauts from *The Sands of Mars* had taken off from one. Space stations were further reinforced in the popular imagination by the movie *2001*, made from Arthur C. Clarke's novella.

Just like in *The Sands of Mars* the station could serve as a rest stop along the route. Experiments there on the physical effects of long-term weightlessness were a perfect way to prepare for the seven-month journey to Mars. The space station could also be a source of income for NASA, many hoped. Astronauts could perform experiments for private companies, something for which we could charge a substantial price and also answer the political clamor for making space exploration revenue-producing. If NASA was actually making money in space, perhaps political enthusiasm would build around space exploration again.

Such a large project would be a complex engineering problem, and involve JPL in working on a human space project for the first time. JPL basically exists to serve the investigative efforts of scientists; we build and fly the machines that make their research possible. For years scientists had been complaining that the humans crawling all over the space shuttle made it incredibly hard to work with. Each experiment had to be human rated, meaning the scientists had to prove that even the smallest instrument was absolutely safe to the astronauts on board.

I once saw a picture of a guy standing next to a stack of paperwork one and a half times as tall as he was. The caption explained these were the documents he'd had to fill out to prove his instrument was safe enough to be placed on the shuttle. We wanted to serve the scientists by helping to make the space station, which was envisioned as being as big as a football field, user friendly.

We also wanted the station to include instrument platforms orbiting near the station but with no humans to jiggle the experiments. Plus, scientists needed a platform orbiting from north to south rather than in an equatorial orbit so they could observe the whole Earth from space. We were most interested in providing the robots to help astronauts assembling the space station and to tend the automated platforms that humans couldn't reach. NASA authorized the design of robots to be called Flight Telerobotic Servicers or FTS.

NASA wanted a robot that could fly alongside the space station assembling pieces or handing tools to the astronauts. To work around people the FTS would have to be autonomous and well behaved. It couldn't grab the tool and swing it so fast that the astronaut would be knocked out. These tasks, which are so simple for humans, required huge advances in robotics.

Each one of those judgments presents an increasingly more complex engineering problem: pattern recognition, interpretation, and decision making. Actual control of robotic motion requires yet another set of skills. Robotics is such an interdisciplinary science that several different teams of engineers must work together to make even a small advance in capability.

Although I'd never been a robotics engineer, through the space station I was learning to love robots. Anthropomorphic robots like the FTS could construct and repair things in Earth orbit, and future planetary spacecraft, especially those crawling on the surface of planets, could use much of the same technology. When JPL was looking for a person to pull the lab's automation and robotics technology activities into a coherent program, I volunteered.

JPL was the lead center in NASA for robotics, but several other centers were working in various aspects of the technology. I saw the FTS work as a way to pull together the disparate NASA efforts. The head of NASA's technology organization at headquarters in Washington was enthusiastic about the idea and I ended up developing a plan for an integrated NASA automation and robotics program.

The program's long-term goals included laboratory demonstrations of the key technologies. The robotics lab was usually humming, literally, when I entered for one of my apprenticeships in robots or to bring visitors to view JPL's progress. I found myself charmed by the toy shop atmosphere.

Robot arms of various sizes and complexities spilled wiry intestines onto the floor. Technicians could make a piece of equipment to order on the lathes and drill presses that were tucked into corners of the lab. Presiding over this mess of activity was Tony Bejczy, the grand old man of robotics at JPL. Tony had worked in everything from a rickety trailer to a well-appointed lab. Times were relatively flush when I managed the automation and robotics program from 1985 through 1987. Our budget doubled almost every year. Tony Bejczy's group was working on a robotic arm for the space shuttle as well as on technology for the FTS. If I was lucky, the engineers in Tony's lab would be running an experiment and I would see an arm pick up an object, turn it around, and fit it into a hole.

In another lab, suspended on a cable from a beam, hung a 5-foot-by-3-foot hexagonal mock satellite that the researchers were trying to teach a three-armed robot to grab. Depending on the day, any one of the several teams involved in this research might be playing pin the sensor on the satellite. Two arms did the grappling. Small infrared sensors embedded in the ends of the claws on the robot's arms measured the intensity of the light reflected from the target's surface. Besides distance, sensors in the robot wrist measured dynamic effort: push force, pull force, and torquing. The stereo cameras on the third arm relayed an image of the mock satellite as it swung back and forth on its cable. The image would come in as a bit stream that the computer on a nearby desk would break down into a pattern, searching for the straight lines that told it the shape in question was the satellite it was searching for. The computer was programmed to recognize the pattern of the lines as well as their relative distance to each other and to the robot. The computer could also "see" the Velcro pads at the base of the satellite, the place where it could grab on with its own Velcro-lined hands.

Although the arms were supple and capable of moving very quickly, accuracy was more important than speed in accomplishing the job. The rudimentary computers that were the robot's brain could take up to ten minutes to calculate the variables, approximate the rate at which the satellite was moving relative to its own speed, and instruct each arm to grab on. The arms would reach out smoothly, Velcro sticking to Velcro, and bring the swinging satellite to a gentle stop. It wasn't successful every time, sometimes because of errors in the vision and sometimes because the arm didn't understand where it was.

Whenever important visitors came to JPL, they wanted to see the robots. Robots with their hands, arms, and eyes are anthropomorphic machines. They made the cutting edge science that was taking place all over the lab more comprehensible. It's akin to going to the zoo and wanting to see the monkeys. Sure the lions and elephants are grand and stately, but the monkeys arc antic and nearly human in their motions and expressions.

Robots are also unpredictable. In the days before the lab mandated a safety zone around any operating robot, one of Tony Bejczy's robot arms reached out and smacked him on the hip. Ever loyal to his machines, Tony defended the robot. "I did not notice the guys were setting it up for something. I should not have been there," he recalled. "The robot did the right thing."

When I led distinguished guests through the robotics lab, I was never sure how the robots would behave. If I was hosting a contingent from NASA, millions of dollars of research money could be riding on a single demo and we rehearsed the event very carefully. Still, you never knew what the robots would do.

Once, the combination of the dark suits the NASA visitors wore and the drawn shades to spotlight the demo changed the light values in the room so much the robotic system became confused. The robot arms flung wildly and the engineers had to hit the emergency stop. They tried it again and the same thing happened. At this point, everyone was so rattled that a software engineer loaded the wrong program for the next demonstration, a two-handed manipulation of a light, foam-filled panel. The robot arms promptly tore the panel apart. The engineers had practiced the demonstration about fifty times, but Murphy's Law always prevails. The NASA big-wigs went away muttering.

We also could never predict what the government would do. Working on the space station turned out to be a frustrating and ultimately unproductive effort for me and the lab. We had bid to be the lead center for the FTS, to work on the robotic platforms, and to represent the scientists as customers of the space station. But JPL has never fared well in the world of human space flight. By the middle of 1985, all of the space station work was parceled out to the other space flight centers. Maybe we were lucky that we didn't get the FTS assignment, as the project was severely underfunded. JPL had estimated the cost of the FTS at about $300 million. The space station program, perennially short on money and badly underestimating the difficulty of the job, decided to spend only $100 million on it. It never got built and the Japanese and Canadians are now providing robots for the station.

The shuttle and station, however, provided foci for much of the robotic research at JPL and every advance is useful. Tony Bejczy, for instance, succeeded in building a force-torque sensor for the giant shuttle arm that let the controllers in the cabin "feel" what they were doing when they grappled with a satellite to deploy or retrieve it. The FTS vision work was applicable to something much closer to my heart—planetary rovers.

4
Fang, Tooth— and Rocky

My lifelong quest to get to Mars had become a source of frustration for me by the time I began my third decade at JPL. Pursuing missions for the government is an inherently frustrating task for all involved. A team of engineers sets out to solve a tough problem for a mission to Mars or the moon or Venus, throwing all their brain power into it, sacrificing time with their families and losing sleep perfecting some small piece of the design. Then suddenly, after years of creative work, intense internal controversy, and passionate disputes, the government pulls the plug. The team disbands and moves on to other projects for which they are supposed to build the same enthusiasm and commitment.

I had arrived at JPL in 1966 thinking I'd be on Mars in a few years. Because of leaving JPL for six months I missed Mariner 9, which established the first Mars orbiter in 1971. Because of Mariner 10 I was too late to get a spot on Viking, which put the first successful landers on Mars in 1976. When NASA became interested in sending a rover to Mars, I finally felt that technology, talent, money, and my career were about to come into rare conjunction. In 1987 I started leading the research into Martian rovers. After Viking, three different groups of scientists competed for who would control the experiments on the next mission to Mars. Meteorologists lobbied NASA to buy a Martian year of weather reports. They wanted Mars Observer, an instrument-laden satellite positioned over Mars that would send back data and photographs, and, also, to fly a network of as many as twenty weather stations scattered around the planet.

The seismologists, a much smaller constituency, wanted to get a look at what was going on inside the planet by sending up seismometers to measure Mars quakes (if there were any). Each Viking lander had carried a seismometer strapped to one of its legs. Mission control realized soon after they landed that the seismometer was recording the lander's shaking in the Martian wind instead of Mars quakes. The seismologists had been cheated out of their experiment on Viking, so they were lobbying to get on the next ship out of port headed for Mars.

Planetary geologists advocated for a mission to collect rocks and soil and return them to Earth. Viking photos showed a planet strewn with rocks, several one or two meters across. Had a lander leg ended up smashing into one of those, the spacecraft would have been destroyed and that part of the mission lost. Along with the felicitous luck of having landed safely in a rock garden came an equal ration of frustration. After the Viking's onboard laboratories uncovered no sign of life in the soil samples taken by the spacecraft's robotic arm, scientists turned their attention to the rocks sitting just out of reach of the lander. The pits and holes in those rocks could be impressions made by bubbles escaping from cooling volcanic rocks. Or they might be sockets dug by water washing over their surface in some ancient Martian flood. Perhaps they held the key to the mystery of what had happened to Mars's water. Unfortunately the Viking landers weren't designed to move and their soil scoops couldn't reach the rocks.

Simply deploying a few instruments, such as a spectrometer to read the mineral composition of the rocks, wasn't considered by some geologists to be worth the expense of the launch. After all, if you could get the real stuff back, scientists could get their big laboratory instruments down deep into the samples and detect tiny traces of material. Then we could learn how old Mars was and what it was made out of. Most of these people thought that a variety of samples from different rock types and locations would be necessary to really understand the history of Mars. Getting a variety required a rover.

JPL's interest in rovers had come and gone several times in the last thirty years. The five Surveyor robotic spacecraft we'd sent to the moon in the mid-1960s were designed to answer basic questions about the surface of the moon. Surveyors had a very specific value for the Apollo program: to determine if it was safe for astronauts to land. Some planetary geologists theorized that the surface of the moon was covered with a fine talcum powder–like substance as much as 10 meters deep. If this were so, the lunar lander would sink out of sight and we'd never hear from it or the astronauts inside again.

When the first Surveyor reached out its scoop to sample some of the soil, the top few inches looked fluffy. Below that it hit ground harder than any encountered on Earth. Eons of meteorite impacts had done the reverse of what scientists had expected. Instead of pulverizing the surface into powder, they had compacted it into a mass harder than concrete.

The Soviet Union flew two robotic lunar rovers, called *Lunakhod* (meaning moon car), in the early 1970s. These rovers, which resembled old-fashioned bathtubs on eight spidery wheels, successfully crawled across the lunar surface, moving during the two-week lunar day and "sleeping" at night. One lasted for several months and traveled 37 kilometers. With only one-and-a-half second time delay to transmit a signal from Earth to the moon, Soviets could drive the Lunakhods from Earth-like radio-controlled cars (although the strain of dealing with the three-second time delay between sending a signal and seeing the results quickly exhausted the drivers).

Mars rovers presented a much greater challenge than rovers for the moon. First there was the time delay between Earth and Mars which averaged half an hour roundtrip. This required an autonomous rover that could plot its own path. If the operator on Earth saw the rover approaching a cliff he could signal STOP!!!! as frantically as he liked but the rover wouldn't hear him until it was already lying at the bottom in a heap. Mars rovers had to be able to take care of themselves. Autonomy required semi-intelligent robots, which required high-speed computing. Unfortunately, computers of the 1980s were crude and heavy, and artificial intelligence was still in its infancy.

JPL engineers had been working on rover mobility since the 1960s, but their first crack at the problem of autonomous control came a few years after Viking. As computers ratcheted up in power and started to shrink in size with the advent of microprocessors in the mid-1970s, the idea of an autonomous sample return mission to Mars didn't seem so far-fetched. Robotics research was progressing quickly. Optimism was high that computers would overtake human thought processes by the end of the century. Computer researchers boasted that within a few years they would be able to program a computer to beat a human at chess. (This of course didn't happen until 1996, so you can see how unrealistic those expectations were.) The first JPL autonomous rover effort was to rig a steel frame on a set of Volkswagen tires and pile a wooden platform with cameras, sensors, and computer equipment. This mass of hardware connected over phone lines to a huge mainframe at Caltech.

Loaded down with all the complicated programming for vision, path planning, and hazard avoidance, and guided by a computer much less capable than the average desktop workstation in use today, the rover was unbearably slow. So slow, in fact, that tests showed it was faster to drive it from Earth even with the time delay to Mars than to let it find its own way around the surface. This first Mars rover program was canceled in 1980 awaiting the new wave of interest in robotics that swept the lab in 1982.

Brian Wilcox was in the middle of the robot vision work and it was his robotics lab that had done the work on grappling with spinning satellites. In addition to working on the technology for robots to service the space station, Brian was working under a military contract to develop autonomous off-road vehicles to scout hostile territory. The military wanted a vehicle that could plan its own path toward an enemy position and then, as its cameras surveyed the scene, send back information about the enemy's numbers, weapons, and position. Even if all the robotic scout did was draw enemy fire, the army would have established where the bad guys were hiding.

It should be possible to apply the same technology to planetary rovers. NASA funded a few rover studies in the mid-1980s as a way of evaluating and guiding this research. As part of the robotics job, I got familiar with the rover mission concepts. By the late 1980s, with the demise of the Flight Telerobotic Servicer, rovers were more and more the focus of JPL's robotic technology efforts.

In 1987 NASA headquarters decided to chip in some money to study a Mars Rover Sample Return (MRSR) mission. I was happy to lead the rover design team that was part of the sample return study. Robotic rovers and Mars and a design team—all my favorite things.

Although there were several ideas for the sample return mission, the common assumption was that we'd plop down a brawny rover at a point on Mars adjacent to several different types of Martian terrain. The rover should be capable of traveling 100 to 1,000 meters a day so that within a year it could ramble over 100 kilometers, sampling a wide variety of geology and mineralogy. Then it would rendezvous with a sample return vehicle and hand over the box of samples to be brought back to Earth.

Based on Viking data, geologists believed that in order not to get hung up on the rocks and ancient flood channels, the rover would have to climb obstacles a meter high and span crevices a meter in width. In one concept the rover would be guided along its path by comparing what it could see on the surface against photographs of the territory around it taken from an orbiter. We envisioned flying orbiters with huge cameras that could detect objects about a meter in size, which was another reason for that one-meter rover obstacle requirement—the rover could just drive over everything that couldn't be seen in advance.

Brian Wilcox was a natural person to get on my MRSR rover design team. He and a few others had been keeping rover research alive—often on a shoestring budget from his military contracts. Brian recalls grousing to some of the older engineers one day, complaining that he needed a vehicle test bed for his army work and didn't have the money to build one. One of them confessed that he actually had a small rover prototype he'd hidden from a succession of JPL bosses. Each time a boss uncovered the old General Motors lunar rover prototype from the 1960s, he told the engineer to throw it out. Storage space was at a premium, he'd say, and it was useless. But each time the engineer would find another place to stash it. He was happy to see Brian put it to use.

When Brian first saw it, the sight of the little six-wheeled vehicle engulfed him in nostalgia. The 5-foot long, three-body Surveyor Lunar Roving Vehicle (SLRV), designed to scout out landing sites on the moon, was the same one he'd driven around the General Motors facility in Santa Barbara at a company open house in 1962 when he was just twelve years old. With its three-segment body, it had looked to young Brian like a big bug as he maneuvered it around with a joystick attached to the rover by a tether. Brian's father was the director of research and engineering at GM's Defense Research Facility. He'd directed a team of émigré Hungarian engineers led by M. G. Bekker who led the world in off-road design. The SLRV was an experiment in climbing capability featuring a flexible spring chassis and six doughnut-shaped wheels. That team also designed the two four-wheeled rovers the astronauts raced around on the moon in 1969 (at a top speed of ten miles an hour), bouncing merrily in the low gravity and throwing up rooster tails of dust into the airless sky.

When Brian looked more closely at the rover he saw that the fabric-covered wire tires were shot and the paint was flaking off, but the body and the linkages between the three cabs seemed solid. Brian's team painted it a cheery sky blue and gave it new tires. They hooked it up to an old computer that was lying around the office and started fooling around with the "Little Blue Rover" in the Arroyo Seco, a dry creek bed adjacent to JPL.

Around 9 o'clock every morning they drove Little Blue out from the rickety old Quonset hut–like building that served as their office at the lab's east gate. Little Blue only traveled a foot per second among the people and vehicles streaming in from the parking lot. The five-member crew stopped traffic for her majestic twenty-minute promenade to the Arroyo. She always drew a crowd of well-wishers whose days were cheered by the sight of the team and their robotic pet. Certainly there was something cute, almost ET-like about its bulbous head with two wide-spaced camera eyes in front. Passersby would stop in their tracks and follow the cheerful procession, watching her as she negotiated the steep down slope past the guardhouse. Nearly everyone who saw Little Blue in action had one comment: "It's so small!"

For the computers available at the time, she really was small. The best computer available, a Digital Equipment Corporation "VAX," was the size of a refrigerator and too big to be carried by the 5-foot-long Little Blue. Cables trailed a hundred yards from the Arroyo Seco back to the lab connecting the primitive wheel-driving computer onboard the rover to the VAX "brain" in the lab which figured out how to follow the path selected by the operator.

There were really three kinds of technologies involved in controlling an autonomous robot. The simplest technology translated a command from an operator into instructions to the robot's various motors on how far and in what direction to move. For robot arms these low-level functions positioned the arms and opened and closed the end effectors or "hands." If the arm was teleoperated, the low-level functions were hooked up to a "master" robot arm. As the operator moved the master arm, the "slave" arm would mimic the master's motions precisely. Even though these were the lowest-level functions, the mathematics of controlling a multijointed arm were very complex. For a rover the low-level functions moved the wheels (or legs or tracks): forward, backward, turn.

The next level of technology was for the robot or rover to plan a "path" to a goal. For an arm this meant reaching out and touching something, such as grabbing a satellite. For a rover it meant directing the machine toward a goal in the terrain. Path planning for a rover involved some sort of ability to sense where it was going and a way to tell when it reached the goal.

Finally, and toughest to automate, was goal selection. How could a robot actually figure out where to go?

Brian Wilcox's work with Little Blue was focused on the latter two categories. It was relatively easy to accomplish low-level control on a wheeled vehicle compared to a walker or a multijointed robot arm. Figuring out where obstacles were in the terrain was much tougher, and a rover intelligent enough to figure out where to go without human direction would be a real challenge. Path planning was relatively easy where there were straight lines, like the edges of a road. For the military autonomous land vehicle program several organizations had developed approaches to road-finding. Brian's team had used a similar approach for their three-armed robot to grapple the spinning satellite in the lab: the cameras and computer had looked for straight edges.

For a robot, finding a way around unmarked terrain was a much tougher job than finding straight lines. Brian's group was working on a vision system that would take images in stereo and then laboriously analyze the images to decide which parts were closer or farther away and which were higher or lower. Then, based on rules programmed into the computer, the rover would decide which routes were safe and finally send the low-level commands to the wheels to follow those routes. This terrible computing load mandated Little Blue's cable connection with a big computer in the lab.

The last problem, figuring out where to go in the first place, was solved relatively simply by a process called "Computer Aided Remote Driving," or CARD. Stereo vision was the key technology, but human brains were used to select the goal. Either aerial photographs or the view from the rover's own cameras were shown on a computer monitor. Operators could look into the scene, find the safe paths, and send commands to the rover with the coordinates to move toward. The rover's own low-level autonomy would then drive it to execute the commands. With CARD the vision system could just look for hazards that the operator might have missed. It didn't have to analyze the whole scene, just the bits along the designated path.

The team videotaped one successful demo where Little Blue ambled slowly through the Arroyo, climbing over relatively small rocks with much thrashing of its three bodies. Suddenly it came to an enormous, white, stream-rounded boulder bigger than the rover itself. The rover seemed to stop in surprise and stare fixedly at the boulder—then after a long pause for calculation it turned and went around the obstacle. The military was sufficiently impressed with Little Blue's capability that Brian got money to develop Computer Aided Remote Driving for a big military superjeep called a HMMV or HumVee. When I took over the rover technology program, including planning for the MRSR rover, I knew this was exactly the kind of operation we wanted on Mars.

JPL wasn't the only place researching rovers. The two main research areas were mobility and control, and while lots of people were working on one or the other, nobody except JPL was really tackling all of the problem. Ohio State University had produced a gigantic, six-legged walker that would move over rough terrain with the mincing gait of a cat. The walking was automated, but it took an operator riding in it to tell it where to go. Many people thought walkers would be better for rough terrain than rollers, but they were harder to control. The Russians had a six-wheeled vehicle similar to Little Blue, only more robust and with big conical wheels. Some people were convinced that tracked vehicles like army tanks were the way to go for mobility.

While the General Motors design that led to the Little Blue Rover was pretty good at rolling over obstacles it had a number of drawbacks. Because the three bodies pitched and rolled relative to each other it would be hard to mount solar arrays and instruments on the rover. Also, the links between its three cabs presented enormous thermal problems for a vehicle destined for the cold. Each cab would have to be separately heated. The links between the bodies housed the cables that sent signals and power from the source out to the wheels. These links would be hard to heat. Flexing in extremely cold temperatures could crack cable insulation and make the whole system vulnerable.

We needed a more stable platform that would still get around in rough terrain. Don Bickler, our MRSR mobility guru, came up with the right idea.

Around the time the rover study was looking for a new way to overcome Martian boulders, mechanical engineer Don Bickler was looking for a way out of the project he was on. He was bored with the glorified paper monitor job he'd drawn on the design of the Galileo project to Jupiter and he's not the kind of guy that handles boredom easily. A restless, wiry man with an avuncular manner, he's trailed everywhere by a cadre of eager young student apprentices who hang on his every off-the-cuff insight. Most nights he can be found rummaging among the antiquated tools in his Temple City garage trying to bang out the solution to one mechanical problem or another that has grabbed his imagination.

His son had just bought a jeep and dragged Don to an off-road vehicle hobbyist show. Don was appalled at the pseudoscientific gadgets the manufacturers were selling to enhance off-road performance. None of them were very well designed, he could tell at a glance. At best they would provide a minimal increase in off-road performance. Despite the mediocrity of their designs, Don saw that these overpriced gadgets were flying off the shelves. What if, Don thought, I designed some off-road accessories that really gave these cars some traction? Or better yet, how about an off-road-capable wheelchair? The son of a friend of his had become paralyzed off-roading in the desert and Don was tinkering with the idea of building him a wheelchair that could climb steps. Either one of these might be a good business and a way out of the boring job he was doing at JPL.

He started complaining to an old friend who had been working on rovers since the 1970s, and the friend suggested Don talk to Brian Wilcox. Brian had one piece of advice for Don: take a look at the work of M. G. Bekker.

Don went to the JPL library the next day and took out Bekker's book on vehicle performance. He knew Brian had been running tests on Bekker's rover prototype and had even seen films of the little rover's amazing stair-climbing capability. While it was true that the thing was great at climbing stairs, one part of the film no one talked about was how poorly it went over bumps. The only part of the video where the rover got hung up was on rocks that were larger than the wheels. If this vision gizmo Brian was working on did the job, rocks the size of steps wouldn't be the problem on Mars. Bumps would. Nature is not a series of steps, thought Don. It's a series of bumps. He thumbed through the Bekker volume looking for something to stimulate his own imagination on how to solve this problem.

Scanning Bekker's equations, Don's mind fell back to his youth and the hot rods he'd worked on back in Chicago. Independent suspension was the sine qua non of hot rods and Bekker was a big fan of it too. It allows the shock of hitting bumps to be absorbed with minimal horizontal reaction. But if you were trying to climb, the higher the front wheels got, the more the springs worked against you. What you needed for a vehicle that had to climb and go over bumps was something that provided the range of movement and great weight distribution qualities of independent suspension but without the disadvantages of the resistance from the springs. Don's eyes fell on a passage in the text about the field tests of Bekker's six-wheel, independent suspension design: "The optimum performance is roughly 95 percent of the maximum climbing ability of a bogie."

A bogie! Of course. A bogie was so straightforward, Don remembers thinking. The bogie, where the wheels are connected to ends of levers that swivel on a pivot, is probably the simplest form of suspension in the world. As a kid Don had seen plenty of bogie chassis supporting the trains in the railroad yard where his grandfather worked. Why not design a bogie chassis? The advantage of a bogie is that no matter what obstacle each wheel encounters, the levers keep the weight of the vehicle evenly distributed. A tree of bogies connected to six wheels could do just as well as Bekker's design in climbing stairs, Don thought. For bumps it probably would be better.

When Don and Howard Eisen, one of the students he was working with, started modeling a six-wheel design on the computer, the problem with Bekker's design jumped right out at them. If a vehicle travels along in a line and the front wheel goes over a bump, the rear wheels actually have to move backward to help it move forward. If he suspended the wheels on a tree of bogies much like a child's mobile, the wheel pivots could be raised or lowered to modify this horizontal motion effect.

Don is not the most articulate of engineers. It's always been simpler for him to manufacture what he's trying to describe. Almost every story Don tells about his many designs and patents includes the sentence: "They just couldn't get what I was talking about, so I made one in my garage that night."

At night Don, sometimes assisted by Howard Eisen, built the Bickler Pantograph, a one-eighth scale model of the chassis he wanted to build for the rover. (A pantograph is a drafting tool composed of a framework of joined rods in the rough form of a parallelogram that enables the draftsman to draw something to scale.) Don and Howard believed that the physics they were demonstrating in this one-eighth scale model were independent of scale and therefore would apply to big rovers as well as small rovers.

Don's garage is a museum of aging technology. He machined most of the pantograph and parts of the rover on a 1910 lathe he bought in 1956 for $15. The machine is so old, he can't buy belts for it anymore and fashions his own from a roll of leather belting and an equally antiquated belt stapling device. Don fashioned the tires for the pantograph from a roll of fiberglass he had stashed on a top shelf since he bought it in 1960. He made the ridges on the wheels, designed to help them grip the Martian soil, out of old dollhouse parts. Don never throws anything away, he admits. On his desk at JPL is a pint-size model of the pantograph he built out of pieces from his son's childhood bed that are still lying around the scrap woodpile behind the shelves in his garage.

Don first built the bogie attached to a half bogie with the linkages to the body hooked on the side. He didn't want an axle interfering with the pantograph's ground clearance. Then he and Howard rigged the pantograph up with little motors hidden inside the cone-shaped wheels and attached a tether from a remote control car to steer it. Even Don was amazed by its performance. Without an axle or springs, it had ground clearance equal to its wheel diameter. The pantograph could cross a crevice equal to 40 percent of its overall length and easily recovered from being tilted at a 60-degree angle. They rigged up a set of steps in the hallway in Building 158 and called me over to see their new toy. The ease with which this little machine handled even large climbing challenges was intriguing to watch.

We started assuming for our rover mission design studies that we could use a large version of the pantograph, but Don and Howard weren't yet satisfied. They wrote some computer programs based originally on the equations of M. G. Bekker and one of his compatriots, but Don and Howard's results showed that their model would far outstrip their predecessors when the design of the bogie linkages was changed. I christened this new design the "rocker bogie" because the wheels were attached to bogies, and because the wheels rocked up and down. Naturally, we dubbed rovers with this design "Rocky." When Don actually built a little working version of the rocker bogie, Rocky 1 was born.

A single design doth not a study make. You need to do "trade studies," looking at a variety of ways to accomplish the mission, so you can pick the best approach for the money. So we gave out two small contracts in 1988/89—one to FMC corporation, which built giant mobile machinery including tanks, and another to Martin Marietta Corporation, which had built an autonomous land vehicle for the military.

The first round of the study was really fun. Both FMC and Martin were very inventive and sketches of kites, hoppers, rollers, walkers, and balloons filled the pages of their first presentation. On most contracts the different companies never work together because they are competing. On this study not only did the contractors share their ideas with each other and us, we shared our ideas with them. Each team came up with a different mobility design: two six-wheeled rollers and a six-legged walker.

Martin's Walking Beam was the most unusual. Borrowing a concept from the Japanese, "Beamer" moved like an inchworm. It had two sections, each with retractable legs. The bigger, outer section was a tripod. It had two front legs connected by a crossbar and a long, horizontal beam extending back from the middle of the crossbar. The second section would start at the back of the beam with its legs retracted and ratchet its way forward. When it reached the crossbar it would extend its legs to the ground. Then the first section would retract its legs, ratchet the beam forward over the second section, and then lower its legs. Martin actually built a quarter-scale model of this giant robot (it was to be 20 feet long and 30 feet high to the top of its camera mast). Little Beamer could climb stairs and move over rough ground as long as it had a well-coordinated operator at the radio controls, but like Scarecrow it didn't have a brain and there is an embarrassing film clip of the walker falling on its nose while trying to walk down a slope.

FMC's Attached Scout used a three-segment body like that of the Little Blue Rover. The Scout featured a large sample-collecting arm on the front body and required the use of nuclear power to run the rover because, as with Little Blue, the three thrashing segments weren't conducive to mounting a solar array on top.

Of course, the JPL mobility design was the rocker bogie. The more Brian, Don, and other mobility folks at JPL played with Little Blue and Rocky 1, the more they realized the wisdom of a rover having six wheels. Movies of testing both Little Blue's six-wheel independent suspension design and Rocky 1 show their amazing ability to climb stairs one and a half times their wheel diameters. A car pulling a trailer is a six-wheeled vehicle but you couldn't get your car over something half again as tall as its wheels because the wheels can't get the traction and flexibility needed to make the climb. The individually powered wheels had the torque and traction to handle most obstacles that came in their way. When the front wheels started to climb and lose traction at the top of a stair, the middle and rear wheels powered the vehicle forward. Once the front wheels were on top, they pulled the rest of the body up. Rocky soon proved its ability to maneuver better in bumpy terrain than Little Blue when Don and Howard took it to the desert and ran it over rocky and volcanic terrain criss-crossed with ditches.

We had to combine high mobility with the ability for the rover to autonomously find its way around in a terrain with no roads or road signs. Although Brian's group had made Little Blue semiautonomous (it could find its way to a goal once the goal had been pointed out by a human), a rover would need a much bigger body to carry its own brain.

Although the FMC, Martin Marietta, and JPL mobility designs differed a lot, the autonomous control systems were surprisingly similar. In retrospect, it made sense. All autonomous rovers have to sense where they are and what their surroundings are like. They have to compute where to go and be able to drive the wheels or legs to get there. Ball Aerospace was interested in providing sensors for the rover, so they were participating in the study on their own nickel. In addition to real technical inputs they sent us a cartoon of how they envisioned the rover. It was festooned with cameras—on the front, on the sides, and floating on a balloon overhead. All the cameras were going "whir, click, snap" and taking pictures of a three-headed green Martian who stood in front of the rover making a peace sign.

In addition to "seeing" with stereo cameras perched high on a stalk above the front crossbar, Martin's Walking Beam fired lasers ahead of it. The laser light would reflect off rocks and return faster than if the beams just hit flat ground. If the laser beams hit a hole the return would be slower because the bottom of the hole would be farther away than flat ground. This was

Beamer's hazard detection system. All the designs assumed that the rover would be able to detect tipping and slipping and that it would have some sort of gyrocompass onboard.

The computer and software were the biggest problems. Even in the 1980s computers were big, slow, and expensive, not to mention power hungry and susceptible to failure in extremes of temperature. Artificial intelligence software was clumsy, complex, and prone to the "mesa effect." Once a situation got out of the range for which the software had been developed, the system would immediately fail to know what to do. A road-following algorithm, for instance, was worthless in a trackless wilderness.

Our three teams pooled their ideas on the control system and they all came out looking rather like Brian Wilcox's concept for autonomous control: let the operator pick the goal, let the rover follow the path to the goal while avoiding obstacles. Since all this was expensive and slow there were many who felt we shouldn't spend money developing sophisticated autonomy at all. Maybe we should just teleoperate the rover from Earth, moving such short distances between commands that the operator could see all the hazards and send the rover on a path to avoid them.

Bill Dias, an expert mission planner, proved that was a bad idea. Bill is a stocky, introverted guy with a slow smile and a quiet, thoughtful way of talking. He'd cut his teeth on the complex problems of balancing demands on a scarce resource when he worked on a program to schedule time for the Deep Space Network. The problem of how we were going to evaluate these vastly different rover designs intrigued him. Which would travel the farthest, do the most science, collect the most and best samples? The surface of Mars was not like the clean emptiness of deep space where all the influences on a spacecraft could be modeled mathematically. It was likely to be rugged, rocky, full of hidden pits and hazards like dust traps, and certainly couldn't be modeled accurately. He developed a software scenario called "A Day in the Life of a Mars Rover." Each step of the rover's activities would be listed and the time each step took could be estimated. A rover that was bigger and smarter would presumably move faster than a small, dumb rover.

Bill started imagining how he could represent a "Day" scenario for a Mars rover. Rovers are the epitome of vehicles with scarce resources. In space the sun is always shining, unless the spacecraft briefly flies behind a planet. On the surface of Mars the days (known as "sols") are about the same length as Earth's—twenty-four hours and thirty-seven minutes to be exact—so about half of each day is dark. No solar power, no light for the cameras.

In fact, one of the big tradeoffs we had to make was how the MRSR rover should be powered. Long, fast romps across the planet would be best powered by nuclear energy. But we quickly discovered that the cost and political risk of launching nuclear power was onerous. Solar power was a much cheaper solution. But solar power meant that we could probably only operate during the day unless we devoted a lot of mass to batteries.

So an important question was: How much work could the rover do during daylight hours? This depended on how big the solar arrays were, how big the batteries were that stored energy for night operations, and how smart the rover was, because that influenced how much power it used.

Another issue was the size of the rover. Did we really need to be able to cross all one-meter obstacles, or should we make the rover smaller and make it able to think its way around them?

Some of the rover concepts that people came up with were so big we designated them as "Godzilla" rovers. The mobility team came up with a cartoon—a great green Godzilla riding on a flatbed truck. The scientists loved the idea; Godzilla could carry every instrument known to man. Another rover concept was caricatured as a "genius." It would be smart and therefore fast. But could we afford either of these approaches?

No one had ever worked through these problems before, but Bill Dias took on the job. For a reserved man, he always seemed to be in the center of a controversy between those who wanted the Godzilla or the genius rover and his own more rational view of what engineers could reasonably expect a rover to do in a day, a month, or a year. Bill's computer analysis tool was called just "Bill's Spread Sheet" but it turned out to be the Godzilla Killer. He could keep track not only of time and distance but of power, the amount of data that could be transmitted, and how long science operations would take. Soon Bill had demonstrated that more smarts were a lot better. In the course of a year a teleoperated rover, no matter how big, would cover less than 10 kilometers and collect only about ten samples. An autonomous rover could achieve hundreds of kilometers and samples in that same time.

When scientists were conjuring (as Bill put it sarcastically) a rover that would go all the way around Mars in a year and send back a picture of every single square inch along the way, Bill told them a kilometer was all they should expect in a day from an autonomous rover. Mars is a sufficiently new territory to science that each meter traveled could uncover something of value, so covering as much territory as you can in a single day was the wrong objective. Although the scientists squawked long and hard, Bill's kilometer-a-day range is still much larger than the figure mission design specialists are using for the rovers planned through 2015. Like my "value function" tool on Mariner 10, Bill's spread sheet was a tool for managing the competing interests of the scientists.

So by 1989 we had rover designs and the tools and technology to start implementing them. By 1991 a representative of the Godzilla school of technology had been built by Brian Wilcox's team with NASA technology funding. It was built, unlike Little Blue Rover, to carry its own brain, which still was the garbage can–size VAX computer that Little Blue had used. This required a chassis the size of a pickup truck. A single rigid platform mounted on a rocker bogie chassis would be the best design for the next stage of semiautonomous vehicle testing, but Brian's task was not to solve the mobility crisis. His assignment was autonomy in a reasonably sized package and he wanted to slap something together and get moving on making it faster and smaller. He asked a graduate student intern to design a chassis with one-meter wheels and weighing in at about 450 pounds.

"Robby" started at 450 pounds and just kept on growing. It had four cameras and two computers: one for sensing and one for control. Mars has no magnetic field so Robby couldn't use a compass to get his heading on Mars. Robby needed a gyrocompass. The only one we could get our hands on easily and cheaply was a military model weighing in at about 150 pounds. But even by 1990 it was obvious that a Godzilla rover was not going to fly.

On July 20, 1989, President Bush announced that we were "going back to the moon to stay . . . and then . . . a human mission to Mars" to land by 2019. We were very excited. MRSR was a perfect precursor to a human mission. We believed that a presidential endorsement was a ticket to success. Hadn't it worked for Apollo, the shuttle, the station? The Johnson Space

Center was ready. They had already formed a team to work with us on MRSR.

All told, Robby weighed in at about 882 kilograms. Nearly a ton just for the rover. Now when people saw it all they could say was, "It's so big." And you didn't get much distance for all that weight. At first the team had to work on it all day just to get it to go 13 meters. No way would NASA pay to send something that slow to Mars. Still everyone on the team believed that if we could get more money, we could take advantage of the incredible advances in computers to get the weight down and the speed up.

Now that it seemed there was a possibility of getting real funding, the rover was suddenly attracting a lot of attention. It would be by far the biggest project ever at JPL and the connection with the human space program gave it vast visibility. The lab decided they'd better review it carefully and assigned a review board of top-flight people. None of these folks were familiar with robotics and one of my jobs was to convince them that we knew what we were doing. I remember a review where I tried to explain how the vision system worked.

"Let's say there's a beauty contest," I said, pacing back and forth in front of the table at which the all-male review board sat. "The rover's job is to pick the handsomest man on the review board." Their eyes widened as I walked toward them with my hands cupped around my eyes, simulating the binocular vision of a robot. I scanned over their faces.

"This system is to select the best rock to autonomously take a sample from. The way it works, the rover takes images of the scene in several different spectra [colors] and analyzes those colors with a program in its onboard computer. Green rocks, for instance, would be very interesting to a geologist because they might indicate unweathered material recently blasted up from deep in the surface by a meteorite hit. So the rover can automatically pick out the best rock, just like beauty contest judges pick the best-looking man. The rover has to match the database in its brain with what it's actually seeing."

I went on, focusing on them. "Now, if I'm a robot judging this beauty contest I have a picture of what a handsome man looks like in my computer." I walked slowly past them, intently staring at each of them in turn. "I match that picture with the contestants, and the obvious winner is . . . Walt!"

Walt was well into his sixties, balding and a bit heavy-set, but since he was head of the review board I thought I'd pick on him. Walt sat up straighter in his chair and chuckled nervously. The audience burst into laughter.

I spread my hands. "And that's how it works."

I got three reactions from the reviewers. One collared me just after the review and quipped, "That was the most sexist presentation I've ever heard."

Walt came up and told me how funny the whole thing was and how it helped him understand how the rover worked. And a few days later another reviewer said, "You really turned the tables on us men."

The scent of money in the air permeated the atmosphere lower down at JPL, too, between the factions that were warring for control of the rover's brain. At the opposite end of the robotics intelligence problem from Brian Wilcox's approach was a small, eccentric band of artificial intelligence researchers led by Dave Miller.

Dave, a prematurely balding genius whose wild black eyes matched his unruly black hair, was really interested in machines that would think for themselves. He would sometimes get so excited presenting his ideas that he'd almost stutter. Dave had gotten involved with rovers almost by accident. In fact, his Information Systems Division had no charter to work on rovers at all. They were supposed to be doing research on using artificial intelligence to control spacecraft.

One of the members of Dave's eight-person team was Rajiv Desai, a native of India who had just completed his doctorate in mechanical engineering, specializing in robotics. He'd built the first robot ever made in the college in India where he completed his undergraduate degree. He was a good match with Dave, who excelled in robot behavior and control. Rajiv was honored to get a job offer at JPL because he would be working alongside our robotics experts. He was certainly surprised to show up for his first day of work in artificial intelligence and discover his department had no robots.

Dave and Rajiv had a fast way to remedy that. They built one. Their first project was FANG, the acronym for Fully Autonomous Navigational Gizmo. It was an industrial robot about the size of a garbage can set on wheels. They programmed FANG to navigate through their office building to pick up and deliver messages. This was actually an important function for the group which, for all JPL's high technology, didn't have email.

Their robotic intelligence group had a completely different take on robotic planning and control than the folks in the robotics section. Dave believed Robby was addressing the wrong question and therefore the computer modeling was all wrong. The question Robby was built to answer was: How do I model the world, distinguishing trees from rocks from craters, so I can navigate through it? Robby's program was based on the model of human vision and perception. As the robotic intelligence (RI) guys conceived the problem, the thought process should be modeled more on insect intelligence. An insect doesn't know what the objects in its path are. It just knows how big they are and that it has to go around them. The real question, they felt, was simply: How can I get from point A to point B?

FANG was a good demonstration of that kind of thinking. FANG would motor along the hallway guided by a stripe on the carpet. If someone had dropped something in its path, it would go around it and make its way back to the stripe to resume the journey. And unlike a lot of the workaholic engineers at JPL, FANG knew when its batteries were running low. FANG would home in on its charger and take a break until its power was replenished.

Some people inside the lab discredited the simplicity of this approach for a rover. First off, FANG was an indoor robot. As traditionally perceived, there is a division between indoor and outdoor robots. FANG was fine within the confines of a hallway, but the outside world was too random.

Dave Miller's group would taunt Brian Wilcox with the idea that the rover didn't actually need to see. It could just poke along like a blind person with a cane. "If it can't see, how will it know where it is?" Brian demanded. "It doesn't need to know where it is," retorted Dave, "if you just tell it where to go." This idea was anathema to every rover design that had preceded Robby and undercut the existing computer structure of the rover.

Brian, on the other hand, found it very frustrating to watch Dave's rover in action. The thing was so stupid. Obstacle on the left, it was programmed to turn right. Obstacle on the right, it was programmed to turn left. As Brian watched it pick its way through a hazardous area he had to stop himself from picking it up and setting it going the right way. It would turn to the left even though observers could see that in doing so it was turning away from a much less treacherous space. Brian knew that because Dave's robots were guided by bumping into things, if you set any of them to run on a conference table they would fall off and die. "You might argue that there are no cliffs on Mars, and maybe there are none," Brian said. "But maybe there are. I prefer to build vehicles that at least if you set them on a conference room table they don't kill themselves in one minute."

The RI group decided to experiment with making FANG even smaller. They built a 10-inch robot on a radio-controlled car chassis and christened it Tooth. They had almost no money, but scraped up enough from various places to get Tooth built.

Tooth was a smart little robot. It was programmed to run away from its base—a lightbulb they'd placed in the center of the room—while it searched the floor for hockey pucks. When Tooth found a puck (and evaluated it to make sure it really was a puck by feeling it with its claws), it picked up the puck, scurried toward the light, and dropped it at the base. The minute the hockey puck was out of its clutches, it fled from the light again. Sprightly, small, and smart, as I saw it.

Early in 1988 I invited Dave Miller to be a member of the MRSR rover team so that we'd have more than one approach to robotics represented in our trade studies. With Dave's approach we could potentially have cheaper, although less predictable rovers, just in case the funding for a large mission with "do-everything" rovers never came through. Just as we had nuclear versus solar power, large versus small rovers, and smart versus dumb rovers, we now had two robotic control schemes to trade off.

With the do-everything scenarios the costs were getting very large. Two orbiters, two landers, two rockets to launch the samples from Mars, two very capable rovers, and two Earth return vehicles—ten separate pieces. Viking, our most expensive mission to date, had four pieces and had cost more than $2 billion in 1990 dollars. By simple extrapolation MRSR would cost $6 or $8 billion, and one independent cost estimate by a NASA support contractor went as high as $10 billion.

Those costs were a drop in the bucket compared to the human mission money that was being talked about at NASA's Johnson Space Center in Houston, Texas. Because of President Bush's speech, MRSR was now being viewed not just as a science mission, but as a major precursor to a human mission to Mars. A number of independent studies led by eminent people like Norm Augustine (CEO of Martin Marietta), Sally Ride (the first U.S. woman in space), and Tom Paine (a former NASA administrator) were bullish on human missions to the moon and Mars. It was the destiny of the United States and of humanity, they said—and I agreed with them. The only questions were when and what the role of the robots would be. I envisioned the robots as scouts for the human explorers, much like Lewis and Clark mapping the American West before the settlers trickled in. I had even published a couple of papers on the theme of robots and humans as partners in space exploration.

Although none of these studies published official cost estimates (which stunned even the most bullish NASA advocates of human space exploration), word got around that they were hundreds of billions of dollars. The Democratic Congress leapt on these figures with glee. They were not about to give a political lever to Vice President Dan Quayle, who was head of the Administration's Space Council coordinating NASA and military space. In the fall of 1990, a year after George Bush's bold statements about humans to the moon and Mars, Congress canceled all funding for studies of human exploration. Almost as an afterthought they canceled funding for robotic exploration as well. Our alliance with Johnson Space Center had backfired and gotten our more modest proposal killed.

Even before our money was cut, I had had the intuition that the pricetag was way too high. I had looked at Don Bickler's eighth-scale model, Rocky 1, as it clambered over very rough terrain. I had watched Tooth scuttle around in Dave Miller's lab. What if we used small rovers to explore and collect samples? Even a small set of samples would be better than none.

There was a lot of skepticism, especially among scientists, that small rovers could be made to work in a real Martian terrain and carry out real, useful science. Those scientists hadn't seen the rocker bogie, however. I got Dave Miller and Don Bickler together and asked them to prove the nay-sayers wrong.

"Why don't you guys put Tooth's brain on Rocky's body?" I asked.

"Well," they said, "can you get us some money?"

I agree to scrape up a few thousand dollars from our dwindling MRSR study money and they agreed to try.

Dave's group had already put together $10,000 to modify Don's original Rocky 1 model, adding steering motors and a remote control. Don was happy to lend Rocky 1 to Dave provided that Dave gave him testing data in return. There was a design called Rocky 2 that never got off the drawing board, but the first version of Rocky 3 piled a Macintosh computer box—containing not a Macintosh but electronics built by the Robotic Intelligence Group—on top of Rocky's chassis. The group found it was cheaper to buy a Macintosh and throw away the innards to get a box than to have the lab's high quality machine shop build them one. Rocky 3 was crude. It looked like a breadbox on wheels and weighed about 50 pounds, so it bogged down in soft soil. But on hard ground it could go 100 meters in a little under an hour and it could climb over rocks and hills. A video of an early test at Mars Hill in the Mojave, a place planetary geologists say is analogous to territory on Mars, shows a ground-eye view of Rocky 3 appearing over a ridge like some movie monster and sliding down the soft slope, encouraged by shouts from the engineers. You can see the feet of a member of the Rocky 3 team following alongside the rover as it surmounts rock after treacherous rock. "Now that's what I call off-roading," he shouts.

But I couldn't help get small rovers beyond that stage. I was completely out of money. The end of the Cold War was having its effect and NASA's budget was going into free fall, after a brief resurgence to replace the shuttle Challenger. MRSR had shut down and I was now in the Exploration Initiatives Studies (EIS) office operating on an ever-more-fragile shoestring.

I helped Dave Miller and Don Bickler successfully lobby for $100,000 in NASA technology money to try and mount a test sample return mission with the next version of Rocky 3. But as Dave and Don prepared the new Rocky 3 the storm clouds were gathering over the robotics programs at JPL.

The battle between the robotics organization for which Brian Wilcox worked and Dave Miller's robotic intelligence group centered around control of the dwindling robotics research money. In a rare (for JPL) political power play the robotics organization won.

I was appalled and fought, along with the manager of Dave's division, to keep the RI group where it was. I believed we'd lose them if they were forced into the robotics organization.

This battle was still being fought when all the parties assembled in the Arroyo Seco in the summer of 1991 to watch

Rocky 3 go through its paces. Rocky 3 trundled slowly to a designated position, scooped up some dirt, turned around, retraced its path, and dumped it into a hopper on a mock lander. Everyone cheered, even Brian Wilcox. Dave Miller and Don Bickler had shown that small rovers could do the job of big rovers. Unfortunately, there was no longer any mission planned to bring rovers of any size to Mars.

Providentially, JPL's manager for space and Earth science was impressed by the success of Rocky 3. He scraped up $2.5 million to build Rocky 4. But Dave Miller wouldn't be involved. After being a key person in the selling of Rocky 4 he was still being forbidden to do the work he wanted to do. He went on sabbatical to MIT for a year and then returned, hoping to resume robotic work. A few months later the inevitable was announced: the robotic intelligence group would now be under the control of the robotics organization. All the RI group's robots and all their other equipment would be transported to the robotics building. Within a year most of the RI group had left JPL, a huge and unnecessary talent drain.

Suddenly I was sick of the whole Mars effort. Not the rovers, not the engineers and scientists, but the political manipulations both inside JPL and in Congress. More than that, I was tired of scrambling around trying to get money to keep my team together. I decided to get out of rovers and on to a bigger and more stable project. Little did I realize rovers would keep bringing me back.

5

Rover Boys
and Girls

pprehension surged through me as I picked my way among the rocks and sand of the Arroyo Seco in my sensible business pumps. More than 100 people, including high-level scientists, NASA and JPL brass, and the press, had journeyed to the Arroyo in June of 1992, on the thirtieth anniversary of the Surveyor landing on the moon to see what Rocky 4 could do. The top-level managers who were mopping their brows in the sweltering June heat wave held Rocky's future and mine in their hands.

If Rocky 4, JPL's newly reconstituted miniature rover, performed as described these people could decide to send our rover to Mars. I had just been appointed head of the next phase for what we were calling "microrovers" and if Rocky didn't work I might be looking for a new job pretty soon. The simple truth was, in the month since I got the job, I'd never seen Rocky go through the demonstration without a glitch.

More than just the heat and the guests were disorienting me. The dry creek bed was almost unrecognizable. Three weeks earlier the Rocky team, following the advice of Viking geologists, had rearranged the sand and painted and repositioned the rocks. Rocky 4 faced an obstacle course that was analogous to the Viking 1 landing site. They'd also constructed a mock lander whose camera would keep track of Rocky's position in the Arroyo.

The Rocky team had set up its equipment in a trailer adjacent to the site for the week of frantic testing that preceded this public technology display. JPL rented a fence to enclose the area, which is actually publicly owned land, and staffed it with security guards so the equipment could stay in place overnight. A crew had erected blue-and-white-striped tents to shade the computer equipment and the dignitaries. If you looked at it one way, it seemed like a party. It could just as easily be a wake.

Amid the rocks and sand stood Rocky 4, considerably slimmed down from Rocky 3. In the seven months since Dr. Lonne Lane had gotten the assignment to turn the innovative little prototype into a rover capable of doing real science, Lonne's team had cut Rocky's weight by two-thirds while adding two science instruments and a scoop in the belly to take a soil sample. I thought the new Rocky looked cute standing on top of the fake lander. Unfortunately, they weren't handing out money for looks.

Lonne stood hatless and pacing as he fidgeted in his dark suit in the broiling sun. Of all the colorful characters at JPL, Lonne is one of the most multihued.

He excels in a crisis and arranges his work life so he can go from one engineering triage unit to the next. In a place like JPL, where many people become the premier experts in their field through deliberate focus on a single aspect of science or engineering, Lonne never wants to do the same thing twice: "Always at deadline and always late," is how he describes himself. "It definitely gives me the feeling of being alive." When I managed the Mission Design Section in 1981, I hired Lonne hoping to use his creativity and energy to reinvigorate the mission analysis functions. In fact I spent a lot of my time trying to help him reduce his huge number of commitments. I didn't succeed.

Lonne is a short, intense man with expertise in developing scientific instruments, and he had had several successes.

Lonne was tapped to pull together Rocky 4 because of his reputation for being able to do tough jobs quickly. Rocky 4 was not a mere technology exercise but an opportunity to work in the forefront of a new direction in space science exploration: small, cheap missions launched in quick succession.

NASA had been formed in 1958 as a creature of the Cold War, to "flex our missiles" and show that they were better than the Soviets' missiles by orbiting satellites, exploring the planets, and, eventually, landing humans on the moon. While the human missions had declined in scope since Apollo, robotic missions were getting larger and larger; the Mars Observer satellite was launched in 1992 at a total cost of almost $1 billion, including a $300 million launch vehicle.

By 1992 the Soviet Union had crumbled and the Cold War was over. NASA's mandate was no longer as clearly defined and its budget was under attack. Dan Goldin had arrived as administrator and his oft-quoted "Better, faster, cheaper" was the new mantra to demonstrate to Congress that we too could get with the downsizing and right-sizing mentality that was sweeping the business world. The first program to try this new concept was Discovery. Discovery missions would be done for $150 million in 1992 dollars, not counting the rockets and mission operations.

The first Discovery mission was MESUR/Pathfinder. MESUR was the acronym for Mars Environmental SURvey, the latest concept for a network of weather stations on Mars long desired by the meterologists. Pathfinder was conceived as a test mission to demonstrate a cheap landing system for the dozen or so MESUR weather stations that would dot the planet and measure global surface conditions. The meterologists hoped to understand the Mars atmosphere and thereby shed light on Earth's weather by gathering data from both the Mars Observer satellite—planned to orbit in 1993—and these weather stations on the ground. With a small rover, Pathfinder could test roving as well as landing technology and deploy a few instruments.

Several colleges and laboratories had their own rover projects underway and many of these rovers were small, just as Rocky 3 was small, because of money constraints. JPL knew how much work I and others had done on rovers over the years and wanted to ensure that if NASA was handing out rover work it came to JPL. With a $2.5 million budget gathered from NASA technology and science study money, JPL overhead, and even the director's discretionary fund normally reserved for esoteric research, Lonne set out to build Rocky 4, the smallest rover that could conceivably be made to perform valid scientific tasks, and to demonstrate it by October 1992. That gave Lonne about eleven months.

The top-level enthusiasm and the fact that others disparaged the project and considered the deadline impossible piqued

Lonne's interest. "For all of NASA's doing things that no one has done before it's more conservative than most investment bankers," Lonne says. "Risk aversion is a religion around this place." Not so with Lonne. He'd just finished building a flight instrument for the Russians. The whole process, from the first crude sketch to the finished flight-ready instrument, had taken Lonne and his team eleven months. The rover assignment was a year-long project and he already had Rocky 3 to start on. No problem.

I was only involved at the very end of the fourth incarnation of Rocky. I had taken the job of project engineer on Cassini, the mission to Saturn that had grown out of the study I'd worked on in the 1980s. But after a year on Cassini I learned that JPL was looking for someone to persuade NASA to fund making Rocky a flyable piece of hardware after the demo. It looked like the best chance left to get to Mars. I was by far the most qualified person who applied for the job but that had never proved a guarantee of employment for me in the past. Besides, the person who got this job would be delivering flight hardware. I'd been turned down for several jobs before with the Catch-22 excuse that, because I hadn't delivered flight hardware, I couldn't get a job delivering flight hardware. I had even once been turned down for a middle management job with that excuse, but the man who was selected over me had no flight project experience at all!

"Uh," I later asked the selecting manager, "why did you choose Jim for the job?"

"Oh," he said blithely, "we want to groom him for top management, so we gave him this job so he could get flight hardware experience." I was amazed. Apparently he didn't even remember the excuse he had used to reject my application.

When I got the rover job I was thrilled but suspected deep

down the reason was that all the good old boys thought the rover would never make it to Mars, so they didn't apply.

My job and Lonne's overlapped by a month and I spent May 1992 getting reacquainted with the rover boys. Most of the MRSR team was there: Don Bickler, Brian Wilcox, and Rajiv Desai and the remains of the RI group. I could see why people had their doubts about Rocky's chances. The rover was having significant problems.

When they started working on the project, the team was promised the chassis would be delivered by February. In April, when I first dropped by, the chassis still hadn't arrived. They were testing out the computer code for behavior, but they couldn't calibrate the wheel revolutions to determine the distance the rover traveled. There were also significant problems with the computer board Lonne had ordered from a local manufacturer.

The board was a wire wrap prototype. Underneath the board, the mess of wires looked like a gigantic plate of angel hair pasta. The computer crashed constantly. The technicians would rush to swap out a chip while tensions flared. It somehow didn't have that calm, steady feeling of a situation progressively becoming more and more focused and controlled.

At the end of April, JPL turned the tension up a little higher by telling Lonne the rover demo would the centerpiece of the Surveyor anniversary in late June 1992. This moved up the project deadline by five months. He could have told his superiors they were nuts and refused to go on, but the challenge got him even more caught up in the rover.

Lonne established a new structure for his team to meet the work speedup. Every morning at 10 o'clock they'd gather in front of the HumVee in Brian Wilcox's lab for a stand up meeting. Lonne told his team at one morning meeting this was no longer just a technology demonstration. It was a launch.

"You've got a gate and a time," he said. "In our case, it's half an hour on June 27. You've got to be able to perform in that half an hour. The window opens and the window closes. If you don't hit the button and go, it's all over with. What you've invested and done is gone. They're not going to come back tomorrow."

He made them commit to accomplishing something significant every day. It's crucial to flight in general and critical work schedules in particular that you don't let a day go by. One day is a significant fraction of the time to launch on any mission. If you don't make quantifiable progress toward the goal of launching every day and you let very many days slip by, you won't get there.

He kept the meetings to fifteen minutes with nothing on the agenda except to answer the same handful of questions. What are we going to accomplish today? Does everybody know what they are supposed to do? Does anyone have a communication problem with anyone else? Any issues, raise them now.

Lonne was financially pressured too. Time was so short, he didn't believe he could get all the parts he needed if he waited even a day. If he did, there was a chance it wouldn't be there by the time a JPL purchase order freed up the cash anywhere from three days to three weeks after he made the order. If it was eight weeks before the company got the part in stock again, Rocky would be dead on the design table. Lonne fought with the procurement department to speed up their leisurely process.

Rocky wouldn't have the sophisticated path-planning capacity that Robby did, but neither would Rocky go bumping around blindly, turning each time it encountered an obstacle.

Brian Wilcox described Rocky as not being blind; it was just in a fog. It could see a few meters in front of itself but no farther. The long-range path planning was in the hands of humans as with Computer Aided Remote Driving (CARD). The lander would send a picture back to operators so they would know where Rocky was. Rocky would also send back pictures from its vantage point. The operators would pick a path for Rocky by posting way points on a grid applied over the scene. When Rocky came up against an obstacle along that path, it had the sense and skill to turn away from it while still keeping the ultimate goal in mind.

Lonne and Brian got into arguments over the cameras. Brian believed it was vital to the operation of CARD that the operator have stereo images from Rocky and the lander. Rocky needed to have two cameras on the front, widely spaced, to match the lander's cameras. Lonne told Brian he couldn't squander his limited mass budget on two cameras. He had to get Rocky down from 15 kilograms to 8. He attached a single lightweight video camera.

The team member with the most trouble-free aspect of this project was Don Bickler. Most of his work was already complete. He concentrated on trying to help Lonne reduce Rocky's weight by lightening the rocker bogie chassis. Based on Don's concept, the engineers and machinists came up with a way of fitting seamless hollow sections together to form a lightweight bogie without losing any of its strength, but he had trouble making the JPL machinists understand what he wanted. As usual, his solution was to build it himself in his garage. This was painful because he had to grind a cutter in his ancient lathe and the grinding debris was damaging to the lathe bed.

The final product of this effort was a beautiful piece of engineering art. The bogie was featherweight and made of luminous brushed aluminum punctuated with a regular series of portholes to lighten the structure and so engineers could get at the wires they subsequently stowed inside. Lonne and Don both proudly displayed prototypes of these in their offices. When they talked about it, they balanced its elegantly turned curve on their index fingers and watched it pivot ever so gently on point. From the looks on their faces, you'd think they were handling a piece by Michelangelo.

Lonne had planned a complicated event for Rocky. After the lander surveyed the scene, the computer would process the image of the Arroyo and a human would plan a path for Rocky. Rocky would set off from the lander and drop off a seismometer, take a reading of the mineral composition of a rock with its spectrometer, scoop up a sample of soil in the tiny shovel strapped to its belly, return to the lander, deposit the soil sample in a little bin, and await the applause. A very impressive set of tasks for such a tiny machine, we all thought.

As the demo approached things were looking worse down at the Arroyo. June was intensely hot that year and the rover couldn't handle the heat. Rocky would work for a little while and then just refuse to go any further. It suffered mysterious software glitches and a bug in the chip that the team couldn't locate. Rocky would sometimes just stop executing commands or stop communicating. In the crush of deadline pressure, the team hadn't kept track of which of the chips lying in the pile were the ones they'd discarded. When they needed to swap out a chip it sometimes took several tries before they got one that worked. It was alarming to see them frantically swapping chip after chip as anxiety peaked. And there was also the problem with the rock chipper.

One of Lonne's showpiece instruments was a little rock chipper, a slender pointed rod about the size of a pencil mounted on a simple cam device that peck-peck-pecked dozens of times a second. Scientists were concerned that Mars rocks might "weather" like those on Earth. Weathering by sun, wind, and water changes the chemistry of the surface layer of the rock so that it isn't the same as the "fresh" rock inside. Weathered surfaces are interesting, but the real geology of rocks is in the fresh material. That's why field geologists break rocks open.

So Lonne gave Rocky a chipper, knowing this was the kind of thing that would play very well to the geologist constituency at the demo. The force of the chipper wasn't much—you could put your hand in front of the point and it wouldn't hurt you—but it worried away the surface layer of the rock. At least that's what it was supposed to do. Actually it would often start off fine and then stop in the middle of its task, requiring someone to reset the computer to get it running again. If that happened at the demo, we'd all be updating our résumés.

Two days before the demo Lonne gave his team a pep talk in an attempt to crack through the cynical shells they'd all formed to handle their disappointments with Rocky. He'd faced these kinds of crises many times before and knew that with directed effort and inspiration, they could rally and pull it all together. I stood at the back of the pack and admired his style.

"We've only got so much money. We've only got so much time," Lonne said. "Anyone who works logically in these constraints is insane. We need to develop our own set of miracles."

The evening before the demo I wandered over to the Arroyo to see if his speech had transformed the atmosphere. It hadn't. The technicians had the computer out and were plowing through the rat's nest of wires trying to fix something. Out on the Arroyo, the crew was plotting a very specific path for Rocky and rearranging the rocks so no big obstacles were in the way. Everyone but me had urgent tasks to do so I did the only thing I could—support services. I helped set up the tent and made sure the guards were in place. I retrieved forgotten items. I ferried people to dinner and brought back food for the workers. I finally left the site with a sinking feeling of dread and the sincere hope that Lonne could lock his set of miracles in place by the next morning.

The next day the tent was crowded, not only with visitors and security guards, but with equipment and members of the rover team. Television monitors were set up with cardboard shades so observers could track the rover's activities even in the glare of the sun. One monitor would show traces of seismicity, movements of the earth that would be measured by the micro-seismmometer Rocky would carefully place on the ground. The JPL microdevices lab had made a breakthrough in engineering. The seismometer measured tiny tremors in the earth, something that normally required huge instruments stashed in the basements of buildings. Another monitor would let people see what Rocky's camera saw, and still another would show the data that the spectrometer would see when it looked for oxidized iron in a rock—what we thought we might see on Mars.

Sealed in a windowless trailer next to the tent were Brian Wilcox and his team, who would pilot Rocky along the carefully groomed path. The trailer was so jammed with computer equipment there was barely room for the consoles. At least they had air conditioning. I occasionally found an excuse to drop into the control trailer when it got too sweaty outside.

In the sun, Lonne explained to assembled press and dignitaries what was going on. At the appointed time, he gave the word to start the demo. Cameras rolled and voices were hushed. Then murmurs started as nothing happened.

"It's okay," soothed Lonne, "it just takes a minute for the controllers in the trailer to see the scene and then plan the path for the rover."

Suddenly everyone cheered as the tiny rover twitched to life. It lurched and, six stainless steel wheels clanking, trundled backward down the ramp. On the front of the rover was a simple arm with a hook from which dangled the cigarette-pack-size seismometer. The lanky young developer of the seismometer watched anxiously as Rocky reached the ground, backed up a couple of feet, and lowered it to the ground.

Then Rocky turned and clink-clanked away toward its first rock. Some crowded around the seismometer monitor as the developer tossed a rock to the ground, an event I later referred to in a report as "a simulated seismic event." A peak darted up in the trace on the monitor. The seismometer had detected the tiny earthquake!

Rocky trundled up to the rock, about the size of a football, and paused as if deciding what to do next. The camera and spectrometer were encased in a shiny aluminum box about the size and shape of a small book. A command from the controllers told Rocky to tilt the camera box down so the rock was positioned right in the middle of the picture on the imaging monitor in the tent. Then laughter broke out from the crowd as Rocky began to peck the rock like a frenetic chicken.

The rover drove an inch or so toward the rock and pecked it for a second or two. Suddenly a faint sizzling noise zipped through the rover. Lonne's eyes flashed down at the little beast still chipping frantically away. The vibration of the prolonged chipping had shorted out the computer board, leaving nothing to turn off the chipper.

I was expecting a quiet gasp from the team when they realized what was going on. The chipper wasn't touching rock at all, just jabbing frantically, endlessly in the air. A cynical snigger was audible from some of the team and several couldn't suppress their outright laughter. I guess weeks of high pressure had had their effect on these guys. The demo had never worked, they knew. There was no reason they could see for it to suddenly be flawless. All eyes were trained on Lonne as they waited for him to admit the problem. Elegant spiel-meister that he is, Lonne just kept on filling air discussing the rover's design features and the purpose of the hyperactive chipper. With an air of careless affection, he touched a spot on the rover (the power switch) and the chipper stopped. Lonne announced that the demo was over.

The crowd applauded the demonstration and officials took to the convenient podium to congratulate the team and one another on this technological breakthrough. Miraculously, Rocky performed just as designed. That was our story and we were sticking to it. In fact it *was* a breakthrough and there *was* cause for celebration. Lonne and his team had proved that a little rover could do some serious science, at least as far as they were able to make it go with the money and time they had.

While Lonne accepted the accolades, the team took Rocky to the technician's tent to figure out what went wrong. One of the computer team members swapped out the bad chip, and by the time the crowd cleared from the site, the team had repaired Rocky. They decided to finally put Rocky's mobility through its paces.

They had been so careful not to test Rocky to its limits lest they break some vital part of it before the demo that the mobility team was incredibly frustrated. All the demos had focused on navigation and science. Rocky had only been allowed to roll over tiny, harmless rocks. Now the mobility team turned Rocky loose in some tough terrain. First they commanded Rocky over rocks that taxed the wiggle-capability of the rocker bogies. On the back side of the Arroyo demonstration site was a trench about a rover and a half deep with sides at a 50-degree angle. They sent Rocky over the cliff. We gasped as Rocky skidded down the steep slope. "Go, go, go," we chanted as Rocky tried to scramble up the other side.

But it was too steep. Rocky's wheels scrabbled fruitlessly, tumbling small rocks down the slope. It looked hopeless, but then, like a persistent insect, Rocky turned toward the end of the trench where the slope was a little less intimidating and thrashed its way out to our roar of approval.

The next morning Lonne and I had a little hand-over ceremony. We shook hands in front of the team. "It's all yours," said Lonne. "Good luck."

I would need it.

We had a small JPL budget to write the proposal and keep the technology development going. I also was supposed to have what was left of Lonne's Rocky 4 demo money. But the demo had proceeded so fast, JPL's antiquated bookkeeping system couldn't keep up. There had been only spotty accounting of Lonne's Rocky 4 money and it wasn't clear how much remained. In fact the confusion about Rocky demo money was to plague us for the next two years.

If the rover was going to be an example of the Better, Faster, Cheaper juggernaut that was making its way through NASA headquarters, I knew we'd have to organize its design team differently from the way space hardware had been developed in the last twenty years. Magnificent missions to Jupiter and beyond were infrequent and every scientist wanted to be part of these "last ships out of port," as NASA Director Dan Goldin called them. With high cost comes very conservative design. You can't cut corners when billions of dollars are at stake.

I'd seen many a mission—I think every mission of that era—where the engineers were left scrambling trying to satisfy the scientists' increasing demands on a very limited spacecraft budget. To get a rover to come in on time and at cost, we needed to manage the scientists' expectations from the very first meeting so we didn't get burdened with some outrageous and expensive requirements.

JPL engineers had to rethink their way of doing business too, I knew. For big missions each department gets a lot of money and builds the best radio or camera or mechanism they can devise, and then the systems integrators bring all of these separate pieces together. This process was one of the reason spacecraft cost so much and took so long to construct. Our little rover wouldn't have the mass, power, or time to take that approach. Finding competent people who would be able to work in a radically different way was going to be a big challenge.

I searched out Kane Casani, an old sailing buddy with whom I had worked on the Mars lander project when I had first come to JPL. He'd just finished flying an Earth-orbiting spacecraft that he and his team had designed and built for $10 million in eleven months. The project was called MSTI (Miniature Sensor Technology Integration) and was a Better, Faster, Cheaper technology demonstration for the Air Force. He knew exactly the kind of people I should be looking for.

"You want people who have been here more than twenty-five

years or who have been here less than five years and nobody in-between," he said as he steepled his fingers and leaned back in his chair.

His reasoning was that the older folks (such as he and I) had worked on space missions in the early days when everything was inherently Better, Faster, Cheaper because such things had never been done before. These people knew that you could build spacecraft quickly and for relatively small budgets because they'd done it. The advantage of young people who hadn't worked on any big missions yet was that they didn't know that what we were talking about couldn't be done. He believed that people in between who had only worked on the big missions like Galileo or Cassini wouldn't be able to make the shift to Better, Faster, Cheaper.

He also advised me to choose the technology carefully. Most JPL missions either invented everything from scratch or used spare hardware from a previous mission because it was already tested as safe for deep space flight. Kane had used a lot of off-the-shelf military flight hardware and only developed new things where he absolutely had to. This had saved a lot of money, but Kane noted he didn't think there would be any available flight hardware small and low-power enough to be used by a 10 kilo-gram rover.

Finally, Kane advised if my team was small we all needed to be more flexible and less attached to hierarchy. He suggested organizing the project along the lines of a basketball team where positions and strategies were defined, but where play execution adjusts to the circumstances. This idea really struck a chord with me because I had long believed that the rigidity of com-mand and control organizational structures made them inefficient. I left Kane's office with my mind filled with the possibilities.

Here was my chance to create the kind of work environment I always knew was possible: a creative climate where anyone felt comfortable to offer an idea knowing it would stand or fall on its own merit. Everyone on the team would be responsible for the whole project, not just his little piece of it, because all had felt their contributions were appreciated. I'd seen glimpses of this during the best times of Mariner 10 but never seen a whole project structured that way from the beginning.

I had a new vision for how the team would be organized and work together. Instead of a hierarchical organization chart with me on top and the others stepping down the page in order of rank, I drew a circle. My metaphor was a biological cell. The work of a living cell goes on inside and the outside is a membrane which passes nutrients through to the inner workings but screens out harmful substances and attaching organisms. I viewed my job as being the membrane. I would make sure the money came in to nurture the work and I'd try to keep the evil forces of bureaucracy and micromanagement from impacting the team.

The team, on the other hand, didn't usually need me to act as interlocutor among them. They could, once jobs were agreed on and money allocated, work with each other as needed. Only when there was a dispute or a problem that they couldn't solve should they turn to me for help. I expected all my team members to be generalists and team players and they thrived on this approach. Now the challenge was to find engineers who would be flexible enough to work with this new kind of structure.

The people I inherited from the Rocky demo made for an

auspicious beginning. Brian Wilcox and his remote driving team were ready and willing to proceed to flight. I'd worked with Brian enough over the years to know his style was conducive to my management experiment.

Don Bickler was willing to help out, but he was now a group supervisor and wanted to have someone in his group lead the mechanical team rather than himself. Also, while Don was a genius he reveled in appearing to be an irascible old curmudgeon (although he was really a cream puff) and I wasn't sure how patient he'd be with the detailed flight project work. I was happy to hire his protégé Howard Eisen, the chubby, bearded New Yorker who had banged out the rocker bogie prototype with Don in his garage three summers earlier. Howard had also been part of the MRSR team. Now twenty-four, Howard had a Master's degree in Aeronautics and Astronautics from MIT and was already a veteran of two Earth-orbiting flight projects including MSTI. I was pleased to have his energy and his intellect on my team.

When you're hiring people for a project at JPL you begin to understand instantly in what regard the institution holds your project. With some projects, people just swarm all over you begging to be included in the mission. With the rover, some of my old friends from the MRSR study were eager to sign on to make a flight version of the innovations we'd been studying. For instance, Bill Dias, the MRSR mission planner, brought his "Day in the Life of a Rover" planning tool and pitched in to define how the microrover would operate. Outside that small circle, I had to use all my persuasive skills, call in a few favors, and impose some guilt trips to get my team together.

I was able to inflict enough guilt on the manager of the robotics organization that he ponied up one of his top engineers, Dr. Henry Stone, to lead the rover navigation and control team. Henry, handsome, blond, and bespectacled, was a thirty-five-year-old researcher who had his Ph.D. from Carnegie-Mellon University in robotics. I knew Henry from my days as manager of the robotics program when he worked on calibrating the accuracy of our robotic arms. In the years since that project had withered and died, Henry had distinguished himself with Hazbot, a small, remote-controlled robot that could be used by bomb squads and Hazmat (Hazardous Materials) teams to go into unsafe areas and investigate explosives and toxic spills. Significantly, he'd built Hazbot cheaply from commercial components.

The organizational structure was flexible within the subsystems as well. Brian Wilcox was Henry Stone's group supervisor, his nominal boss, but on the rover team Brian worked for Henry developing cameras and software. Don Bickler and Howard Eisen had a similar relationship. It gave me a warm feeling to watch people working together without needing a strong hierarchy.

I was both managing the team and leading the systems engineering effort that was pulling the design together. I thought I was doing fine, but the divisions that Howard Eisen and Henry Stone worked for thought I needed help. Their divisions were historic rivals. The mechanical guys believe that if you have a robust chassis, as Rocky most certainly had, you don't need a very big brain. The controls guys want to build the smartest brain they can. They proposed Bill Layman, probably the best all-around engineer at JPL and maybe the best in the world, as the only person both sides trusted to represent their interests fairly in making design trades.

My attitude toward this proposed addition to the team was

not open-minded. Instantly I feared that with Bill around I wouldn't get the credit for flight hardware. But when I entered the room for my first meeting with Bill I left my paranoid assumptions at the door.

There is something about Bill's manner that puts everyone immediately at ease. Bill is a tall, laconic fellow, extremely unflappable, unfailingly reasonable, and very creative. He has no management aspirations whatsoever because the politics and the organizational headaches don't interest him at all. He just wants to keep working on interesting technical problems. Bill said he'd make sure I got my flight hardware ticket punched.

As I was building the team, the NASA Science Office announced it would fund a demonstration of a low-cost entry and landing system with Pathfinder before it would commit to the MESUR network of Martian weather stations. The man heading up this challenging assignment was Tony Spear, a charismatic leader known more for his blunt talk than his social and political savvy. Tony had a pretty tall order before him. He was to land safely on Mars for $171 million; in equivalent dollars Viking had cost $3 billion twenty years earlier. My job was to convince NASA and Tony to give our rover technology demonstration a ride to Mars on Pathfinder. The rover added a completely new element to what was already a wholly unconventional situation. Never before had NASA approved a project where two spacecraft would be designed separately, funded by separate departments, and then be expected to harmoniously accomplish a task.

Getting an institution such as NASA to change even one element of how it does business is an exceedingly difficult task. Here we were trying to get them to change everything. I had a choice. I could either be discouraged and expect that the institution was so bricked in that it couldn't absorb this magnitude of change. Or I could blithely assume that if you removed the right brick, the whole wall would tumble and we could start afresh. As I woman doing something no woman in NASA had ever done before, I was trusting my instinct to choose that one brick. I just kept right on building my team.

We still needed someone to develop the power and telecommunication subsystems. Bill Layman spotted Ron Banes, a very senior engineer who was at loose ends, and we recruited him to work on powering the rover. He was close to retirement and no one seemed to be able to find the right slot for him. On the other end of the experience scale we got Lin Sukamto, a young engineer from Indonesia, to lead the radio but we only had enough money to pay Lin to work half time to find us a cheap, flight-qualified radio. Little did we realize how immense a chore that simple sounding task would become.

Rocky wasn't the only rover vying for a ride to Mars. Other organizations with rover designs wanted theirs considered. The Planetary Society held a "Rover Expo" on the mall next to the Air and Space Museum in Washington, D.C., on Labor Day weekend of 1992. Rocky 4 was on a pretty tight design schedule so we offered up Rocky 3 and Brian Wilcox escorted Robby to the Expo.

There were all sizes of rovers under the big tent on that hot summer weekend. An MIT undergraduate student had a little six-legged walker called Genghis, and a more sophisticated walker called Attila had been spun off from MIT to a little company called IS Robotics. Another group of students at MIT had developed a small six-wheeled rover which they gave me the honor of naming—I called it MITy. There was also a tiny tracked vehicle called Treader which was brought in by the same Dave Miller who had designed Rocky's control concept.

Ames Research Center was putting an autonomous control system in a Marsokhod (Mars car) they'd borrowed from the Russians. Marsokhod was relatively large—about the scale of the Little Blue Rover—and much heavier. The Russians themselves brought a tiny replica of the Marsokhod—about the size of Rocky 4. And finally there was a competitor to Rocky from within JPL. Brian Wilcox's group had built a little four-wheeler named Go-For which had the charming capability to do flips and right itself if it got stuck in rugged terrain.

The most impressive and impractical was 20-foot-high Ambler, a walker built by a team from Carnegie-Mellon. Ambler was so huge that one visitor exclaimed as he saw it standing at the edge of the demonstration sandbox, "What a great gate for the Expo!" Carnegie-Mellon had also brought Dante, robotics legend Red Whittaker's eight-legged, bright purple spider, which was being prepared for a daring climb into a volcano in Antarctica. Red Whittaker was famous for such exploits. Red had built robots which had helped clean up Chernobyl and Three Mile Island. But all Red's robots were like Red himself, large and robust. He scorned microrovers.

Robby loomed at the other side of the 30-by-50-foot enclosure, which was filled with sand mixed with red pigment to look like the surface of Mars. A large photograph of Mars taken by a Viking lander formed the backdrop for the sandbox. Rocky 3 looked like a midget next to Robby, and even next to Marsokhod, but it delighted the ten thousand people who came to see the robots run.

Although the Expo wasn't really a test, some very interesting things came out through the demonstrations. Genghis' and Attila's tiny pointed feet quickly sank into the loose sand and they "swam" on their bellies rather than walked. Treader bogged down when too much dirt piled up in the tracks. Sandia's Ratler got easily hung up on rocks and Brian Wilcox's Go-For had to be carefully managed by an operator to right itself after turning over. Of the microrovers, Rocky 3 and the MIT students' MITy were the best performers and the only ones that could use sensors and intelligence to avoid obstacles rather than climbing over them.

To fend off the clamor to substitute another microrover for Rocky, I wrote a paper that analyzed the readiness of the various candidates for flight, and projected the cost of substituting another concept for Rocky at this point. Based on the results of the Expo our arguments were convincing. The June demonstration had jumped Rocky ahead of all the other concepts.

I came back from the Expo optimistic about our chances, given the quality of the competition, if we could only get some more money to really get to work. Just at the moment when I had my team up to full staff and the chances looked good for solid monetary support from headquarters, Tony Spear gave Lonne Lane $65,000 of his project money to design a rover that would compete with mine. Lonne twice tried to turn down this assignment but he now worked for Tony—and Tony was adamant. He said, as the project manager, he needed to have an option. I suspected he was acting on his negative view of me and my unconventional team. He just wanted to get rid of us so he could concentrate on his own tough assignment. For my part, I was beginning to think I'd never make it to Mars.

6
Better,
Faster,
Cheaper

ony Spear, the project manager of Pathfinder, is a ruddy, barrel-chested man who walks the JPL halls with a fist full of pencils to record ideas that occur spontaneously to him under any circumstance. In the middle of a meeting with high-level managers from JPL and NASA, I've seen his eyes light as he gets an insight into some problem that he's been concerned with and rapidly jots notes and sketches, oblivious to the glares of others.

Tony is charismatic and inspiring, qualities that certainly were essential to bringing together the Pathfinder team. As a person who he saw as in the way of his achieving success with Pathfinder, I was not inspired. My job was to get him to do something he didn't want to do—fly the rover. In that first tempestuous year before Tony finally accepted the fact that the rover—my rover—was going to Mars on his spacecraft, our yelling matches occasionally spilled out into the hallways of Building 230, making our colleagues exceedingly uncomfortable. Our personality conflict was so intertwined with the project's management problems that it was difficult for me to separate his attempts to kick the rover off Pathfinder from his desire to never see me in his office again.

Our first intense skirmish came when Tony decided he was going to build a rover of his own to avoid flying ours.

When Mars Rover Sample Return died, the Mars science community scrambled to develop a cheaper way to get to the planet. As the NASA bureaucracy batted around ideas for the next mission, one concept emerged as the clear favorite. The weather scientists at the NASA Ames Research Center took the fairly old idea of a network of Mars weather stations and gave it a new twist: simplicity. Instead of multiple instruments on a few Viking-size landers there would be just one instrument—a weather station. Ames sold the MESUR concept to NASA by offering up an absurdly low cost estimate. Even with twelve to twenty weather stations, Ames said, MESUR would only cost $200 million. NASA enthusiastically supported this ridiculous figure—in fact held it up as an example to the other space science labs—and was considering allocating money for Ames to develop MESUR.

In 1991 JPL recovered MESUR in an intra-agency political battle by pointing to our charter and our vast experience in managing planetary exploration projects. We wouldn't commit to a $200 million pricetag, however, until we established if that figure was realistic. Tony had recently finished leading the operations for the Magellan project, which used radar to map the

heat-blasted surface of Venus. Since then Tony had been studying ways to implement Better, Faster, Cheaper missions which
made him the logical person to look at MESUR. By 1992, just at
the point when I was looking for a ride to Mars for the
microrover, Tony was in charge of both MESUR and Pathfinder.

The rover wasn't the only wannabe hitchhiker. The seismol-
ogists and the geologists, who had hoped to load the Mars Rover
Sample Return rover down with instruments, were looking at
MESUR and Pathfinder in a whole new light. Their question
about Pathfinder was valid: Why was a project funded by the
NASA science office not doing any science?

The best way to gauge if Pathfinder landed safely was to fly
some instruments along with it to see if they work after the
descent, the geologists argued. Scientists were trying to get it to
carry a seismometer to find Mars quakes, a spectrometer to analyze rocks, and a neutron spectrometer to test for water in the
soil, as well as a camera to look at new Martian vistas. And we
might as well have a weather station while we were at it. Suddenly Pathfinder was no longer a simple landing experiment.
The "last ship out of port" mentality that NASA administrator
Dan Goldin derided was alive and well even with missions that
were supposed to be small, cheap, and frequent.

Besides trying to find the money to build the rover, I had to
get Pathfinder to agree to fly it to Mars. Lonne Lane was now
Pathfinder's science and instruments manager, so any rover on
Pathfinder would be in Lonne's domain. Lonne saw my team as
unnecessary. If NASA wanted a rover, why didn't they just give
him the money to build one? Tony and Lonne made no secret of
the fact that they thought my group was at best superfluous to
their mission and at worst dangerous. After all, where was our

flight hardware experience, especially mine? How could we be depended on to deliver a functioning rover on schedule?

"What I bring to the table, what Tony brings to the table is what I'll call a good set of intuitions," Lonne lectured me. "I've got plenty of scars and knifewounds to show from the learning curve of hardware disasters. Mistakes you've made. Mistakes others have made that you've tried to correct. Mistakes that nobody's been able to correct and you die. I don't think until you've actually bled on the floor and been sliced up that you really understand the magnitude of certain decision pathways. This is not the place to teach you flight hardware."

From Tony's point of view, if the rover failed, it would be more than just a public relations disaster for Pathfinder. The rover would have cost him at least 10 kilograms of mass on his spacecraft and could end up diverting talent and time he needed to make his mission succeed.

Furthermore, he believed that it would cost him more than $2 million to integrate the "free" rover into his spacecraft. Tony decided that he wanted to take that same $2 million and build a tethered rover. With a tether, the rover wouldn't need its own power, communications, and perhaps not even a camera, all of which could be provided by the lander. At least if he had it attached to a tether, he was sure he could get even a very simple rover off the lander to drop off a seismometer, examine a rock or two, and send the information back. But if the rover was tethered, its brain and muscle and voice would be on the lander testing nothing for future freely roaming rovers. The NASA Technology Office wouldn't sink money into a rover on a leash. If Tony got his way, my project was sunk.

"Tony, take the free rover. Why spend your science money?"

I asked him, but saw I wasn't getting through. "You can't build anything useful for $2 million."

Even Lonne told him frankly he was out of his mind.

"Why drive yourself off a cliff?" Lonne remembers asking Tony. "You know what the answer is already. It's going to be an untethered rover."

"I'm not going to take no for an answer," Lonne remembers Tony saying. "I want you to do this. I want you to cost it. I want you to figure out what it's going to take to make it happen. It's an assignment from your boss."

"Okay," Lonne responded. "But I do it under duress."

Lonne and I had a long history and we had developed a lot of respect for each other over the years. Although Lonne didn't originally believe in the tethered rover, he played to win, and I was just as intent on flying a rover that would lead to longer range rovers in the future.

My dispute with Tony about the tether brought home how precarious the rover project was both financially and with the bureaucracy. Although we were second on the NASA Technology Office's list of projects for the fiscal year that started in October 1992, the technology people wanted some kind of promise from Tony that if they spent money on the rover he'd carry it to Mars. No such promise was forthcoming.

Despite my lack of money, direction from on high, and mandate, I had to proceed "as if." As if I represented the best mission concept in the country. As if I was just about to get the money to start bending metal on this concept. My favorite quote from the early space station days was my colleague's: "It's better to beg forgiveness than ask permission."

This was something with which I had vast experience. With the space station, MRSR, and the Exploration Initiative Studies, there had come times when it was abundantly clear that no one at NASA and few at JPL believed we could get the money to go ahead. Still, it was my job to continue to sell. After all, if the politics of space did an abrupt about-face, the project might be in vogue again. I would keep selling until I was thoroughly convinced it was just wasted motion, and then I'd try something else.

For the rover, the feeling was different. The cost wasn't too high. Engineering the rover was challenging but, with skill and some luck, not impossible. Although the technology offices of NASA and JPL backed the rover, many scientists sided with Tony. If there was money or mass, they wanted to spend it on instruments, not on the rover that would deliver them. In itself, the rover didn't have any really sexy instruments that could guarantee its passage to space. We could do some soil mechanics experiments with the wheels but only a few scientists were interested in that. The reserved ticket to ride was for the Alpha Proton X-ray Spectrometer (APXS).

This spectrometer peppers the surface of a rock with alpha particles (the nuclei of helium atoms). Each particle is either absorbed and re-emitted as a proton or X-ray, or bounces back into the detector. The mix of protons, alphas, and X-rays detected gives a reading of the elemental composition of rocks, the holy grail to the geologists. Best of all, the APXS was almost free. The Germans had volunteered to provide the alpha and proton detectors so all the United States had to pay for was the X-ray portion.

If the scientists weren't going to go for the tethered rover to deploy the APXS, Tony was angling to install an arm on the lander instead of flying our rover. Scientists knew arms would work. Simple arms had flown on Surveyor, better ones had scooped the soil around Viking, and very sophisticated arms had been constructed for the space station in the JPL robotics lab. A long arm could reach rocks with the APXS and would cost less than integrating the rover with Pathfinder, many scientists believed. Tony commissioned Martin Marietta to design an arm and they estimated building it would cost $2 million—just what Tony was willing to spend to get rid of the rover! My team needed to find a way to convince the scientists the rover was the way to get to rocks.

First we tried to get Tony to abandon the idea of the tether. The rover team rallied together to present to him a point-by-point comparison of a free-ranging rover with one on a leash. We filed into the conference room, charts in hand, and took our seats facing Tony. He scowled, ready not to be impressed. I was up first with a carefully worded, unbiased comparison between the tethered and the free-ranging rovers which we hoped would serve as the starting point for a rational discussion. Wrong, we soon discovered. Tony did not believe we could produce an unbiased analysis.

Our backup plan was to shift the rest of the presentation to the capable hands and cool head of Bill Layman, our chief engineer and the man with the most widespread technical credibility on our team.

Bill noted that even the best of tethers would hold the rover back from getting to some interesting rocks just a few meters out of its reach. What if the tether got snagged on a rock? What if, in the course of the rover's ramblings, it ended up running over the tether? A tether would have to be light or too much power would be required to haul it around. That meant that the teeth on the rover's tires could damage it by running over it. Plus, a rover highly integrated with the lander would add more cost and risk to the lander itself than would an independent rover.

By the time Bill began disputing the $2 million Tony claimed it was going to cost him to accommodate the rover, Tony was no longer listening. His head was bent down as he furiously jotted notes on the pad of paper. He just couldn't believe we would really be unbiased.

Oddly, Tony and I could have shared a lot if we had been willing to work with each other. Both of us felt that we weren't getting much help from our management. Tony called his project team a Skunk Works after the famous Lockheed advanced aircraft builders. "For a while there I was wondering if I did stink," he recalls. "It seemed like we were all alone."

Both of us had many bosses. Even before I was assigned to the Pathfinder project, I had three bosses. The one I considered to be my real boss was Murray Hirschbein, my sponsor at the NASA Technology Office, who controlled my money. JPL found it necessary to give me two more internal bosses. And Tony Spear and Lonne Lane thought that if my rover was supposed to piggyback on their project, then I must work for them—five bosses in all.

JPL's director for flight projects decided the whole project needed more oversight. He brought in a hard-bitten group of senior mission veterans he called the "Red Team" to review the project. Tony established his own additional review board as a way to get more direction and feedback. In addition, every project undergoes standard periodic reviews by NASA headquarters to ensure it's progressing on schedule and within the budget. Instead of the normal two or three reviews, Pathfinder had about twenty-five reviews in a two-year period. As Howard Eisen said: "Never have so few been reviewed by so many." Bill Layman estimates in our first two years we spent 75 percent of our time preparing for reviews. When you focus on getting reviewed, you deflect energy that should be used to get on with design and answer the questions we already knew we had to deal with.

The difficulty of the early Red Team reviews for my rover team (as well as for the lander team) was that we were so early on in the process—only a few months along and not yet fully staffed—that such reviews were premature. I was supposed to come up with supportable cost estimates when my team was still asking the fundamental questions that govern the mission: What must the rover do? How much can it weigh? How big can it be? How are we going to conduct the project? The competition between Tony, Lonne, and me put my project in another bind. Back in the days of Rocky 4, Lonne had told the NASA Technology Office that he thought that JPL could design and build the rover for about $10 or $15 million. No matter which way I looked at it I was sure we'd need about $25 million and I was still working on a way to reconcile the two estimates. Besides, I knew Tony and Lonne would be trotting out the $2 million tethered rover at this review. We'd look pretty bad if we couldn't even bring our rover in for $25 million.

To get a cost estimate I broke the work of building the rover into four subsystem teams, rather than the normal eight or ten, to save the cost of integrating them into a functioning system. Then I estimated how much time and money and how many people would be needed to build each subsystem. Finally I sent my estimates out to the team leaders—cognizant engineers, we call them—hoping for a match with Lonne's $15 million estimate.

When the answers came back from each area the total was

far more than $15 million. We had to start over again with a more reasonable idea of the minimum the rover would need to do on Mars.

Pathfinder mission studies told us a lot about the needs and limitations of the mission. We had a first-level cut at how the rover could carry science instruments, and some crude ideas about technology experiments to prove that small rovers could actually work on Mars. I wanted above all else not to overcommit. If a few days on Mars would meet the needs of the sponsor, we'd design a rover capable of surviving a few days.

Tony was insisting that both lander and rover should operate for at least a month, with hopes of lasting a year. I believed that from the moment we landed on Mars, we could be dying, so we needed to start work as quickly as possible. With the mission to the moon, the Apollo engineers had used the slogan "man, moon, decade" to encapsulate their criteria for a success: bring a man to the moon and returning him within a decade of Kennedy's pledge. My synopsis was "soil, rock, lander." If we could do one soil experiment, take a reading of the composition of one rock, and take one photograph of the lander, we would have satisfied the sponsor. Everything else was gravy.

Using Bill Dias's "Day in the Life of a Rover" software tools we concluded that the rover could carry out its basic mission in a week, so we made that the basis of the design. If you took a simplified rover as your starting point, then a lot of the design costs could come down, starting first with the number of people required to make it work.

In addition, I gave guidelines about how we would build the rover. Since the rover was an experiment we didn't need as much documentation. We would build real hardware instead of developing computer models. Essentially, we would be perceived as being more risky than the old way of doing business because we wouldn't have such an extensive paper trail.

The guidelines included a schedule that told the engineers how much time they had to design, test, and build their piece of the rover. So that, in turn, told them how many people they would need to do the job in the required amount of time. People equal money. The schedule also told them when to buy equipment. Everything in the schedule was driven by working backward from the launch date in December 1996. The planets wait for no one.

Gradually we whittled the costs down, but after two passes I was convinced that we couldn't do the job for less than $25 million. In fact, the estimate at the time of the Red Team review was closer to $30 million. We'd need another go-around with the team to get it in the $25 million bag but there was no time to complete that task before the review. Our only hope for meeting the mass, cost, and power limits was to show the review board how we would do things differently from the way anyone had ever done them before.

For example, adapting commercial motors to power the wheels was on the face of it a cheaper solution than building and testing motors of our own design. So even if we weren't 100 percent sure how much this solution would cost, we were fairly confident that it would be in the neighborhood of what we estimated. For some of the electronics and controls, Henry Stone had suggested that we could buy spare electronic parts from Cassini, which was finishing up its design phase, instead of buying them individually from contractors. This was a way to save us a considerable amount of money and time and surely an idea the review boards could endorse. We weren't going to spend millions on flight qualified radios, but hundreds of thousands on commercial radio modems. All our electronics would be stashed in one cheap, easy-to-heat box instead of scattered about the rover creating separate thermal problems. As for cameras, we were going to make our own out of a few chips and connectors.

Some of the team may have thought that this fresh approach would be cause for praise by the review board, but I knew better. I'd been through many reviews and knew that our whole approach would appear risky to experienced flight project people.

As my team and I filed into the conference room I could see how the deck was stacked against us. The Red Team was a distinguished bunch, twelve people, most of them with twenty-five years or more of experience building flight hardware. All of them were prepared to cast a critical eye at the way the rover team was doing business. After all, we were saying we were going to do everything on the cheap and faster than anything at NASA had ever been done before. Their decades of experience and intuition told them that what we said simply could not be done.

I was first up and made a final try at defusing the cost issue.

"I don't intend to present costs," I said. "But we'll show you our design and how we plan to cut back to get into the $25 million bag."

The review board chair interrupted me.

"Donna, we expect you to present cost data," he said. "I don't want you just to tell me how you're going to do all this. I want you to tell me how you're going to bring it in on budget. That's the purpose of this review."

"Okay," I said, "but you won't like them."

I turned to the team.

"You guys go get your cost estimates and stick them into your presentations." I plowed ahead with the review board picking at my every word like vultures. When I finished, Bill Layman came on, describing the overall system design.

Offstage, Henry Stone grabbed me by the arm. White-faced, he whispered, "That was a bloodbath!"

I grinned at him. "Naw, just your typical JPL flight project review."

Even though we showed our plans for getting the costs down, the review board leaped on our numbers. It mattered not that I *knew* that the costs wouldn't fit and told them so. They had to make sure that *I* knew that *they* knew.

After the first Red Team review the team assembled as usual in the Pathfinder conference room. Henry Stone was despondent. He didn't realize that being viciously attacked in such reviews was normal. The review board's job was to make sure that we hadn't overlooked anything, to make sure that we weren't doing anything dumb. Howard, Bill Layman, and I weren't quite so worried but Lin Sukamto was almost as depressed as Henry.

"Come on, Henry," I said, "lighten up. It's okay."

He peered at me owlishly through his glasses.

"It was a bloodbath," he muttered.

"No, no. Look, they didn't tell us to do anything we hadn't already planned to do," I said brightly. "They didn't find anything that we hadn't already figured out."

I looked around at the whole team.

"This is *good!*" I put my hands down on the table and stared until I had made eye contact with all of them.

"Now we've just got to do the hard part: get the money in the bag," I continued. "It looks to me like the best way to save money is not to build so many test models."

Our original plan had been for each of the major teams,

control and mobility, to have a rover model to test their designs in parallel.

Howard was brisk. He leaned back in his chair, tapping on his pad of paper with a pen.

"If the mechanical team can have Rocky 4 for a while we can change out parts and get a mechanical testbed while Henry's putting together some computer simulations and getting his design together," Howard said.

Henry squinched his eyes up and vibrated the skin above his eyebrows with his fingers, his habitual stress reliever.

"Okay, but I've got to have a model before too long to start building up a whole system so we can develop the software," he said.

Bill Layman leaned forward.

"Trade the model back and forth. Start with Rocky 4, take the brain off because it's going to have to be completely redesigned anyway," he suggested. "You mobility guys can probably make a lot of progress with some fairly cheap modifications while Henry and Ron are starting their design."

I jumped up and drew a horizontal line on the whiteboard.

"Okay, let's look at a schedule." I put months across the board: November, December, January . . .

I chewed on the end of the marker.

"What if we call the Rocky we've got Rocky 4.0. Howard, when can you have Rocky 4.0 converted to a mobility testbed?"

Howard ran a hand through his curly hair.

"Oh, it probably won't take more than a couple of weeks. If we take the computer and instruments off we can do a lot of testing at real Mars weight."

I drew a small triangle on the horizontal line for a milestone.

"Let's say that you get that finished by December. We'll call that version Rocky 4.1. You can hand Rocky 4.1 to Henry and he can turn it into Rocky 4.2 by putting a commercial computer on it so he can start software development."

"Rocky 4.3 can have an upgraded computer, something more like the flight version," Henry said. "We'll need to put the sensors on it—the cameras and the accelerometers that will sense tilt, and the odometers for the wheels."

I pointed at him with the marker.

"We can meet our objectives if all the rover does is bump into things like a bug and work its way around them," I said.

Henry leaned back from the table in horror. Brian Wilcox looked stunned; with that one statement I'd just obliterated a decade of his research, the research he was hoping to send to Mars. I understood how he felt but I also understood we now had no choice but to be slow, stupid, and simple.

"You can't do that! It's too risky," Henry declared.

I looked at all of them.

"Look, guys, we have $25 million, and that's all we have. Risk is just one of the things we have to take into account. Performance is another. If we have to move slower, we move slower," I said. "If we have to be stupider, well . . . We'll be just as smart as $25 million will allow."

Ron Banes spoke from his habitual position in the back row.

"How are you going to power these testbeds?" He waited for us to look at each other. "We've only got 0.2 square meters for the solar arrays on the flight rover. That's not much power. About eight to ten watts. That will influence the whole design. When are you going to start simulating how the rover will really work with solar power? How many test solar arrays will you need?"

We hadn't thought of that.

"Well, let's count up how many testbeds we need, " said Bill Layman. "We need to have one that's just like the flight rover so we can practice building one before the real thing."

We set up an intricate schedule for the Rockys and the two other models we committed to building: the System Integration Model (SIM) and the Flight Unit Rover (FUR). Each time Rocky was radically improved, it got a new number. By the time we had scheduled all the way through Rocky 4.5, and the FUR, we were no longer licking our wounds. As Bill Layman would say, we had a problem so hard, our bruised egos disappeared. Later we were united in victory.

Lonne had had the morning of rover Red Team day to make his presentation on the tether, while we had the afternoon for the free-ranging rover. Lonne and his team had been very creative in the three months that they'd had. In fact, they had two designs: a rover with the same performance as ours, except tethered, and a tiny, four-wheeled kiddie car he called an Instrument Deployment Device (IDD). His own cost estimates showed that the rover similar to ours would cost about $18 million—almost as much as our free-ranging rover and would be much more expensive to integrate with the lander. Even the little IDD, which could barely deploy an instrument within a few meters of the lander, would cost more than $2 million.

Within a couple of weeks we had our descoped rover project within the $25 million limit and were able at the next Red Team review to convince them we had a chance of doing the job. Poor Lonne. The second review board essentially told Tony to cut it out and focus on his own problems. The idea of a tethered rover remained alive for another year, but only in the background. Now we could tackle the next hurdles for our free-ranging rover.

For me, our Monday morning rover team meetings, when all

these creative people came together to make the trades that defined the rover, were the highlight of my work week. The atmosphere was charged with inventiveness and energy, making up for the hours I spent dealing with politics, wheedling NASA for money, and fending off Tony's efforts to scuttle the rover. The energy generated by these meetings buoyed me for my many late nights of laboriously adding up the money and doing the puts and takes of liens against the budget.

I know in the beginning some of the team saw these meetings as a necessary evil. They'd rather have been back in their labs or at their computers creating something. But meetings were the only way to break down the physical distance and form our identity as a team. The rover team was scattered around JPL. The control team was packed into tiny Building 107 where the Martian sandbox lived. Mobility was on the second floor of Building 158 with Bill Layman. Lin had a minute space in the corner of a lab in the telecommunications division. Ron Banes had to travel to another building to talk to the people constructing his power hardware.

Designing the rover was like working a giant jigsaw puzzle where six or eight boxes of puzzle pieces—representing all the solutions others had tried on previous missions to Mars—had been dumped onto the table. We had to pick out those that would fit together and could be squeezed into our tiny margins of mass, power, and money. The pace of the meetings was rapid, the intensity level high, the adrenaline flowing. Everybody offered ideas, drawing things on the board and on pieces of paper. Sometimes we'd jot things on sticky notes and move them around. To an outsider it might have seemed as though we were arguing, but these were the sounds of a group creating a product.

I seldom sat at the head of the table but usually in the middle of one side or the other. Move around, keep 'em guessing, break up the hierarchical pattern. The others would arrange themselves around the table. Howard and Henry liked to be center stage as their vociferous negotiations dominated the meetings. Ron Banes would almost always sit in the second row away from the table, although I'd frequently urge him to move up and mix in; he'd look thoughtful, study his fingernails, and sometimes appear to be asleep, but if we headed off on the wrong track on a power issue, he would speak up.

Lin Sukamto would wait patiently for the bluster to stop before offering her opinion. This was her first flight project job, but she proved to be a determined and innovative contributor to the team. Short, dark, and stocky, with a shock of black hair and the sweet face of a person much younger than she was, you'd never pick her for the kind to win an argument against the forceful personalities of Howard and Henry. Lin would calmly stick to her guns during technical arguments. Through these meetings she came to understand it was possible to disagree and be heard even if your voice was soft. "Sometimes that makes them listen harder," she said.

I'd usually start the Monday meeting by reporting on what was happening with regard to the money, the volatile political environment, and with the Pathfinder project as it affected us. Bill Layman would go over the system level state-of-the-rover, and Bill Dias would tell us where the mission stood. I stressed that we didn't want status reports on the subsystems, which we covered in the lengthy email I'd construct each Friday and send to the rover team, the Pathfinder team, and our many managers.

The focus of the meetings was on problem solving. If a plausible technical solution emerged, we'd take that concept as far as we could with Bill Layman as the arbitrator. Bill is completely open-minded and has great instincts. He's not one of those engineers who studies something ceaselessly until he's got a foolproof design. He sets up what he calls the "straw man" design—a design he's absolutely not wedded to, but which seems like it's solid enough in its basic elements. When some-one comes up with a better idea, he's happy to knock the straw man down. With his well-honed instincts and vast experience, he's usually about 80 percent right in the direction he takes. When team members got the nod of approval from Bill, they felt as though, as Henry Stone once described it, they'd "gotten the blessing from the Messiah." Bill had this amazing ability to take an engineer's proposed solution, turn it upside down with a few well-placed questions, and still allow the engineer to leave the meeting thinking he, not Bill, had solved the problem.

My interaction with the team wasn't confined to these meet-ings. When I got a free hour I'd drop in on one of the labs so I could get to know the junior team members and see what diffi-culties they might be facing.

Every time I'd go down to visit the mobility team I'd find them picking apart motors to figure out which one would be the best on Mars. They disassembled five or six different motors before they discovered the strengths of a powerful little fishing reel–size brush motor made by the Swiss company Maxon. They liked the fact that the motor brushes were made of precious metal, which is more hardy in space, and they liked the capaci-tor that dissipated excess energy in the motor. The only prob-lem was when you took the capacitor down to minus 100 de-grees, it sometimes shattered, leaving shrapnel inside the motor. With a few modifications to compensate for the flaws, Howard Eisen believed, these motors would be adequate on Mars. He called Maxon's U.S. representative to discuss these modifications. The Maxon guy told Howard he was nuts to ask for changes. Maxon sells its motors in lots of 500,000 for use in the aircraft industry. Howard was asking for special work for a meager order of 100.

I realized this was not the kind of negotiation we could conduct by phone and fax. In order to convince the CEO of Maxon that it was worth his while to make expensive changes on his $100 motors, we'd need to rely on personal charm and invoke the mystery and romance of space. I was scheduled to give a talk in France about machine vision for which the conference was paying my travel. I couldn't negotiate about motors but Brian Wilcox and I could write the paper and coach Howard on machine vision. I told Howard to present my paper and, while he happened to be in the neighborhood, drop by Switzerland and pay a call on Maxon.

Howard flew into Lucerne and spent the day sightseeing. The next day he took a train to the tiny Swiss town of Sachseln where Maxon headquarters are located. He carried with him drawings of the rover and the way Pathfinder might land on Mars, as well as an X-ray of a shattered capacitor to illustrate what he wanted the company to modify as well as some of the data his team had developed on the motor. After all, Maxon was a huge motor manufacturer and twenty-five-year-old Howard wanted to be well prepared for his meeting with the head of the company and its chief engineer.

When Howard sat down with the U.S. sales representative and the company's lead engineer he unfurled the exhaustive report he and his team had compiled on the subtleties and performance of this little motor. The technical discussion— engineer to engineer—went smoothly. The Maxon engineer was amazed by how well Howard knew the motor. When the president of Intergalactic AG, Maxon's parent company came in, the tone of the meeting changed. The president was concerned that modifying these motors for such a small order would be too much of a drain on the company's resources. This was Howard's cue.

The day before, Howard had visited the Swiss transport museum, Verkerhaus, which is mainly full of old trains and carriages. He was naturally drawn to the exhibit on space exploration which featured precisely one item: a latch a Swiss company had made for a weather satellite.

Howard switched from talking about motors to remarking on how much he'd enjoyed visiting Verkerhaus. The president responded that everyone was very proud of the museum and he was a big fan of it as well. Howard observed how small the space section of the museum was: that one tiny latch. He suggested that in three years, if the two of them could come to an agreement, Maxon could rightly augment that display with its electric motor, the one that propelled the rover around Mars.

That pretty much completed the negotiation for Howard. By the time he left Sachseln he'd walked the factory floor with the chief engineer to establish that there was a way we could determine the history of all the motors, persuaded them to let him see the technical drawings of the motor design, convinced them to make the modifications we wanted and to send us the performance report the company generates when it tests each motor. Maxon found that there were easy ways to accomplish the modifications that increased the motor's reliability in the harsh Martian environment. In the end, Maxon increased the price of each motor by less than $10.00.

Definitely worth the money we spent to send Howard from France to Switzerland.

My team was working together effectively despite our lack of money and institutional support. We had only $500,000 to spend for FY92, but Rocky 4.1 was already working with a new, more flightlike computer and with a better navigation system than Rocky 4 had demonstrated in June. The mechanism for getting us some more money was the Rover System Requirements Review.

Headquarters had decided to distribute the $25 million over the four years of our project in the wrong-size chunks. We had too little in the first two years and more than we could spend after we had delivered the rover in 1996. We desperately needed to move more money into FY93 and 94 and, if we could pull off a good System Requirements Review, Murray Hirschbein might be able to get the situation fixed.

The System Requirements Review is akin to a marriage ceremony in the world of spacecraft design. This is the review where JPL answers the question: Can we do what the mission requires at this cost? while NASA asks: Is the mission worth doing at this price? We could have certified our collective commitment to proceed through an exchange of email, of course, but it wouldn't have had the same significance as this institutionalized ritual of spacecraft affirmation.

Unlike the Pathfinder lander team, which was still considering different design options that could only be shown via charts, when the rover was being reviewed, we could simply place Rocky on the conference room table and tell it to move. When we put Rocky through its paces in our Mars sandbox it went a long way toward convincing skeptics that we knew what we were doing.

After a successful Rover System Requirements Review we had a contract with NASA and a promise to get us $2 million for the remaining six months of the fiscal year, plus the remaining $23 million in future years. Tony and the HQ Science Office had also promised at the review to fly the rover if we met the requirements.

But all was not yet rosy between Tony and me. When Pathfinder was given the go-ahead as a flight project, Tony took the opportunity to advertise for a new rover manager. I cried foul. Why was he advertising my job? I had competed for the job of building a flight rover and won it fair and square.

Tony got around that problem—he made everyone compete for their jobs. Lonne Lane would have been my only real competition, but he had left the project to work on an instrument to fly on the Russian Mars 96 mission. With Lonne out of the picture Tony had no excuse to pick anyone else to manage the rover. He was stuck with the rover and me.

Fortunately we had one very prominent scientist rooting for us. Former Viking scientist Hank Moore had been one of the scientists who ached with frustration when the Viking couldn't get to the rocks just a few meters beyond the lander. He had a grandfatherly love of the rover which he referred to as "the sweetest thing on six wheels."

Having such an eminent planetary geologist in our corner was a huge boost. He and Matt Golombek, the energetic Pathfinder project scientist, published a paper about the likely density of rock at the landing sites we were considering. They estimated the probability of an arm actually reaching a rock with the APXS to be much less than 100 percent. After that paper was published, scientists slowly came to accept that with the rover carrying the APXS the science of the mission would be better. When the scientists started saying nice things about the rover, we were a step closer to becoming a main focus of the mission's success.

In March I moved onto the second floor of Building 230, the windowless operations area that housed the Pathfinder project. I had decided that moving onto the same floor as Tony's operation could foster cooperation and allow me to keep an eye on things to avoid being blindsided. We had yet to settle who would pay the cost of the lander accommodating the rover. The government required us to keep the rover and lander money separate. So, after a lot of discussion and haggling, the Pathfinder and rover teams agreed that, rather than attempting to account for every dollar, we would exchange equivalent services. The lander would do all the functions necessary to integrate the rover, and the rover would carry the APXS. The costs for both functions were, as far as we could tell, about equal. This "barter" system worked very well.

Tony was worried that the spacecraft wouldn't have enough money to do its difficult job. His review boards had relentlessly reinforced this fear. As much new technology was being invented for the lander as for the rover, and staffing was progressing much more slowly. Not only did Tony need more money to solve the lander's already known problems, he needed a big reserve to solve the "unknown unknowns" that he knew would lie ahead.

He had already cut the budget for the ground system—the set of computers, software, and people that send commands to the spacecraft and collect the data during flight—and the budget for science instruments right down to the bone. In his search for still more money for the spacecraft he cast a jealous eye on the tiny pot of rover money. One day in June he called senior members of his team and me into his office allegedly to discuss the barter system, but in fact to demand money.

"You have to give me $2 million," he said to me. "I need that money to integrate the rover into the lander."

"You're nuts," I said, knowing $2 million was our entire budget for the year and we didn't even have it in our bank account yet. "Your team and I have a barter system going here that's working just fine. I'm not giving you a dime."

"I'm the project manager and you have to do what I tell you to do," Tony bellowed, turning red in the face, his curly gray hair practically bristling.

"Congress allocates our money," I shot back, my voice rising at the hubris of this move. "It would take an act of Congress to change that."

"This is an order," he commanded.

"You're just trying to get rid of the rover by taking all our money." I flashed into a fury.

We yelled back and forth, getting louder and more profane as everyone else in the room stared at the walls and ceiling, trying to ignore our unprofessional behavior.

Finally, Tony's big, amiable information system manager ambled in from his office next door. He cleared his throat and Tony and I swung around to look at him.

"Could you guys keep it down a little?" he said calmly. "I'm trying to meditate."

We drew back from our face-to-face stance and took deep breaths, but we both still seethed.

"This is a headquarters issue, Tony," I said. "It isn't your money. It isn't science money. It's technology money."

"Your damn rover is going to sink my project," Tony grumbled.

I believed just the reverse was true. Rocky gave the project a public presence beyond any JPL project in recent memory. The rover was exceedingly popular with the public and therefore increasingly popular at JPL. Rocky's sandbox was quickly becoming a standard stop on the JPL tour. Much like other robotics experiments, a functional Rocky put our scientific and engineering advances into a comprehensible, accessible form.

The little rover was photographed for a semihumorous spread in the April Fool's issue of *Road and Track*, which featured a chart of Rocky's design elements identical to the charts the magazine uses to rate the performance of an automobile. It cited Rocky's top speed as 0.0037 miles an hour. *National Geographic* also featured an item on Rocky that year which depicted me as the happiest woman on Earth because I got to spend a good part of each day playing with the rover. Well, it was at least partially true.

I was usually the tour guide for the increasing stream of guests to the sandbox in Building 107, from visiting classes of schoolchildren to U.S. senators. We'd rigged it up as a faux Mars with lava rocks scattered around and photos from Viking 1 as a backdrop. This confused some guests, who asked: "Are those real rocks from Mars?"

Some version of Rocky, bristling with wires and cables, was usually on the floor or stacked up on a crate reacting to the commands that programmer Jack Morrison was sending into its tiny computer brain.

To save money we had used a very low capability but flight-qualified computer, an Intel 80C85 that we had bought cheaply from Cassini spare parts. Brian Wilcox complained that its 8-bit-long words were too short for efficient programming, but Jack seemed to relish the challenge. He would type in a line of code, the code would command the rover's wheels to rotate or turn, and Rocky's sensors would measure the amount of turning. Patiently Jack would tap away, day after day, getting the rover's response to each sensor input to be correct. He needed a whole rover system to program the computer because of the heavy interdependence between what the rover "saw" and "felt" with what it did. "See" a rock on the left, turn right. "Feel" yourself tipping too much, back up and try again.

Jack, a good-looking fellow with dark, prematurely graying, wavy hair, also has an impish sense of humor. To demonstrate the rover's reaction to the laser light-striping hazard avoidance system, he programmed one of the Rockys to talk. There were five laser stripers. As each one flashed its red stripe across the sandbox, a computer voice would intone "right," "left," or "center," depending on which lasers were turned on. Visitors would often jump during hazard avoidance demonstrations, startled by the synthetic voice.

I had developed my own spiel to entertain the visitors and myself during these demonstrations. The thing that most interested people was the rover's size.

"That's full size?" they'd say in amazement.

"Yep, this is full size," I'd answer. "It's all we can afford."

"The rover is about as smart as a bug," I'd start off. "When a bug comes to an obstacle it doesn't think 'Aha, this is an obstacle. If I turn and move forward I can avoid it.' The bug just bumps into the obstacle, turns a little, bumps into it again, and keeps doing that until it gets around. The rover doesn't have to bump into the obstacle because she has the laser light stripers that stripe out across the ground and two cameras in front that can see the stripes.

"If the stripes are nice and straight the rover knows that the ground is flat and it's okay to move ahead. If the stripes wrinkle, she knows there's a rock. If the stripes disappear, she knows there's a hole or a cliff and she'll keep turning away until there are no more obstacles and then move ahead. If she tries three times and can't get around the obstacle, she'll stop and call home for help.

"We operate on a peak power of 16 watts at high noon on a summer day. Most of the time we operate on about 8 watts, which is about the power of the nightlight in your bathroom."

In the year to come it would be clear that, contrary to Tony's fear about the rover sinking his project, it was helping to keep his project sold. MESUR got canceled as too costly, leaving only the single Pathfinder lander. Without MESUR or the rover attached, Pathfinder was just a landing technology demonstration. Who would want to spend $171 million, plus $50 million or so for a rocket, just to prove we could land on Mars again? Pathfinder alone, as I saw it, had little sex appeal. Everyone—the public, the press, the review boards, and the scientists—loved the rover. With the rover attached, the Pathfinder mission was hard science with cover girl appeal.

7

Bending the Glass Ceiling

s I motored down Oak Grove Drive on my way to work the last week of August 1993 I was amused to find a pack of protesters near the entry gate to JPL. One had a sign that said "NASA Face Up To It!" and several waved gray, smudged reproductions of the helmeted "face" the Viking orbiters found on the Plains of Cydonia in the far north of Mars. Because of the lighting angles this weathered rock formation looks to some like a shadowy profile of a sculpture from some ancient civilization and has stimulated a belief among a few people that intelligent Martians constructed it. The believers come out to remind us of "the face" every time there's a significant Mars event taking place at the lab. That day their arrival was inspired by the mysterious silence of Mars Observer (MO).

A few days earlier, while the mission operations crew was pressurizing the fuel tanks for MO's blast into Martian orbit—our first brush with Mars in seventeen years—they lost contact with the spacecraft. If we didn't hear from MO today, there was a pretty good chance it was lost for good. Protesters were waving placards and Congress was scratching its chin about next year's NASA budget, but at JPL it was like a death in the family.

The previous Saturday's maneuver to increase the pressure in the fuel tanks for the thirty-minute thrust that would put MO in orbit was a routine procedure. Mission operations had sent up a command to turn off the radio, which could suffer a punishing jolt from the shock wave that travels through the spacecraft when the pressurization begins. At consoles scattered around mission operations, the engineers had waited for a signal back from the spacecraft, something they should have heard after about twenty minutes. When thirty minutes went by with no response, they clustered, speculating about what could have gone wrong, tension rising.

Glenn Cunningham, the MO flight project manager, was in his office four floors above mission operations listening to the NASA voice feed as he ate some take-out Chinese food. At the half hour mark, he called down to the mission control room where the engineers were brainstorming solutions for contacting MO. Command the computer to switch to the backup. No, don't send commands because that automatically triggers the backup program. Glenn believed there was a chance less than 0.001 percent that something had gone awry in the pressurization and blown MO up. But when an hour had passed with no sound from MO, Glenn asked his mission manager to declare a spacecraft emergency. He called the Deep Space Network and asked it to use its largest antenna to scan for the frequency MO's transmitter was to use if the spacecraft was disabled. Days passed, hundreds of commands were sent, and they heard nothing.

This Tuesday Glenn was hosting the orbit insertion event anyway, hoping the spacecraft would execute the commands to burn the engine despite the silence. Before they shut off the transmitter, the mission ops crew sent the sequence of commands that directed the insertion sequence. There was no real reason to believe the spacecraft was gone just because it didn't have a signal. MO might successfully go into orbit and then click back on. Everyone believed it was just a problem with turning the transmitter on again. Glenn placed his hopes on JPL's astonishing history of reclaiming spacecraft everyone had written off as lost.

JPL hadn't lost a spacecraft since 1971 when a faulty rocket caused Mariner 8 to splash into the Atlantic just after launch. JPL engineers learned how to nurse a wounded spacecraft along on Mariner 10. The Voyager missions to the outer planets had given everyone anxious moments, as when Voyager 2 encountered more vibration during launch than we expected which made its onboard computers switch the electronics into an unexpected configuration. Both Voyagers, thanks to some brilliant engineering, were still working more than fifteen years later. Within the last year the lab had made an excellent mission out of Galileo despite damage to its large antenna. The engineers had figured out a way to send back almost all of the science data on its small low gain antenna. Each day, after fruitless attempts to make contact with MO, Glenn stood alone at the podium in

Von Karman fielding sometimes hostile questions from the press. He refused to entertain suggestions that MO was silent for good.

MO was a magnificent mission in the grand old style. At a cost of nearly a billion, including spacecraft, instruments, and launch vehicle, it was designed to furnish more data than any scientist could analyze in a lifetime. It had a $22 million camera capable of taking thousands of high-resolution images a day, a laser altimeter to build a Martian topographical map, gamma ray and thermal emission spectrometers for geological content and history as well as instruments to measure Mars' magnetic field and gravity. All those scientific hopes and dreams were riding on that spacecraft as well as the twelve years of work some engineers had invested bringing it to life.

For the orbit insertion burn I joined not just the press but the friends and families of the MO team jammed into Von Karman Auditorium. If it didn't work, if we didn't hear from MO, we'd know the minute Glenn did.

At 2:40 P.M., the precise moment when MO was to signal its rendezvous complete, a silence fell over the auditorium, a silence so profound it blanketed the JPL campus. Eyes throughout the lab fixed on a red, white, and blue graph on the labs' television monitors. Any movement on that graph would indicate we had a signal. After seven minutes of excruciating silence, the voice of NASA flight control crackled through.

"We have come up negative in our search for a signal," the voice announced. "We will continue the search."

Glenn was so poised, so honest in the middle of this tragedy that he earned the admiration of all of JPL, NASA, and even the press. Two thoughts kept coming back to me as I watched my friend endure the grilling alone. If I were a high-level manager at

JPL, I would never let someone who worked for me take the rap. I knew I'd be up there with him or her. At the same time, I knew that if the rover wouldn't move or couldn't communicate on Mars, I'd be up there just like Glenn, all alone.

The old saying at the lab is: We're only two failed missions away from closing the lab and we're a single transistor away from failure. My mission was up next. I suddenly felt MO and the rover heavy on my shoulders. Perfect timing. Almost everything my team was trying that was new was suddenly running into trouble and we were running out of money fast.

Congress was refusing to pass the U.S. budget, even though October marked the beginning of the fiscal year, so JPL's cash flow was delayed. For a few months that year, JPL was so in arrears to the vendors that we couldn't order parts. When money finally did flow at headquarters, the NASA bookkeepers sent our rover money to the Science Office instead of the Technology Office. We couldn't get our hands on it until they figured out a way to transfer it back. Besides that, the funds phasing for the rover meant we were very short of money for fiscal year 1994. To top it all off, JPL's bookkeepers couldn't seem to figure out how much money NASA had sent to JPL for the rover. NASA was holding up the money already allocated to us until that got figured out. We were in imminent danger of closing down. If the team dispersed, I'd never get them back. The rover would be dead.

Fortunately I had a meeting scheduled at headquarters. I was racking my brains, trying to figure out some way to bring in money, when I ended up having coffee with the deputy manager of NASA's Mission Assurance Office, the people who certify spacecraft will work. All of headquarters was still buzzing with theories on why Mars Observer failed. My companion was very interested in understanding risk. Every spacecraft design involved risks. How do managers decide which ones to take?

An idea flashed into my head.

"The rover would be a great model for a study on taking risks," I said.

His face lit up. "How much would you need?"

"One hundred seventy-five thousand dollars per year all the way through operations," I suggested, pulling a number out of the air.

Done. Phew, that was a close one.

Shortly after we got the money and started working on analyzing the risks involved in building the rover, Mission Assurance loaned us a couple of consultants. One of them asked a question that opened our eyes to something we and the review boards had skimmed over. Our baseline telecommunications design relied on a small, commercial radio on the rover to communicate with another one on the lander. The lander would then relay the rover's messages to the Earth.

"You're not testing the modems very much?" asked the consultant.

"Well, no," admitted Lin Sukamto. "We don't have the money and the review board said that we should just go with them."

"Let's see," mused the consultant. "A failure of either radio and you lose the rover mission, right?"

We nodded.

"These are commercial radios, right?"

Nod again.

"So you're betting your $25 million that a $700 radio is going to be just dandy on Mars?"

We got his point.

We needed only a walkie-talkie style UHF radio to send data and photos a few hundred feet to the lander for transmission to Earth. Also we absolutely did not want a big radio that would need more than the trickle of power available from the solar panels.

Basically Lin's job sounded impossible. She needed to space qualify a low-power radio that was strong enough to withstand launch, entry, and descent and the radiation bombardment on Mars for her total three-year budget of $750,000 including parts and labor. Her only path seemed to be to find a commercial radio modem and test it and modify it for Mars. And it couldn't be a voice radio—it had to be a radio modem to communicate with the rover and lander computers.

Radios, as do all other electronics on a spacecraft, have to withstand the radiation of space. The aerospace jargon for something that can withstand radiation is "rad hard." As no spacecraft had ever used radio modems before, there was no rad hard modem. One problem with a modem's electronics being bombarded by radiation is that it can "latch up." When an electronic part latches up, it develops a short circuit and power flows through it as through a penny in a fuse box. If it latches up in space, you can't fix it. Power running unchecked generates heat and can damage or kill the part.

Lin had chosen a Motorola modem for its low cost and reputation for ruggedness. JPL's electronic parts people kept our costs down by identifying, just by long experience, parts susceptible to latchup. All but two of the modem's many electronic parts seemed okay. Those two were proprietary to Motorola and unfamiliar to our parts guy so we had to test them. Lin's technician sanded the top off the suspect parts to reveal their silicon chips and metal guts. Lin, the technician, and some parts people took the modem to the particle accelerator at the Brookhaven National Laboratory in New York to be bombarded with radiation. The parts instantly latched up.

They brought the modem home and after a few weeks of agonizing analysis returned with it to Brookhaven to see if long-term latchup would ruin the modem. Radiation hit the part and it latched up but nothing burned up! Even after an hour of running with a latchup, once the modem was turned off and on it worked fine. We were amazed. All we had to do was to turn the modem on and off periodically, something that Jack Morrison, the programmer of the rover's brain, could easily write into the code.

After that, we decided to stay with Motorola. But just like with the Maxon motors, we needed to make our handful of modems a little different for space and we didn't have much money to pay for it.

Lin didn't waste her time with the hierarchy of the Motorola corporation. She hunted down the plant in Illinois that manufactured these commercial modems and spoke directly with the lead engineer about her technical inquiries. He had made a career of building modems for commercial use, but Lin intrigued him with an engineering problem with a wee dash of stardust on it. Engineer to engineer, buddy to buddy, and unauthorized by his managers, he helped her determine how to modify the modem for space. Lin ordered some more modems for test and evaluation.

When the modems arrived, Lin opened up her order and found silvery, cigarette-pack-sized modems that looked identical to the previous ones. She gave one to the mechanical team so they could chuck the silver box and wrap the modem with stronger and lighter fiberglass. When the modem was stripped of its shell, though, Lin discovered it was completely different inside from the one we'd just spent thousands of dollars testing and modifying. Different parts, different arrangements, but the same part number. After a frantic series of phone calls, she discovered the batch she'd received had been manufactured by an entirely different plant from the originals. And, by the way, Motorola was just about to discontinue the line.

When Motorola executives got wind of Lin's quest to find the last few of the original modems, they were alarmed that we wanted to fly commercial modems to Mars. Motorola sent us a letter informing us that with our modifications they would no longer guarantee performance. And could we please not use them because Motorola didn't want the bad publicity if the modem failed. Lin went right ahead testing the modems and trying to uncover the last few of the original design.

The modems were the rover's mouth and ears but it also needed eyes, and our clever new cameras were causing trouble inside JPL. We needed stereo cameras that could withstand Martian temperatures but video, as Rocky 4 had used, was unnecessary. There's not a whole lot moving on the surface of Mars, and the rover itself would lose a race with a snail, so we didn't need, nor could we afford, the power to transmit live video of a static scene.

Brian Wilcox's solution was to take images with a charged couple device (CDD), the basic imaging chip in the average home video camera. JPL's camera group shook their collective heads. A CCD wouldn't hold a picture long enough for the rover's painfully slow computer to read out the image. Brian's idea was to take advantage of the incredibly cold Martian temperatures to hold the image on the CCD longer than you could on Earth. In fact it took Sojourner fifty-three seconds to take an image. The final design for each of Brian's cameras—an aluminum box with a lens, the pins to mount it, and the five chips connected to the computer—weighed in at 27 grams or just about one ounce.

The "camera" Brian's team devised wasn't, strictly speaking, a camera at all but more of an optical sensor. While Brian opened negotiations with Kodak to purchase off-the-shelf CCDs that were packaged for cryogenic applications, a firestorm broke out in the lab about whether we should be allowed to build our own cameras for the rover. The instrument building section wanted to make the camera and the scientists seemed much more confident that those engineers could produce a camera that would work. JPL's optics group offered us a camera with its own electronics, a processor better than the one that ran the rover, a memory chip, and a separate interface with the spacecraft. It was a wonderful camera but it was expensive, heavy, and power hungry, and we couldn't afford one like that for our measly five images a day. I told Brian to plow ahead with his idea.

While the cameras were built to withstand the cold, the electronics and batteries had to be warmer than minus 40 degrees. Howard Eisen was having a hard time with the Warm Electronics Box or WEB, as I called it. On a normal spacecraft the radio alone would be the size of the 2-foot-square rover. Somehow Howard's mobility team had to fit the modem, the APXS electronics, the computer boards, and the batteries in an 8-by-10-inch box. In buying commercial electronic parts to save money we'd ended up with a different voltage for every device. As electricity poured off the solar arrays it was filtered through one of five different power converters, all of which needed a place in the increasingly cozy confines of the WEB.

With commercial insulation the box got too cold. The team built walls of fiberglass honeycomb and filled the chambers with silica powder. While this method kept the temperature within the right range, with the powder the box weighed in at 3 kilograms, double the 1½ kilograms we wanted it to be. Our 16 kilogram total mass allocation included not only the rover but the ramps to get the rover off the lander, hardware on the lander to communicate with the rover, and all the tie-down, cables and pyrotechnics that would hold the rover to, and then free it from, the lander. We needed every gram.

The mobility team tried another solution—instead of building the box of honeycomb, build two thin fiberglass walls, one inside the other, just like a thermos bottle. Tiny Z-shaped strips of fiberglass held the walls apart without adding a lot of weight. Then insulation could be layered between the walls. They hit upon the idea of silica aerogel, which is 99.9 percent air surrounded by a delicate matrix of silicon. Aerogel is amazing to look at, a mysterious, almost invisible substance like a hunk of frozen smoke. But the commercial silica aerogel, even in sheet form, was still too heavy. Was there a way to get the aerogel to be lighter? Although the WEB passed a preliminary design review, the team knew there must be something better out there, so they just kept on looking.

Even if we could get the WEB to work it looked like we might not have any electronic parts to put in it. When we first started working on the rover, Henry Stone and I met with the spacecraft manager from Cassini, to ask him if we could buy some of his spare electronic parts for the rover. He'd agreed that we could have any that he didn't need. We'd sailed through the rover design reviews with a loud pat on the back for such a simple and low-cost solution to the problem of affording expensive electronics on a minuscule budget.

Once Henry finished his design, using Cassini spares right down to the rover's central processor, he placed his parts order and was refused. Cassini's parts guy had believed that there were lots of spares available. Now he discovered that there were only a few and the project wasn't giving them up.

When Henry arrived at the Monday morning rover meeting the next week he was still shaken by the news, unable to believe how he'd let the project down. We'd had an agreement, or at least we'd thought we had. Now, not only would buying parts cost us $300,000 more than we had planned to spend, the effect on our tightly coordinated schedule was devastating. With Cassini parts Henry would have been able to walk across the lab and pick them up. Now that he had to order them his schedule was blown. Just that day Henry had ordered a flight-qualified relay switch, a minor part on a spacecraft, and the electronics house told him it would be a year before it was available.

After Henry announced his dilemma, a hush fell over the room almost like a moment of silence. There were no recriminations, no blame, no shouting. Everyone knew Henry had done his best, but we had another problem—to rework the whole schedule.

"Okay, Henry," I said, "what's Plan B?"

Henry offered a solution: build another prototype so he could perfect the software on commercial hardware while he waited for the flight-qualified parts to dribble in. Again I had to figure out how to lay my hands on a few hundred thousand more dollars.

I was dispirited when I left that meeting, dragged down by

the worry about money. We were working hard but things were going wrong, as they always did on a flight project. Out there on the distant horizon of FY96 was more money than we could spend, but now, in 1993, we were almost broke. I was going to go hard after the money at the next review, but that was a few months in the future. There was plenty to be happy about: We were on Pathfinder (or at least we hoped we were). We were going to Mars. We were overcoming all the obstacles and excitement was building. There was still a long grind to go, but we had a plan to get there. What we really needed now was a party.

Some of the best times I remembered from Mariner 10 had nothing to do with the spacecraft and everything to do with goofing around together after work. Socializing after work builds a stronger team. For instance, Henry and Howard defused hostility by sailing together. My house was the perfect place for a party and has seen some great ones over the years. I live up a ravine next to a dry stream bed in the foothills of the San Gabriel Mountains. Nestled thus, my house has a sort of protected, nurturing feeling to it. The parties had tapered off after I'd married and settled down to family life. At this point, my marriage had dissolved fairly amicably after many years of trying to make it work and I was a single mom. It was time to make my house my own again.

The rover potluck was held on a blazing hot October Sunday afternoon. My non-air-conditioned little house was pretty warm, but the big old California oak trees provided some shade for the house and the kids played in the sprinkler I set up on the neglected brown plant life I euphemistically refer to as "the lawn." Most of the adults ended up inside.

We played a new videotape that I had cobbled together from rover test videos and bits by JPL's public information department for news releases. The highlight of that tape was a stellar performance by Howard in the spiel-miester tradition of Lonne Lane. Howard was demonstrating how the rover would stand up when it first got to Mars. Unfortunately the rover's batteries were low and the "stand-up" was painfully slow and incomplete. Undaunted, Howard talked on and on and on as though everything was happening exactly the way it was planned. The look on Howard's face inspired deep belly laughs from his colleagues. Tam Nguyen, Jack Morrison's partner in programming the rover, also took a lot of kidding. Part of the video showed Henry earnestly explaining the control and navigation subsystem. Tam's entire job was to look intently, but wordlessly, at what Henry was yakking about.

Conversations around Don Bickler were exceptionally animated as Don practiced his curmudgeonly manner—making dogmatic technical statements so people would argue with him. Howard and Henry sat on the couch, swigging beer and exchanging comradely barbs. I could feel a sense of pride and solidarity from the team as I circulated, getting in on a conversation here, a joke session there. As Henry later observed, when you ask most people what they're working on they describe the camera or the computer they are building, just that little piece. When you asked anyone on our team, the answer was: I'm building the rover that's going to Mars. I felt renewed spirit after the party, something I needed to draw on for the unanticipated flaps that always seemed to await me whenever I thought things were going pretty well.

How is it that sometimes the most innocent impulse can become the thing that gets you in the most trouble? I had had this bright idea a few months before the party. We'd have a contest to name the rover and bring some publicity to the project. The Planetary Society had agreed to do all the work of running the contest so it wouldn't cost us anything. I made up the rules. Students were asked to name the rover after a heroine who had blazed a trail for humanity (although I took a considerable amount of razzing from the male members of the team for deciding to name the rover after a woman!). The name had to be supported by a 300-word essay describing the deeds and virtues of this historical figure and how these qualities would help her explore Mars. This contest would mark the first time an American spacecraft was named after a woman. Typically they are named after mythological gods such as Apollo or Mercury, prominent scientists such as Cassini or Galileo, or heroic imperatives as with Challenger or Enterprise.

I knew enough about NASA to realize that one person's splendid idea becomes a bureaucrat's appalling faux pas. I looked carefully at the NASA regulation governing the way things get named. It said very clearly that major missions, and only major missions, must be named by a NASA committee. The rover was not a mission, it was an experiment and merely a passenger on the Pathfinder mission. So this contest couldn't possibly be a problem, I thought.

When one manager in the NASA Science Office at headquarters got wind of my contest, he went into an uproar. He ordered me to stop the contest. But it was too late—the Planetary Society had already sent out the contest instructions and school kids worldwide were sending in essays. Some teachers made it a class project. We ended up with 3,000 essays from all over the world with the authors ranging in age from five to eighteen. Ten members of the rover team volunteered to help the Planetary Society staff read and evaluate the essays. After several late nights, we had narrowed the list to ten names, with

Sojourner Truth the clear favorite. Valerie Ambroise, a twelve-year-old girl from Connecticut, ended her winning essay with: "Sojourner will travel around Mars bringing back the truth."

Now we had to get NASA to accept the name. I pointed out to the Science Office person that this wasn't a science rover, the Technology Office was paying for it and should name it. Murray Hirschbein, our Technology Office sponsor, agreed to be the deciding official. He also liked the name Sojourner Truth, and so the flight rover was christened. The spare, SIM, rover got the runner-up name, Marie Curie.

The NASA Science Office wasn't through with us, though. When JPL got its report card from NASA for 1993, the rover team was given a black mark for the Name the Rover Contest because it was undignified and had not "followed proper procedure." So much for new ways of doing business, I thought.

While we were having troubles on the rover, the lander was in even more trouble. Tony had decided to use all the inheritance that he could from Viking: the same heat shield shape that I had worked on in the sixties and the same parachute type that lowered Viking to the surface. Pathfinder would be coming straight like a cannonball through the atmosphere instead of going into orbit first as Viking had so parachutes needed to be tested for higher speeds. On an early test the lead engineer was poised in a helicopter over the desert ready to tumble the mock lander out the door and rip the cord that released the parachute. As he leaned over to look out he accidentally dropped the lander before the rip cord was attached. Smash. Scratch one lander model. Scratch one lead engineer who quickly moved on to a private company.

The airbags were another problem. Mike O'Neal and Tom Rivellini, two of the young mechanical engineers that Tony had rounded up, came up with the idea of using airbags to cushion the final fall instead of retro-rockets. We later found out that the Russians were planning to use airbags on their Mars 94 (later the doomed Mars 96) landers and they said that they had used airbags to land on the moon in the sixties and seventies.

Mike O'Neal had also borrowed from the Russians the idea of a lander that unfolded, although the Russians used a sphere that opened up like a segmented orange. Mike's concept was to use a simple, flat-sided pyramid.

The airbags were made out of a bulletproof vest material called Vectran.™ They had to be inflated instantaneously just a few seconds before the lander hit the ground, but how would the lander know when it was about to hit? The lander team tried triggering the inflation with timing, but there were too many uncertainties in the density of the atmosphere and the speed of descent. They added radar to determine the distance from the ground but only military radar was cheap enough and they weren't sure if it would work right. The radar had to detect the exact altitude even when the lander was swinging back and forth below the parachute.

At first Tom Rivellini wanted to have the airbags deflate quickly. His team devised patches that would blow out on contact with the ground, quickly spilling out the air. On testing, they found the patches didn't rip open fast enough. The airbags retained enough air that the lander bounced. By the time it hit ground again, the airbags were deflated and the lander smashed. Tom's team finally decided to just let the lander bounce along like a superball and deflate the airbags when the whole thing came to a stop. But with every change the airbags got heavier and mass was a huge problem for the lander.

As the system got heavier more atmosphere was needed to

slow it down. The heat shield couldn't get any wider or it wouldn't fit into the launch vehicle, so the trajectory had to get shallower to make the lander travel through more atmosphere before the parachute opened. The parachute couldn't open until the speed dropped enough. A shallower trajectory meant that the navigators had to be more accurate. Too shallow and the lander would just skip out of the atmosphere like a flat rock skimmed over a lake. Too steep and it would burn up or auger in, making a new crater in the battered surface of Mars.

The navigators agreed to go in at a shallower angle than they had planned to allow the spacecraft mass to increase by nearly 100 kilograms, but at the rate the spacecraft was gaining weight, that wouldn't be enough. The lander manager was desperate. At one point he tried to force us to fork over half a kilogram of the rover's 16 kilograms.

Once in the Martian atmosphere, the parachute couldn't slow the heavier lander down enough for the airbags to properly cushion the final fall. The lander team added rockets fired by radar which would slow everything to a dead stop just before the airbags inflated. More than fifty separate pyrotechnic events had to work perfectly for this complicated scheme to succeed. For two years project review teams were on the verge of saying: "You can't do this."

The only benefit of the lander's troubles from my point of view was that Tony had so much to worry about that he worried less about me and the rover. All our rover problems looked soluble if we could get our money moved forward.

By this time Rocky 4.3 wasn't looking much like a rover at all. When I took visitors by for the rover stop, our messy prototype still got oohs and aaahs for its performance, but also got giggles on its appearance.

We were using commercial computer boards which were almost bigger than the rest of the rover. Flat flex cables linked the sensors with the actuators that made the rover's parts move, and the cables were wrapped between chassis and computer so that Rocky looked like a woman with fat curlers in her hair. The chassis was getting old and tired and periodically a motor would have to be replaced. The mobility team was spending a lot of time tinkering with the motors and the APXS.

The APXS head had to be aligned precisely against the surface of a rock; it really couldn't take an accurate reading at a slant. Our initial cheap designs of a mud flap that would engulf the rock surface while the APXS took a reading didn't quite meet the specifications. Neither did the first couple of egg-beater designs which featured three bendable struts—much like those of a tripod—that would secure the APXS in place. There wasn't much room on the front of the rover, which was crowded with the two cameras and laser striping hardware. Yet putting the APXS on the back required putting another camera on the back of the rover so we could align the APXS correctly, as well as turning around a lot to get anything done. This one simple instrument turned out to be far from free.

By the time we were testing our final deployment design Rocky 4.3 was definitely rickety. The wheels jittered back and forth before each move. Jack Morrison hadn't got all the bugs out of the driving program yet. The rover looked like it had palsy as it inched across the sandbox, turned, backed up, and pressed the spectrometer against a rock. Visitors laughed at its antics, but it worked.

By now I'd added a few wry comments to my rover spiel to reflect the problems we were facing.

"The rover and lander talk to each other over these little

radio modems," I'd say, pointing to the modem on the rover. "They cost about $700 apiece—commercial radios from Motorola. Motorola told us that if we take them to Mars they're out of warranty. [Pause for laughter.] So we are spending about $500,000 testing and repackaging and qualifying them to go to Mars."

I used other cost comparisons too. "Pathfinder is about the same price as the movie *Waterworld.* [Pause for effect.] And the rover's total price is about a year's salary of a star professional athlete."

By early 1994 the rover's situation started to change.

Our long struggle over the minicameras was ended when Brian Wilcox handed Bill Layman and me a picture from Rocky's perspective of Jack Morrison's room in Building 107 next to the sandbox. It was grainy but it looked plenty good to our eyes. He'd taken it with the CCD camera his team had just devised. The rover's slow computer read the image at Earth temperature, not even at the cold temperatures the Kodak people thought were required to keep the image from fading.

"That's the camera we'll be using on Mars," I said, smiling.

Bill smiled too and pinned it on his bulletin board.

"That problem just went away," he said.

A WEB solution was also found. After a lot of sniffing around the lab, the mobility team had uncovered a scientist who was making silica aerogel for a mission to fly close to a comet. The aerogel would capture comet dust. This aerogel weighed only a third as much as the commercial stuff. The scientist worked his magic in a special little oven that would turn out diaphanous blue cubes of aerogel that could be sliced into flat rectangles and layered between the walls of the WEB box. When impregnated with gold paint the box not only absorbed heat better from its surroundings, it gave the rover a nice look.

Constructing a thermos box lined with specially fabricated aerogel still wasn't enough to keep our electronics warm in the minus 100 degrees nighttime temperatures on Mars. Although we had a letter from Headquarters forbidding the Pathfinder mission from using nuclear power, the mobility team had long ago decided that we would probably have to use RHUs— radioisotopic heater units—pencil eraser–size bits of plutonium encased in invulnerable film-canister-size containers. I resisted the RHUs until the team proved they were absolutely necessary because I was afraid our few grams of RHUs would get caught up in the antinuclear phobia that was plaguing Cassini. Cassini had spent about $25 million—the entire budget for the rover— just fulfilling the documentation requirements for the 44 kilograms of plutonium they flew.

The procedure for flying a tiny amount of radioactive material ended up being not as onerous for such a small amount. Still we had stacks of forms to fill out with accompanying reams of calculations to certify that the RHUs wouldn't contaminate the atmosphere if the spacecraft blew up on launch. The Department of Energy, which regulated and furnished the RHUs, even fired the canisters at brick walls and steel plates to certify they wouldn't break up on impact. Eventually, we got the approval, and in the process pioneered a new process for getting RHUs approved for space flight—one that will save future missions a lot of money.

There was a bright side to the control team's parts problems too. Before investing a lot of money in the expensive flight parts, the team wanted to be sure that its design was good. That meant that the power design had to be good because the electronics were tightly coupled to the power parts. And the power design required that the mobility design and the operational strategy hang together. We needed a review before we could move ahead. A critical design review (CDR) is by tradition a precursor to investing money in flight hardware. Our CDR was scheduled for May but in January Bill Layman and I offered up a scary proposition. If we moved the CDR up to February, and if the control team's design passed, the parts could be bought in time to make the launch schedule. I gave the team a week to think about it. They said yes.

As the CDR approached, I must have beamed with confidence as I walked the Pathfinder hallways. That's the only reason I can think of for the JPL director for flight projects pulling me aside and suggesting I take my team through a dry run before the review board met. He looked very nervous.

"We don't need a dry run," I said blithely. "I don't care if our charts don't look great. Our design will convince the board that we're ready to go. I'm sure of it."

"You're not scared enough," he said, scowling.

"Why should I be scared?" I asked.

"You just ought to be," he growled.

We had loaned Bill Layman to the lander team to help them with their mechanical design. The lander manager then talked Bill into chairing all the lander's detailed review boards. Since it wouldn't help the rover if the lander didn't make it, I approved all of this. In return I asked the lander manager to chair our rover CDR review board. It would get him up on the curve about the rover, force him to understand the rover's interface with the lander, and maybe make him friendlier to the rover.

The CDR went off very well and set off a series of reviews for our subsystems, all of which we sailed through, relatively speaking. Henry Stone fired off his order for parts and started counting the hours until they'd arrive.

After a lot of gnashing of teeth about the modems, Lin Sukamto and I decided to use our connections with Motorola's space division to help us with the modems. The Motorola plant in Phoenix makes flight-qualified radios and does a lot of business with NASA and JPL. Lin and I flew out to Phoenix and appealed to the space people to intercede with the commercial plant in Illinois. Instead of just opening a bin and grabbing six modems at random to send to us, we wanted them to go through and select the six with the best workmanship. Motorola finally found thirty and we bought them all.

Then the control team started getting some of the parts they ordered. Things were really moving, including our relations with the lander.

For me one of the best moments in perfecting our rover design was when Howard Eisen figured out a way for the rover to have absolutely no electrical connection with the lander. The rover needed to turn on just three times before it left the lander—during launch and just before landing so we could check her health, and finally at the moment Pathfinder settled safely in its landing spot. Howard was so afraid that a physical connection with the lander might fail to release, clamping the rover to the lander for all time, that he hit on the idea of placing a magnetically activated little device called a reed switch on the rover. When we needed to turn the rover on, the lander would activate an electromagnet positioned directly underneath the reed switch. When the reed switch closed, it connected the rover's own battery to its brain so it could send data via the modems to the lander's radio and thence to the Earth. The control team also designed the computer logic so that the rover would come fully alive only when its accelerometers sensed Mars's specific gravity.

By May 1994 our spirits were soaring as the rover easily passed all its reviews. Tony Spear was getting friendlier and friendlier. Rather than vanquishing him in some bureaucratic maneuver or design triumph, it seemed as though we were wearing him down through our string of successes. He had to admit we were actually making the program look good. The scientists were starting to say, "Wow, we can do neat things with this rover." They'd chosen some experiments we could do with the wheel tracks to test the density and loft of the soil. And we were meeting all of our schedules, coming in on budget, on our mass, and not making trouble for anybody. We were even helping the lander out by sharing buys of parts and supporting some of their design work, and sharing our chief engineer.

In return the lander engineers voluntarily solved one of our problems. We needed some way to get the RHU-generated heat out of Sojourner's belly while she was buttoned up inside the highly insulating lander. That was solved when the lander team, completed by Bill Layman, now the lander's chief mechanical engineer, allowed us to use the lander's fluid cooling loop. Coolant would swirl through pipes in the lander, carrying the heat generated by the computer and radio to radiators and thence to space. Bill directed that the lander add a "cold finger" inserted into the rover's WEB. The cold finger would be withdrawn when the rover stood up in the cool breezes of Mars.

In May we were conducting one of the mission's periodic

tests at Mars Hill in the Mojave. Every now and then we'd get together whatever aspects of the mission that were most in need of a tryout and all caravan out to our spot in the desert that is analogous to the terrain on Mars. This time Lin Sukamto came along to test out the modems.

Tony Spear was sure to be a hard sell on modems. He's a radio guy and had worked on the radios for Mariner 10. He was very skeptical that some cheap piece of commercial hardware would make the grade for flight. Tony paid his own way to attend the test and observed the proceedings from a hilltop some distance from the test site.

Lin had her modems attached to two laptop computers. The test started out with Lin and Henry Stone 5 meters from each other, likely the average distance the rover would be from the lander on Mars. When that transmission was successfully received, Lin sent Henry 50 meters away. Now she had Tony's interest. Henry sent the signal, which was easily received. Lin and Henry decided to take it to the limit. Henry went over a few sand dunes, out of Lin's sight. They were so far apart they each had to have someone signal by waving their arms when they were ready to conduct the test. Henry sent the signal and his spotter waved his arm. A few seconds later, with Tony watching, Lin received it. She leaped up in triumph. Tony scrambled down the hill and embraced her with a big fatherly hug.

The team brought back a momentous picture: Tony giving Lin a congratulatory handshake. That was the moment when I knew he had accepted the rover and our arguments were over. Tony later said when he was out in the desert watching my team working so hard he believed he had done the right thing in harassing us with the idea that he was going to substitute a tethered rover for ours. "I could see on their faces, they were going to show Tony," he said. "They were doing the best work of their lives just to prove me wrong."

I smiled. If he wanted to believe that, it was fine with me.

My relations with Tony improved significantly after that modem test in the desert. We really had nothing more to fight about. At a JPL panel that I, as president of the Caltech Management Association, had set up on Better, Faster, Cheaper, he actually embraced me onstage and told the audience he couldn't do his job without me. At that point I thought: He's got so many problems of his own, we must be looking pretty good to him.

A few weeks later he went on a business trip and came back with a present for me, a Marvin the Martian T-shirt. I gave him a big hug and told him how much I appreciated the gift. All he could do was shake his head and mutter: "I can't believe I did that."

Periodically Tony had these big parties for the project at his house in Pasadena where he set out a great spread of food and cleared the garage for everyone to dance. From that summer's party I actually have a photo of me dancing with my former nemesis wearing my Marvin the Martian T-shirt. Fleeting happiness for us, because there was big trouble ahead.

The failure of Mars Observer caused a reassessment of the whole path NASA was taking to Mars. We could continue going on the same way with an orgy of exploration every twenty years or we could try something new. There was much more consensus, especially with the enthusiasm for cheaper missions, for having a more systematic and frequent string of missions. With careful planning and steady funding from NASA, JPL believed that it could conduct a systematic program of Mars exploration with each mission costing only a fraction of a Mars Observer or Viking.

Support built around the idea of making a Mars program, something we'd never done before for planetary exploration.

I was amazed when Congress actually funded the Mars Surveyor Program. The program was first to launch a new orbiter in 1996 to recover the majority of the lost Mars Observer science. Then it was to fly two missions every opportunity—every twenty-six months—all for $150 million per year, about the cost of a major motion picture. Glenn Cunningham was picked to manage the first mission, later christened Mars Global Surveyor. The search began for a Mars program manager and I applied.

I felt as if this was the job I'd been preparing for all my life. I'd been thinking about how to explore Mars for more than two decades. I'd had papers published and had already written strategic plans for a sustained program of Mars exploration. The rover was also far enough along and doing well enough that I could legitimately claim that I knew how to deliver flight hardware. Still, I didn't think I'd get the job. Everyone believed that either Tony Spear or Glenn Cunningham was a shoo-in.

I was so shocked when the director of JPL called me into his office to tell me the job was mine that my mouth fell open. He swore me to secrecy because in a couple of days he was going to make the announcement himself.

I was having a hard time keeping my mouth shut, but I was succeeding until I found myself in a private meeting with Tony. We were in his long narrow office, he sitting at his desk, me leaning against it with my arms folded as we talked.

"Do you know who got the program job?" he asked.

"Uh, I don't know," I muttered, not meeting his eyes.

He could tell I knew something so he kept after me. Finally I admitted I did know. "But I can't tell you."

"It's you, isn't it?" he asked. "You've got to tell me."

"Yes, but you can't tell anybody," I said, regretting it instantly.

Shock came over his face and silence filled the room.

"How do you feel about this?" I asked him.

"I don't feel very well at all," he said.

"Look Tony, I really want to work with you," I said, deeply affected by his somber reaction. "Nothing should change. We're in a good relationship now. We're working well. Why should anything change?"

"Well, now you're going to be my boss," he said. "I've got to think about this."

A few days later we had an all-Martians meeting at Von Karman Auditorium. It was impressive to see how big the team had grown from my modest little study groups of five years before. There must have been 300 Martians jammed into the room. I got there just as the meeting was beginning and sat in the back row, surrounded by the rover team.

The room was buzzing because no one knew why the JPL director had called us all together, although many were speculating there would be an announcement about the program job. The director explained what a great opportunity this program was for the lab and for the exploration of Mars. Everyone nodded and smiled in agreement.

"I've called you together to announce that I've picked the program manager," he said. "It's Donna Shirley."

I was startled as the whole room suddenly rocked with applause. The rover team went completely nuts, hugging me and clapping and hooting, but everyone else—Pathfinder and Mars

Global Surveyor alike—was applauding and cheering too. As soon as I could break free from the rover team, I made the long walk up to the podium to shake the director's hand. I must admit I was embarrassed but it was much better than winning the Miss Wynnewood contest! The director looked in astonishment at the celebration. "Well," he said, "it's obvious that this is a popular choice."

I stood at the podium surveying the room full of my good friends and long-time workmates. My eyes filled with tears and I got a lump in my throat.

After running a long gauntlet of handshakes and hugs, I got back to my office and had a surprise phone call from Glenn Cunningham.

"I wanted to congratulate you and let you know that I'll give you my full support," he said.

"Wow, Glenn, thanks," I responded, truly grateful. "Actually, I thought you'd get the job."

"I didn't want it," he said. "Remember when we were working on the Mars studies after MRSR died?"

"Sure."

"You told me I wouldn't like that kind of job—studies and marketing—and you were right. I learned my lesson."

He told me the JPL director had actually called him in to ask why he hadn't applied for the position.

"I wouldn't be good at it," he had said. "Donna *would* be good. I think you should give her the job."

Within a few days my desk was piled with congratulatory notes. The announcement of my promotion had been sent out and the lab tradition is to send you congratulations written on a copy of the announcement. There were comments like: "You make a statement for womankind," from a woman I'd worked with. And another from a good male friend: "Hey, you've left glass all over the floor from that shattered ceiling."

Tony Spear, however, had boycotted the announcement meeting. He couldn't bear to watch me, as he saw it, be elevated above him. I didn't worry too much about it. Tony was an emotional guy but I was sure that he'd come around if I handled things right.

I sat in my chair, drinking it all in. My office was windowless, but in my imagination I could see a red dot in the sky. I'd finally gotten my chance to lead the world to Mars.

8
Launch!

My assignment in 1994 was to spend at least the next ten years exploring Mars, an opportunity that hadn't been offered before in our universe. Unlike the last-ship-out-of-port mentality of sending a huge craft weighted down with every instrument we could cram in the payload, we could systematically explore the planet every twenty-six months with each mission building on the knowledge acquired by its predecessors. We could send our robots to sniff out the planet's history and to see if we could find any signs of life at locations all over the planet.

There were thousands of interesting sites to investigate. Pathfinder was heading for a flood plain. With the next missions we could explore areas that looked tantalizing, like dry lake beds.

Could life have flourished in shallow seas on Mars? Maybe we could find fossil slime around the edges. Say we dropped some instruments into Valles Marineris, a 2,500-mile-long gash up to 5 miles deep just south of the Martian equator. Could life be hanging on somewhere in that crevice? Or could we visit the two places on the planet where we know there is water ice, the polar caps? If liquid water were to be somewhere, say inside the rocks as in Antarctica, life could be there too. It was hard to know where to start.

Certainly no one at JPL had any experience building a program. They were used to building projects one at a time. Each flight project had its own science strategy. Galileo: go understand Jupiter. Magellan: go map Venus with radar. Each of these individual missions also had its own spacecraft design, its individual instrument designs, its own operations system, and its own management structure. With a program, we could share.

The first thing to develop in a shared mode was a strategy for the program. I had a great opportunity to go to the scientists and ask: How can I help you?

There are three prongs of research about Mars: Life, Climate, and Resources. If there was ever life, what happened to it? Is it still there? If there wasn't life, why not? Mars started out much like the Earth and had water at one time. Why wouldn't life have burst forth there as it did on Earth? The search for life has profound implications. If life did start on Mars under very different conditions than on the Earth, then life is probably prevalent in the Universe. If life didn't start there maybe the fragile reservoir of our small blue planet is unique.

In looking at climate, we want to know why Mars turned into an icicle. Four or five billion years ago three very similar rocky planets—Mars, Earth, Venus—spun out into radically different fates. Venus, with its runaway greenhouse effect, turned into hell—lead will melt on its surface. Mars lost most of its atmosphere and went into an age-old deep freeze. And Earth turned out just right. Some scientists even call this the Goldilocks effect.

Mars's atmosphere is thin, but it still has weather. Global dust storms, perhaps stimulated by Mars's dramatic temperature fluctuations, rage periodically over the surface. At the equator the temperature can go from 0 degrees Fahrenheit in the daytime to minus 150 degrees Fahrenheit at night. On the poles it can plunge to minus 280 degrees. Water vapor lingers in the atmosphere. Some summer mornings clouds form over the Tharsis bulge obscuring all but the tops of its massive volcanoes. Martian valleys are sometimes shrouded in fog at sunrise. Besides just scientific curiosity, Mars weather studies could help us back on Earth. Mars weather is simpler than Earth's and as a result could help us improve our weather models.

Resources, the third and final major area of interest, has to do with sending humans to colonize Mars. If we were actually to send explorers there, they'd need water and shelter. The atmospheric pressure is like Earth's at 130,000 feet. Astronauts would need to wear pressurized suits. Even in space suits they couldn't stay very long on the surface because of the constant bombardment from radiation, charged particles, and the unfiltered sun. Are there lava tubes in the surface that might serve as shelter? How hard is the soil, if they had to bury their habitats?

I woke up as always in the middle of the night with my mind full of thoughts of exploring Mars. But now I wasn't just worrying about Sojourner and Pathfinder, I could envision wonderful possibilities for the fleet of spacecraft that we planned to send. I had the job of my dreams, better even in some ways than the

one I envisioned when I read *The Sands of Mars* in the tree
outside Auntie and Unkie's house. The first few weeks after I
got the job were the happiest of my life.

For someone with visions of the future the Mars Science
Working Group (MarsSWG) meetings were fascinating. This
group of scientists had been in place since the Mars Rover Sample Return days. They were chartered by the NASA Science
Office to plan scientific strategies for learning about Mars. Now
their job was to develop a strategy for learning about Mars on
the cheap, a little at a time.

The current chair of the MarsSWG was a wiry young geologist from Cornell. He and I conferred.

"We need a strategy that will fit into a budget," I told him.
"Can you get the MarsSWG to focus on the science content of
the program instead of trying to design the missions?" Scientists
were notorious for trying to out-engineer and second guess the
engineers.

"I'll do my best," he said.

His best was very good. He displayed an interesting combination of diplomacy, scientific know-how, and firmness over the
course of a few months, to develop a strategy that made scientific sense and looked doable.

The main theme that cut across each of the "life, climate,
resources" science objectives was water. Life needed it, climate
was driven by it, and future human explorers would need it not
just to drink but for spaceship fuel. So the MarsSWG developed
a water strategy. Pathfinder, if it landed in the right place—say
at the mouth of a river valley—would get a glimpse of a place
where water had been. The payload of the failed Mars Observer
had been carefully selected to map and understand the planet
from orbit, including looking for water on the surface and in the

atmosphere. The five instruments that were riding on Mars Global Surveyor (MGS)—due to orbit Mars two months after Pathfinder landed—would help in the water search, and we might be able to fly the other two instruments that had been on Mars Observer in 1998 and 2001.

The MarsSWG wanted the 1998 and 2001 missions to focus specifically on the search for water as part of a "volatiles and climate" theme (the most interesting volatile being water).

In 2003 it would be the turn of the weathermen and seismologists. The European Space Agency (ESA) was planning to fly a mission called InterMarsNet which would feature a very large orbiter, bristling with instruments, to map the planet. They wanted the United States to fly some landers with weather instruments and seismometers. It would be a less far-flung version of the MESUR network.

And, of course, all the scientists wanted a piece of the rock— a sample return. I argued vigorously against putting a sample return in the science strategy because there was no way it would fit in our $150 million per year budget. Wistfully, the Mars-SWG added a 2005 mission to "prepare" for a sample return. Then they attached a rider to the whole strategy: if there should miraculously be more money we'd sure like a 2005 sample return.

Armed with a science strategy that was endorsed by the NASA Science Office we were in good shape to plan future missions. Fabulous opportunity. Incredible luck. Chance of a lifetime. But also a big responsibility. In addition to being in charge of planning the new Mars Surveyor program I had inherited Pathfinder and its problems.

Most of the mechanical elements of Pathfinder weren't finished. A lot of things were failing when tested and the mass was going through the roof. It looked as though Pathfinder was growing to the point that it would be too heavy to enter Mars's atmosphere safely. The budget was dwindling and one could predict many liens waiting in the wings as the team finished the design.

The biggest problem was the airbags.

Tom Rivellini, a young, gray-eyed engineer with a permanent five o'clock shadow, searched the country to find a vacuum chamber big enough to test the hardiness of the airbags in a Mars-like atmosphere. He and his team had been playing around with three-lobe airbags attached by cords to a three-eighths scale model in a small vacuum chamber in New Mexico. This 6-foot-tall bundle of model airbags were made of a bullet-proof vest material. The engineers set the airbags in the chamber and a slapped a flat plate on them at 60 miles an hour to simulate crashing into Mars and see if the bags would pop. They worked just fine.

Then Tom and his team strung a cable between two mountain peaks and sent the airbags down on a trolley weighted with a 30-pound sandbag. When the trolley hit some bumpers, the airbags would drop to the ground on a separate cable at 30 miles an hour. This was how they found out that the supposedly sturdy material—wasn't. It cracked. The airbags were fine for the first drop, but subsequent bounces were risky. Each time they were inflated, they'd crack at a lower pressure than before. Finally they just blew up. The next set of tests needed to be with full-scale airbags of a different material, and dropped in more Mars-like conditions.

After calling around to the different NASA research centers, they found Plumbrook Station near Cleveland, Ohio, which is run by NASA's Lewis Research Center. Plumbrook is the world's second-largest vacuum chamber—100 feet in diameter and 120 feet high—and was built during the Apollo program to test out nuclear power plants for colonies on the moon. The facility had been mothballed for years until shortly before, when NASA started testing rocket shrouds there.

Tom and his crew built a 60-foot-by-40-foot platform that they could tilt at a 50 degree angle. Onto this platform they bolted jagged rocks each coated with a different color chalk. They planned to haul the airbags—with an 800-pound mock lander inside—up to the very top of the chamber and drop them on the slanted platform at 55 miles an hour. Attached by ropes to the side of the platform was a big slack net to catch the airbags after the first bounce. Bouncing back on the platform could smudge the chalk marks and they'd never know which rocks did the most harm.

After some quick calculations, the engineers determined that dropping the bags 120 feet they'd hit the platform at only about 30 miles per hour. What were they going to do? There was no taller vacuum chamber in the world. Tom and his team had already figured out how to solve this problem when he met with the head of Plumbrook Station to ask to test there. They'd attach giant bungee cords to the bottom of the mock lander which was suspended 100 feet in the air. Then they'd winch the bungee cords tighter and tighter like stretching a huge rubber band. When they had the tension on the cords just right, they'd let it go and the airbags would slap the platform at exactly 55 miles per hour.

The head of Plumbrook told Tom he was insane, but said yes.

They decided to start off with two layers of another, more

resilient bulletproof vest material sewn together with special thread by a company in Delaware that sews space suits.

The huge volume of the airbags had to pack down into four segments the size of thin pillows. This shape had to be folded perfectly or the rockets they were using to inflate it quickly would burn through the airbag before it inflated. After they perfected the fold and the mechanism for attaching the rocket to the airbags, the airbag inflation worked perfectly every time.

On the day of the first test Tom was very excited to at last see a full-scale model of his airbags. The airbag contractor team started inflating the cheerful yellow airbags to 1 pound per square inch (psi) for the first test. That's not a very high pressure compared to the average automobile tire inner tube at 44 psi. As each fold in the airbags expanded it made a little "pop." Tom was beside himself with tension. He jumped with every pop. By the time the technician announced the bags were at 1/2 psi Tom thought the bags were full enough. The surface was so rough and tough he skinned his knuckles when he rapped them on the outside of the bag. At seven-tenths of a psi, "POOF!" the airbags blew a seam.

The source of the airbag material's strength is the fact that it is highly resistant to stretching. This same quality means that if its seams aren't perfectly straight, they rip open.

Two weeks later the team was back with airbags sewn in a new manner which inflated without bursting. They cranked the airbags up to the roof, attached the bungees, and let fly. When they entered the chamber, the bags looked fine from a distance. The policy after a test was to inspect every inch of the airbag, every stitch of the seams. They found fine tears through the second layer of the bag. Then they uncovered shards of glass on the platform. A lamp in the chamber had exploded before the test, unbeknownst to them. If a tiny shard of glass was causing this kind of damage they needed to rethink the material. They needed more mass and Tom was dreading asking spacecraft manager Brian Muirhead for it.

The Pathfinder team was spread out in a maze of offices and cubicles on the second floor of the Spacecraft Operations Center building. They were always charging in and out of each others' offices to confer. Many decisions were made in the hallway. Tony Spear was one of the most persistent wanderers.

The upside of someone who wears his heart on his sleeve is that when he's happy to see you he spreads it around. As Tom Rivellini trudged down the hallway to Brian's office he encountered Tony and some other Pathfinder colleagues. The minute Tony spied Tom, a big paternal smile burst over his face.

"Hey, Rivellini, how's it going?" Tony said slapping Tom on the back. "Hey everybody, this whole project is riding on this guy's shoulders. Rivellini, you'd better do good!"

Tom gulped and went to see Brian.

Brian gave Tom some money to try out different materials. To see just how far off they were on the first of the new materials, the team decided to test the bags at full pressure. After this test the engineers watched in horror the video taken by a camera mounted on the airbag. Where did the airbag go? They rewound that piece of tape four or five times before they realized they were looking through the airbag. It had exploded. A gash ran all the way across on one side and there was a huge shredded patch on another spot.

The airbags weren't looking very promising but the rover was coming along fine. However, I needed to turn it over to someone else now that I was trying to build the Mars Exploration

Program. The logical person, now that Bill Layman and I were both working other jobs, was Jake Matijevic. Jake, a former mathematics professor turned roboticist, had joined the rover team in early 1993. He'd been working on broad rover systems issues in support of Bill Layman's systems engineering of the rover but his first love was math. His happiest moment so far had been working out a difficult mathematical problem having to do with how many errors the radio modems could tolerate when they talked to each other between rover and lander.

But because Jake had the curse of never having delivered flight hardware I thought I'd better stay as the rover team leader, at least nominally, until things settled down and Jake would be perceived by our sponsor and the Pathfinder project as a competent manager. I made Jake my deputy and joyfully handed over to him the job of keeping the books. He could make the budget balance in a fraction of the time that I could.

Tony was still upset that I was his boss. How could I win him over? I undertook to help him with some of Pathfinder's problems. The Critical Design Review was coming up and Tony had handpicked the toughest review board possible. Led by Jim Martin, the former Viking project manager, it was loaded with former Viking people, all of whom believed it was impossible to land on Mars as cheaply as we were attempting. We had thought the Red Team reviews were bloodbaths, but I'd never seen a board so hard on a manager as Tony's handpicked reviewers were. They nearly sputtered with incredulity at the number of things that still seemed iffy with only a few months to go before Pathfinder had to start building real flight hardware.

They also criticized Tony's management process. The NASA headquarters manager for Pathfinder was especially insistent that Tony have some better way of managing his schedule and budget. To the review board it all looked very ad hoc. Several of them took me aside and said I had to make Tony hire a deputy to straighten out his management. Tony had a very hard time accepting a recommendation from me so we argued over it for quite a while.

Although the problems with Tony and Pathfinder generated the most adrenaline, the opportunity that was most exciting to me was creating new management paradigms for JPL and NASA. I was working hard to make the Mars program a model of Better, Faster, Cheaper on the management side. I thought we could save quite a bit of money just by being more efficient and less luxurious. I cut several big offices in half, had a single secretary for the office staff, and started looking for ways to integrate things. In the big projects of old each mission had had its own business staff, but I hired a single business operations manager for the whole program. I also took a hard look at MGS and Pathfinder to see if they could share any services or equipment, but both of them were too far along and their missions were too dissimilar to benefit from reorganization. For future missions such as Mars Surveyor 98 I could start them off sharing operations services with MGS and save a substantial amount.

I upgraded the quality of the staff, often hiring women and minorities that had been overlooked by the establishment. We put all our business operations together instead of each project having its own staff. Money saved. We combined all the outreach functions into the Program Office. More savings.

And it changed the dynamics of working together. A couple of months after the whole staff was in place some of us were meeting about how to distribute our advanced study money among the different projects. Things were just zooming along, everyone was in agreement, nothing but constructive conversation. Suddenly we realized: we were all women! I'd never been in a JPL meeting without a single man present. In fact, I'd rarely been at a meeting where there was more than one other woman besides myself. I felt I had demonstrated that if you really just picked the best people a good percentage were likely to be the oft overlooked minorities.

The next project in the pipeline was Mars Surveyor 1998, which was to fly an orbiter and a lander. Mars Surveyor 98 was a two-for-one sale. We had to fly two spacecraft for the price of Pathfinder. Amazingly, there was a contractor who made a successful bid to build both orbiter and lander—Martin Marietta, who was building the Mars Global Surveyor (MGS) spacecraft. By making two spacecraft, even with different missions, Martin believed they could do it for the available money. One spacecraft would orbit, carrying the infrared radiometer from the Mars Observer payload that wouldn't fit on MGS, plus a small camera. The lander would land near the south pole and look for water in the soil.

I had to be persuasive with JPL's Executive Council to get John McNamee selected for Mars Surveyor 98 project manager because he (guess what) hadn't delivered flight hardware, but I finally succeeded. John immediately introduced a number of cost-saving management innovations. Instead of the usual detailed specifications for the spacecraft procurement consisting of hundreds of pages, Surveyor 98 had a thirty-page Request For Proposal that basically said: "Here's $100 million to build two spacecraft. Tell us what you can do for that." Headquarters tacked on several other requirements. The spacecraft, in addition to being half the cost of Pathfinder and MGS, also had to be half the mass. Headquarters was requiring Mars to be the guinea pig for a new, small launch vehicle that would be only half the size and cost of the rockets launching the 1996 Mars missions.

In spite of the challenges, Mars was coming together on all fronts. I was surprised when the deputy comptroller of NASA, a man noted for his irascible nature, praised me publicly for my management innovations. After a presentation where I showed how we had reduced our costs precipitously while keeping our projects on budget and schedule, he said: "The Mars Team has gone a long way toward convincing NASA headquarters that JPL is serious about new ways of doing business." Despite the praise from that tough audience my efforts went unacknowledged back at the lab. No one in the other JPL organizations was impressed. My economical style, which had cut overhead by half, was a curiosity but not a model for managers who were used to judging the power and importance of their organizations by the number of people under their control.

At least the scientific community was getting the Better, Faster, Cheaper perspective. Even though they wanted a sample return—and for good reasons—the scientists I was working with as program manager were much more realistic than the ones I'd worked with on Mars Rover Sample Return, even though some of them were the same people. They knew Better, Faster, Cheaper was not going to fund a huge rover and bring back dozens of samples. Some said, I'll just take a handful of dust. Another said he'd be happy with a single pebble. Or air, one said. I'll take a tiny cylinder of atmosphere and I'll be happy. But sample return of any kind was still beyond our reach.

The debate about where Pathfinder would touch down was underway, also driven more by constraints than by possibility. When the mission kicked off, project scientist Matt Golombek assumed he would be able to use a wealth of detailed photographs from Mars Observer to help him pick a good landing site. When MO failed, he brought in Viking scientist Henry Moore to help him interpret the twenty-year-old data from Viking and Mariner 9 along with some dust storm information from Hubble and old-fashioned telescopic observations from Earth. Hank Moore developed a lot of the data we use to evaluate the surface of Mars. He was nearing seventy, and had finally retired from the United States Geological Survey. Hank's stock in trade is a dry humor. He and the more tightly wound Matt made quite a wonderful pair of opposites.

Both Pathfinder and Sojourner needed to land between 10 and 20 degrees latitude north of the equator for maximum exposure to the sun. Higher or lower than that and they couldn't stay warm or get enough power to the solar panels. That single restraint cut out 90 percent of the planet. In the remaining 10 percent strip Matt and Henry looked for plots of land slightly below the hypothetical sea level of a planet without an ocean. The entry, descent, and landing system needed all the air it could get to decelerate it. The lower the landing site, the more atmosphere it would pass through.

The most delicate part of the landing was getting a good fix for the radar, the instrument that cued each of the many actions required to land safely. The parachute would open at 5.5 kilometers. In the subsequent fifty-five seconds, the lander would drop 4 kilometers while fixing its radar on the surface to cue the retro-rockets and the airbag inflation. If the surface was too high, there wouldn't be enough time for the airbags to inflate before the lander hit. This constraint cut the territory down to just 4 percent of the surface.

We couldn't choose a windy spot, either. At 12 meters above the surface solid rockets in the backshell would bring the lander to a dead stop while the radar cued the airbags to inflate. Strong winds buffeting the parachute-backshell-lander would swing it crazily like a triple pendulum. If the rockets fired while it was tilted too much, it would shoot sideways until the rockets were spent, sending it way off track and into a place much different from the one we'd picked.

Matt and Hank had to consider the slopes on the surface too. A steep slope could confuse the radar or make the solar array less effective. The land below had to be smooth enough to reflect the radar signal back. "There are some places in that latitude where if I only had one spacecraft, I would not send one," Hank said. He was referring to a place west of Olympus Mons that scientists call the radar stealth region. Radar waves sent there from Earth go in and never come back. The ground could be porous like a sponge or it could be simply an enormous pile of dust. The radar wouldn't get a reading to cue the airbags and Pathfinder would disappear into the void.

The territory we knew the most about was Chryse Planitia, where Viking had landed. Ares Vallis, a smooth portion of Chryse Planitia, offered the much coveted "grab bag site," which, because it was situated in the outflow channel of an ancient flood, perhaps would have many different types of rocks scattered among its teardrop-shaped islands and braided channels. Scientists hoped that there they could read the composition of rocks from the ancient crust and ridged plains as well as whatever else had washed down a billion years ago. But not everyone wanted to go there.

Matt held a workshop in Houston in the spring of 1994 and invited the entire scientific community to offer suggestions. After eliminating the spots that would harm the lander or rover, he was left with ten to consider. He put together a comparison he dubbed the Chart from Hell because it was so complicated. On it, with assistance from Hank, he listed all the data they could muster on these locations: likely atmosphere, terrain, rock density, slope, and effect on the lander. For his entire twelve-year career at JPL, Matt had been the study scientist on missions that had never made it beyond the study stage, so he had a lot riding on this site selection. "This is what you go through when you're flinging a quarter-of-a-billion-dollar piece of hardware at Mars," he said, referring to the Chart from Hell.

While technical progress was being made on Pathfinder, I was still worried about the management. I was putting in eighty hours a week and still not keeping up with my workload. Finally, I admitted to myself that I'd have to give up even nominally leading the rover team. Jake Matijevic was doing fine. He was great at detail and had developed a total understanding of the design. I was a little nervous, not because I didn't trust Jake and the team, but I wondered if they'd have trouble with both Bill Layman and me gone. But they proceeded smoothly. I felt proud that the team I had put together could get along just fine without me—it was a bit like sending your child off to college.

Pathfinder had another big review coming up and I was apprehensive about how hard the board would be on them. Review boards can be like an angry pack of dogs. When they sense a weakness, they attack. Pathfinder had followed up on only a few of the many improvements the board had suggested in previous sessions. I decided that instead of criticizing Tony's organization and methods, I could lend those talents to him. My proposal had to be carefully worded, however, so he didn't see me as trying to tell him how to do his job. I came into his office fully expecting he'd be threatened by my offer to help.

"Tony, I know you like to call these firestorms down upon

yourself, but it's really hard on the troops," I said. "Why don't we try to get a lot more organized? Tell you what, I'll take notes during the review to make sure that we have a set of concrete actions to follow at the end of every day instead of this random reign of terror."

Tony looked at me skeptically, but merely said: "Oh, fine."

Every day, all day of the three-day review I was there with my laptop, taking notes and recording every specific suggestion the board made. My college training in journalism was coming in handy—I could type like a son-of-a-gun. At the end of each day I printed out my list and distributed copies to the board members so they could get consensus on the recommendations— such as the idea that Tony hire a deputy to document the project and attend to the schedule, tasks that Tony despised. By the time the three-day review had ended, I was able to hand Tony a succinct list of items for him to act on. To my surprise, he was grateful.

"None of my other managers have ever done anything like this for me," he said. "That was really great. Thanks."

The review board's report made it clear that he had to get more organized. He finally appointed a deputy to organize the budgets, schedules, and documentation and things started to get a lot smoother. Pathfinder started coming together technially, too. The parachute and rockets were working nicely and the review board's suggestions had helped a lot in fixing the radar that would trigger the entry, descent, and landing system. Still there were problems. One was with the radio. Pathfinder's radio system was behind schedule and over budget when a new manager was pulled in to fix it. She installed better management of the contractor, dug into the design, and got it back in the box to make the first delivery of flight hardware on time.

But another part of the radio's problem was political. NASA headquarters was demanding that Pathfinder have a backup transmitter. The all-important data on the entry and landing needed to be sent back at all costs, even if the primary radio failed. Tony couldn't afford another radio, either in money or in mass, and he was getting a lot of conflicting inputs from JPL's radio people about whether it was possible to cheaply make a little emergency radio that would just send back that key entry and landing data.

I was at headquarters, being browbeaten by one of the managers because Pathfinder still didn't have a backup radio. Tony had been negotiating with JPL's radio engineers for months, but nothing definite was happening and we were running out of time to put new hardware into the lander system. I decided to take things into my own hands. I called the manager of the telecommunications division where the radios were designed and demanded that he straighten his engineers out. Could we get a million-dollar emergency radio or not? The division manager rolled up his sleeves and after an all-night design session promised that they could quickly build a very small, high-tech radio that would fit the bill. Then I had to convince the headquarters manager that just getting the most important data back was enough, and certainly all we could afford. Done, and done.

One of the last things to work out were the airbags. Tom Rivellini was a very worried young man. Each time he added a layer to the airbags he increased the spacecraft mass by between 10 and 15 kilograms. His best guess was that he was going to need four layers of the stuff to ensure that the airbags wouldn't explode on impact. The spacecraft manager told him he'd get no more mass. Tom was also starting to run out of money to test his airbag ideas. Each test took two to three days to run and cost between $20,000 and $30,000. The team brainstormed four different combinations of fabric and, since they could control which side of the airbag hit the platform, they made a set of airbags with a different arrangement of materials on each side.

After each test Tom would call Brian Muirhead, the spacecraft manager, with the bad news, no matter if it was three in the morning. Tom was watching the video monitor on the eighth test. When the airbags hit the rock-coated platform, the red chalk dust that marked the rocks was flying everywhere. "Brian, the airbags look like something out of the O.J. trial," Tom said during the late-night phone call. The tests helped the team close in on the final solution. They wanted to make a set of airbags where some sections were reinforced with several layers of material and other parts had only two. This had better work, Tom thought, because we only have this one test left. This test was to qualify·the airbags for flight.

In contrast with previous tests this one went just as the team had expected. There were tears in the airbags but nothing that would endanger the lander. In the end the airbags, which in Tom's initial design were a single layer of material weighing 15 kilograms, had four layers and weighed 85 kilograms, or 25 percent of Pathfinder's landing mass.

There was a moment in the troubled journey of Pathfinder when everything started falling into place. By January of 1996, less than a year before launch, the project received its first positive review. The airbags and the rest of the entry, descent, and landing system had tested out. The computer software still had a few bugs but it was essentially sound. Instead of attacking Tony, the review board was dumbfounded by a different kind of incredulity. "This is such a turnaround," said one reviewer.

"Wow, I didn't think you could do it," said another. "You have a chance to make it."

Matt Golombek and Hank Moore had been working with their Chart from Hell steadily since 1994, trying to narrow down the sites to just a few choices. From the initial ten, they'd come down to just three: Ares Vallis, Tritonus Lacus, and Isidis Planitia, a site in a basin in the western hemisphere. Hank and Matt had pretty much settled on Ares Vallis because, despite the fact that it was a familiar piece of Mars, it offered the best chance for doing useful science. To impress the other members of the landing site committee that Ares Vallis would be rich in its choice of rocks, Matt led us on a field trip to the Channeled Scablands in eastern Washington State, the place on Earth most similar to what Pathfinder would discover in Ares Vallis.

The Channeled Scablands are a bleak but interesting place. Between 17,000 and 12,000 years ago glacial Lake Missoula burst an ancient ice dam and floods ripped through the Columbia River Valley and out to the Pacific Ocean. The force of the water, equivalent to draining one of the Great Lakes in the space of a few days, yanked rocks from the mountains carrying them throughout the plain below.

As we walked through the flat, rock-strewn expanse at the mouth of the Scablands flood channel, it was easy to see why an equivalent place on Mars would be a great site for a geologist or a rover. To the north was a remnant of the great waterfall that had drained Lake Missoula. To the south stretched the surface over which this gush of water flowed, fanning out before it washed into the Columbia River Gorge. The part of the fan near the mouth of the flood is littered with gravel and rocks up to several meters in diameter. The number and variety of types and sizes of rocks was impressive to behold. The "monster of rocks" loomed as big as a house. I imagined Pathfinder appearing overhead, first as a puffy cloud, growing larger and larger as it hurtled toward the ground and then smashing against the craggy plain at 40 miles an hour with a tremendous bounce.

Tom Rivellini and Howard Eisen were there to look at the possible effect of the rocky plain on airbags and rovers, respectively. Howard had brought a crude model of the rover, to try its mobility in a realistic terrain. Video crews were on hand, as well as the local Washington papers, and they were delighted when Tom and Howard had to spend half an hour with inadequate tools trying to fix one of the rover's wheels before it could creep over the surface. Once it got moving, though, it showed that it could handle an amazing variety of rocks and gullies.

A month before launch, NASA certified Ares Vallis as the landing site, agreeing with Hank and Matt that it offered the best chance for the rover to reach the right rocks to do good science.

All during 1996, as Pathfinder and Sojourner were rushing to launch, so was Mars Global Surveyor. MGS was scheduled to launch a month earlier than Pathfinder, but MGS would arrive at Mars two months later because it was on a different kind of trajectory. At launch the rocket basically throws the spacecraft off the Earth in a slightly bigger orbit than Earth takes around the sun. At certain times Mars will be just at the point where the spacecraft and Mars orbits will intersect. Pathfinder took the fastest route. It was a light spacecraft and depended on the Martian atmosphere to slow it down before it hit the planet. MGS was heavier because it had to carry fuel to slow it down to get into Mars's orbit. It needed to arrive at Mars with a lower speed so less fuel would be needed to slow it, so it was supposed to loop outside Mars's orbit and hit the planet on the way back in.

MGS was built by a contractor in Denver; Pathfinder was assembled at JPL. MGS was also on a much shorter schedule than Pathfinder, only twenty-five months. By using spare parts left over from Mars Observer the MGS contractor was able to make the tight schedule. Careful management by Glenn Cunningham, who was the leader of MGS, resulted in an underrun of its $154 million budget by over $7 million. Pathfinder spent nearly every cent of its $171 million, but didn't overrun.

MGS and Pathfinder actually left for Cape Canaveral, Florida, at about the same time. MGS used a new travel technique—it flew in a giant military transport. Pathfinder took the conventional route—a truck convoy.

Three months before the Pathfinder launch Howard Eisen and some others from the rover team transported the rover to Cape Canaveral in a specially packed airplane cargo container. For months the team had been testing and retesting different elements of the system in a clean room to minimize the contamination of the rover. The rover was protected right down to the rocker bogie, which was wrapped in special antistatic tape.

Once it arrived in Florida, the radioactive heater units (RHUs), the pencil eraser–size pieces of plutonium that would keep the rover warm on Mars, had to be placed inside the rover. These little bits are under the control of the Department of Energy, which delivered them to the Cape for the final assembly.

The day the Department of Energy delivered the RHUs, a big black eighteen-wheel truck pulled up outside the Spacecraft Assembly Facility escorted by a fleet of unmarked vans. A dozen guards leapt from the vans brandishing machine guns. From inside the truck, another group of guards wheeled out a 25-gallon drum that contained the itty-bitty RHUs. One of the rover technicians made the mistake of trying to cut through the line of guards to get to the bathroom. He found himself face down on the concrete, tackled by a DOE guard. Although our RHUs were not weapons-grade plutonium, the government took the same security measures as if they were, to the amusement of the rover team.

When the team received the new APXS they were supposed to send to Mars, an initial test revealed that it produced false readings. The team was frantic. They needed to close up the spacecraft but they couldn't do so until they got an APXS whose readings they could trust. The engineers and the scientists were at war with each other over the problem. The engineers were adamant that they not hold up the launch of the spacecraft because of one instrument. The scientists felt equally strongly that they shouldn't launch the spacecraft unless they had the APXS because it was the reason the rover was going in the first place. The rover team decided to use the APXS they had been using to test the rover because they knew that one would work.

After the APXS crisis was solved, the Pathfinder team was ready to close the rover up inside the lander. Bill Layman and another very senior engineer had the job of final check. They went over the spacecraft with a fine-tooth comb. Everything seemed okay but when the three petals were pushed together to seal the spacecraft up, they didn't mesh perfectly. Even though the gap was only 50/1000ths of an inch, everyone worried that this small difference might prevent the lander from opening up on Mars. During flight the three petals were held together by a mating bolt. To open them, a small explosion shoots the bolt into a bolt catcher. Unless the petals matched up perfectly, the bolt might snag when it was fired and jam the petals together.

For three days the engineers worked frantically devising a way to make sure the bolt wouldn't snag. They had no computers with them in the assembly facility so they holed up in a meeting room and calculated by hand the clearances of the petals, their opening dynamics, and the speed at which the bolt would exit. In order to understand how stiff the petal was and how it might spring out in lighter gravity, they tested it by hand. One engineer pulled on a petal with a 50-pound fish scale so they could gauge the stiffness of the petals and confirm their clearance. Oh, the high-tech world of spacecraft engineering!

In the end they decided what the petal needed was a new bolt guide with a larger clearance. The team designed the new piece and had it manufactured at JPL. Three days after the problem was discovered, an engineer was on a plane to the Cape with a new part in his hands that he'd just machined. When the new part was attached, the petals closed smoothly with good bolt clearance on the last day possible before launch.

The final closing of the lander took place in the dark. The rover was designed to turn on when the solar panels detected light so the team didn't want to start it up by assembling it in a well-lit room. With just one light on in a distant corner of the room, Howard Eisen and his team carefully took off the wrappings that had kept the rover clean during the painstaking task of assembly. They stripped off the film that protected the solar cells. Howard held his flashlight at the side of the rover and examined each solar cell to ensure none had broken in transit or assembly. Then they sealed up the petals knowing the next time they'd see the rover it would be in a photograph driving around on the surface of Mars.

"Meteorite Find Incites Speculation on Mars Life" read a headline in *Space News* on Monday, August 5, 1996. "The prospect that life once existed on Mars is being raised following analysis of a meteorite recovered on Earth," the article began. Within two days the story had swept around the world. The human imagination was sparked by the idea that an alien life form, long speculated about but never proven to exist, might finally have been discovered.

Within two weeks, at the direction of NASA headquarters, we had replanned the whole Mars Exploration Program to focus more on life and less on climate and resources. The basic strategy was to fly orbiters to look for likely past or present habitats, then to send rovers to the best sites to collect and store samples. Finally, a sample return mission would bring them back to earth. MRSR all over again but at a fraction of the cost. Even so, all of the programs with sample returns were much more expensive than the current program.

We didn't hold our breath waiting for the extra money. We had launches coming up.

On November 7, we were ready for the second attempt to launch MGS. The first had been scrubbed for weather. At about 4 A.M. the Delta launch vehicle, with the MGS spacecraft tucked into the shroud on top, was rolled away from the structure that had supported it while it was being put together. The vehicle stood, shining in artificial light and then in the rays of the morning sun, next to its "gantry," which allowed liquid oxygen fuel to be loaded at the last minute before launch. MGS project people came out to the pad at 7 A.M. to admire the vehicle and have a group photo taken.

At noon I watched the launch from a crowded viewing area a

couple of miles from the launchpad. The loudspeaker counted down, joined by the crowd. At exactly noon there was a brilliant flash and a roar and the loudspeakers announced, "We have ignition!" The rocket rose on a column of smoke and flame and arced through the cloudless sky. We could see six solid rocket motors fall away in little trails of smoke at just the right time. We cheered until the rocket disappeared into the blue, then we ran back to the bus and went back to the control room.

Every event was tracked by different tracking stations around the Earth. Everything happened exactly on time and we cheered each success. The solid rockets burned out and dropped away. The first and second stages ignited and then shut off. The rocket "coasted" in a "parking orbit" for almost an hour before the third stage burned to send the spacecraft on its way to Mars. Then the spacecraft separated from the launch vehicle and was on its own. There were several anxious minutes until the Deep Space Network tracking antennas heard the spacecraft's own signals . . . but then there they were!

There was an orgy of handshaking and hugs all around. Glenn Cunningham had a huge grin. The spacecraft team at Lockheed Martin in Denver began studying the telemetry from the spacecraft. Some of the early results were puzzling. One of the solar panels hadn't unfolded completely. The engineers concluded that it was probably not a serious problem, and they had plenty of time to fix it before the first trajectory correction maneuver scheduled for thirteen days after launch. They turned out to be wrong.

The Russians were also trying for Mars in this opportunity. At first their November 9 launch looked beautiful, according to the news. But the next morning we learned that the fourth stage of the launch vehicle had only burned for a short time. The spacecraft had separated from the fourth stage, and had probably fallen into the Pacific Ocean.

The Russians' Mars 96 was a huge orbiter with twenty different instruments from many countries and it carried four landers. The mission was originally supposed to be launched in 1992, but had to be delayed first to 1994, then to 1996 because of lack of money in the Russian space program. If it had worked it would have been a wonderful complement to MGS and Pathfinder, but now it was a total loss.

Pathfinder launched at night almost a month after MGS. The first night it was delayed by weather. On the second night we got four minutes away from takeoff and a computer glitch canceled the countdown. By the third night we were all exhausted from all the days without much sleep. December 4 was a clear night with only a thin sliver of a crescent moon. As I entered the building to await the launch I noticed Mars just above the crescent to the left. Weather wouldn't be the problem tonight, I thought, gazing at the planet that had consumed my professional life for thirty years.

This night the countdown proceeded flawlessly and the rockets fired right on schedule. As it cleared the launchpad, I could no longer stay in my seat. I ran out of the building and joined a crowd who had the same idea as me. I stood shoulder-to-shoulder with Tony Spear watching as the rocket roared right over our heads and then off into the horizon, a big ball of flame in the night sky. We tracked it with our eyes as it climbed into the heavens, shrinking smaller and smaller as it appeared to leap over the moon and head straight for Mars.

9
Landing!

Pathfinder hurtled out of the Martian sky at 3 A.M., Mars time on July 4, 1997, smacking against the surface of the planet at 50 miles an hour. The force of that first bounce sent it 50 feet back into the air. It bounced more than fifteen times in its two and a half minute ramble, traveling more than half a mile before it came to rest almost on top of the place we'd picked for it to land.

By 4:30 P.M. Pacific time on Earth, both the sun and the Earth had risen on Mars and we had our first photos of the rocky desert landscape where Pathfinder had rolled to a stop. Project scientist Matt Golombek was beside himself with the scientific possibilities offered in the territory where Pathfinder had landed. To the southwest of the lander stood a place we later called the Rock Garden, a piece of land where rocks were crammed together over 30 percent of the surface and offered a stunning variety of samples, just as he and Hank Moore had predicted. Most astonishing to those familiar with the flat terrain of the Viking landing sites were the conical twin peaks that stood on the horizon. As the camera panned around the horizon even the first pictures showed that the terrain was much more varied than where the Vikings had landed.

Some rocks had sharp edges and flat forms that were consistent with having been hurled from an impact crater or a volcano. Other rocks were rounded and were all tilted in the same direction as if they had been positioned by rushing water. To make it easier for the team to understand which rock they were referring to, the scientists quickly named them. The lander camera team leader started it off by naming the rock nearest to Sojourner after a bawdy sailing song: Barnacle Bill. Barnacle Bill, the rock, looked lumpy, as though it was covered with sea life. Only a few meters away sat a large, lumpish boulder which was christened Yogi because to at least one scientist it looked like the nose of a bear. Within hours the scientists were jostling for position in front of wall-sized prints of the lander's pictures and demanding to name the rocks. The crush was so great that one young scientist was given the policing job. He would approve the names and put a sticky note with the selected name onto the picture. Squash, Half Dome, Wedge, Cradle, and Flat Top got stickies. Stimpy and Ren were named after cartoon characters, and there was even a Scooby Doo, a flat white area which later proved to be more likely a dried-up mud puddle than a rock.

The lander also got a name. Tony Spear announced at an early press conference that NASA had decided to christen the lander the Sagan Memorial Station. "I wonder if Carl Sagan is smiling on us," he mused. Carl, a scientist who had done much to popularize space, had recently succumbed to a rare blood disease. Sagan and Sojourner now communed together on Mars, a strange juxtaposition. At first they weren't speaking very well. There was a problem in transmitting between the Sojourner's modem and the modem on Sagan.

When the modem signal became intermittent and then stopped there was tremendous pressure on the rover telecom team to solve the problem. Lin Sukamto had just, the day before, flown in from Europe to join the operations team. After delivering the radio system she had married a Dutch citizen and moved to the Netherlands, but came back for the first week of operations. She was under a lot of stress. After that whole year of agony the team had gone through—tracking down the last few modems of this kind—meticulously testing them might cause them to break, ruining the mission. During those first hours of the mission they had very little data on how the modem was operating to help them diagnose the problem. All the rover data had told them was the modem's temperature, voltage, and current at that one point in time. Because the rover and lander weren't talking to each other the team couldn't analyze the signal to see if the temperature on Mars was affecting its quality or frequency. The team was confident, reminding themselves how many other elements of the lander or rover could cause this problem. Still, Lin was very troubled.

Tony Spear, on the other hand, was seldom to be seen after his initial triumphant jig in the control room. He'd excused himself from most of the press briefings, saying they didn't interest him. For months before the landing his sleep had been interrupted by dreams of the Pathfinder smashing into a thousand pieces at the landing. The dreams were mixed in equal part with visions of success. When it succeeded he had no desire to share his pride and relief. "I wanted to live that moment with myself," he said later. After all the hubbub died down, he retired to his office and sent email to all the naysayers who had told him that Pathfinder would never work and he should get out while he could. "What do you think now?" he taunted. That was Tony's sweet success.

Tony also wanted his team to get credit for their triumph. Brian Muirhead, now the deputy project manager, Matt Golombek, and Jake Matijevic for the rover plus Hank Moore and other scientists and engineers were the press conference stars. Tony's main press conference appearance was weeks later, after everything was working perfectly, and it was to be his swan song. He had already started working on other projects and was leaving Brian Muirhead in charge. A reporter asked him why he hadn't been at more press conferences. Tony explained, "Since the mission was a success I wanted the team to get the credit." He looked around the auditorium. "If it had failed there would have been just one old man up here explaining it."

"And one old woman," I shouted from the audience. I had always told Tony that I'd support him if the lander augered in or the rover didn't work.

On stage, Brian Muirhead leaped up and brought in a large sign that declared, "We Love You, Tony." The audience in Von Karman Auditorium was packed with Pathfinder people who applauded and cheered as Matt and Brian presented the sign to Tony. I joined in the applause.

As the sun turned the Martian sky salmon pink on the second sol—July 5—the rover was talking again. Apparently, the rover's communications problems had been caused by a temperature difference between the rover's modem and the lander's. If the temperatures were different the frequencies were different and they couldn't communicate. But now the temperatures had stabilized and when the rover woke up on sol 2, as it should, the modems' frequencies were close enough to communicate. Also, the lander's computer had reset itself in the night. Everything started to work. The lander camera popped up to its full height about 5 feet above the surface of the lander and took a human-height look around at the scene. Suddenly the rocks didn't look as big as they had with the camera's chin pressed against the top of the lander's electronics enclosure.

The rover team commanded Sojourner to stand up to her full one foot height, freeing herself from the lander, and to back down the ramp. Sojourner spent four minutes sauntering down the ramp at the stately pace of half an inch per second and finally placed her six wheels in the thin, dry soil of Mars. We pieced together an eight-frame, black-and-white video of the brief journey we'd been waiting five years to make.

The rover team was ecstatic. "We feel like we've been invited back to the party," declared a rover controller. "Life is complete," enthused the lander chief engineer.

And Tony Spear declared: "We're verging on near miracles, my wonderful team."

"The images that you see today show a perfectly deployed rover that has driven down a perfectly deployed ramp, making its first track in the soil of this planet, opening a new era of exploration," exulted rover team leader Jake Matijevic at a late-night news conference.

Where to go first? The target was obvious. All Sojourner had to do was turn and back up a few inches and the Alpha Proton X-ray Spectrometer should be smack on Barnacle Bill. Its interesting holes and dark color indicated it was native rock rather than a meteorite, and relatively free of red Martian dust. It couldn't have been a better candidate for analysis if it had been purposely placed there, just off the end of the ramp. Our first spectrometer reading showed Barnacle Bill to be similar in composition to lava found in the Andes Mountains, with more silicon than scientists had expected.

Less than a week into the mission, we had our first traffic accident on Mars. Jack Morrison, who had written much of the rover guidance software, was driving Sojourner to Yogi with stops along the way to scuff her wheels in the soil for the technology experiments that were the reason the NASA Technology Office had paid to send her to Mars. Jack instructed Sojourner to take a wide left to avoid a hazardous overhang on the front of the boulder. Once in a safe place, he ordered her to turn around and back up to the rock. Sojourner overshot the target by four inches. Instead of backing up to Yogi, which was over twice her height, she backed onto it. She ended up with one wheel cocked up on the side of the rock, causing the hazard avoidance software to order her to stop moving. Before the team could order Sojourner to adjust her position, the lander had a communications problem and the commands couldn't be sent to the rover.

Meanwhile the lander camera team was working on getting the best panorama of the territory around the lander. They had already taken the "Gallery Pan," a full, 360-degree color view around the lander. Now they were trying for the "Presidential Pan," which was to have a wider range of colors. A software bug was preventing them from completing this view, which they intended to present to President Clinton at an upcoming ceremony at the White House.

I was glad of the delay. I didn't want the picture we were

going to give to the president showing Sojourner's back wheel cocked up on a rock. The men on the team were convinced this proved Sojourner was really a male rover. The team teased Jack a little, threatening to revoke his license to drive on Mars, but they let him off with just a warning once the Pathfinder team fixed the communications glitch and Jack got Sojourner off the rock. Sojourner was decorously at Yogi's side with the APXS correctly deployed when the camera team was finally able to complete the panorama.

On Earth we were communicating, too. Our outreach manager had foreseen that a lot of interest in Pathfinder would show up in hits on our Web site and we were ready with mirror sites all around the world. It was barely enough. On July 8 we had 47 million hits, a record for the Internet. By the end of the week we were over 150 million, and within a month there were over 500 million hits. Enthusiasm for the rover was expressed not only in the frenzied Internet attack and the media coverage but in people's desperate search for Hot Wheel rovers. Mattel had come out with an action pack featuring the Pathfinder spacecraft, the lander, and a tiny but perfect rover, but the toy stores couldn't keep them in stock. I got pathetic e-mails from grandmothers who appealed to me to intercede for their grandchildren and find them a rover toy, but I couldn't get even enough to give my own clamoring stepgrandchildren.

As Sojourner and her Earthbound helpers were gleefully exploring, our other mission to Mars was in crisis. It was discovered shortly after Mars Global Surveyor's perfect launch that one of its two solar panels had only partially opened.

During launch the solar panels were tucked close to the body of the spacecraft like the folded wings of a bird. After the spacecraft cut free from the launch vehicle it stretched open its solar panels in a complicated, double-flip maneuver. When the solar panels had extended, on one of the panels the shaft of the damper—designed to ensure that the panel didn't open with a jolt—had evidently broken. A small piece of it had lodged in the joint, preventing the panel from extending fully. This was like having the damper on a door break and jam into the hinge. Instead of being locked into place sticking straight out the panel was bent at its shoulder at an angle of 20.5 degrees. During cruise, when Glenn and crew were supposed to be relaxing, they were working frantically to figure out how to fly the wounded spacecraft without breaking off the panel and losing the spacecraft forever.

While the Pathfinder team were happily examining the Martian rocks and soil, MGS was debating their very grave choices. I was present for many of their meetings, not really to help Glenn decide what to do, but to stay informed and show my support for his decision. I needed to be armed with the latest information for my numerous press interviews. And if the spacecraft failed, I intended to be standing alongside him on the podium taking the heat.

The MGS team was organized into three geographically dispersed groups: the spacecraft team of our industrial partner, Lockheed Martin, was in Denver. The mission designers, navigators, and managers were in Pasadena. The scientists were at their home institutions in northern and southern California, Arizona, and Maryland. So communications were electronic. The meetings I attended were in the MGS conference room, which featured a computerized projector and screen, teleconferencing and fax facilities, and a big television screen that constantly displayed an animation of the actual configuration of the spacecraft.

All the attention of the spacecraft team was focused on figuring out how to fix the solar panel or fly the mission with it
broken. They commanded the spacecraft several times to shake
gently in an unsuccessful attempt to free the trapped debris and
to understand the nature of the problem. It was like working
blind. They only had the data from the normal spacecraft sensors. No rover was there to peer at the damaged panel and the
MGS cameras could only look out into space. Slowly they
pieced together a plan.

Because we'd had to save money by using a small launch
vehicle, MGS couldn't carry enough fuel to burn to get into the
right mapping orbit. It had to "aerobrake" from a large, forty-
five-hour, elliptical orbit down to a circular orbit that would
circle the planet over the poles every two hours. Once in the
right mapping orbit the instruments would always look down at
a line on the surface where it was always 2 P.M. when the spacecraft crossed the equator, a time when lighting was just right for
the instruments. Aerobraking involved skimming through the
top of the Martian atmosphere, just enough so that the few
molecules of gas the solar panels encountered at high speed
would drag against the spacecraft and slow it down a little.
Slowing the speed made the orbit smaller, so bit by bit over
months the orbit would be reduced to the circular, polar orbit
that the instruments were designed for.

Now that strategy was in jeopardy.

The MGS team worked smoothly, many trained by years of
being together on Mars Observer. Glenn is a highly disciplined
man who appears unruffled in a crisis. His team reflected this
disciplined and low-key approach. When I sat in on MGS meetings, I noted the difference in tone from the raucous and more
emotional discussion my rover team had, and the even more

frenetic environment of a Pathfinder team meeting. Glenn's calm exterior and my years of history with him led me to expect he would make a well-reasoned but conservative decision. I thought he might opt to save the spacecraft over risking it to rescue the science. Instead his team found a middle way to save both spacecraft and science.

The Lockheed Martin team, having done many tests and run endless computer models, concluded that the bent solar panel was weakened, but could still withstand the stress of aerobraking if the solar-cell side of the panel was faced into the feeble wind so that aerodynamic pressure would hold it tight against the debris in the hinge joint. In fact, the force might push it back into position. If the panel latched properly the mission could proceed as planned.

The biggest nail-biting event for the MGS team was not the orbit insertion, but the process to pressurize the fuel system two days before insertion. Mars Observer had been lost during this event four years earlier. This time the process worked perfectly and the MGS team relaxed a little.

On September 11 at about 6:30 P.M. I was once again on CNN, dressed in my lucky red suit, commenting on the orbit insertion events. The MGS navigation team chief laid out the sequence. The engine would start burning just before the spacecraft disappeared behind Mars from our point of view. It was a nerve-racking twenty minutes or so before a plot on the screen in Von Karman Auditorium indicated that we'd reacquired the radio signal. The timing made it clear that the burn had worked perfectly. After fourteen years of trying, a spacecraft was in orbit!

The atmosphere in the MGS mission control area was much

more sedate than Pathfinder's landing had been but it was obvious that the MGS team was just as happy. A celebratory gesture had been planned—they'd all bought red baseball caps that they now donned. My daughter ran over to my bag in the corner of Von Karman and pulled our caps out and we jumped excitedly up and down in front of the camera as we put them on. On the monitors the MGS team could be seen passing out celebratory success peanuts.

The next stressful time was the first aerobraking pass. The team let the spacecraft loop around Mars in one forty-five-hour orbit before trying to aerobrake. Then they held their breath and directed the engine to burn a little, slowing MGS down and letting it dip gingerly into the atmosphere. Each aerobraking pass is only a few minutes long. The spacecraft flies like a badminton shuttlecock with the solar panels swept back for stability. After the pass the engineers fell ravenously on the engineering data that had been sent back. Everything seemed to have worked fine. The jammed solar array had wobbled a bit as the spacecraft swung up and down from the aerodynamic forces, but nothing bad had happened. Maybe the mission was going to be all right.

The next two passes also went well and the team was gaining confidence, but on the fourth pass the solar panel started to give. At first it looked like it was, indeed, finally going to swing into the right position and latch, but suddenly the spacecraft team discovered that it had really gone past the latched position. It was like hyperextending your elbow. The Martian atmosphere had unexpectedly "bloomed," increasing the density dramatically even at the altitude of the spacecraft, applying an unexpectedly high force to the panel. When in doubt, with a

$200 million mission, be cautious. Glenn made a rapid decision to pop the spacecraft up out of the atmosphere until his team could understand what had happened.

After seven days of analysis the Lockheed Martin engineers decided that the hinge was still jammed, but that the solar panel's supporting structure, called the "yoke," had probably cracked when the damper broke after launch. There was fear among the spacecraft team that the whole yoke could break if aerobraking continued, tearing the solar panel off the spacecraft. The mission would be lost.

Glenn had a terrible decision to make. Should he stop aerobraking, condemning the spacecraft to be in a highly elliptical orbit forever? The scientists pushed hard for continuing to aerobrake. Their instruments were all designed to work in a circular, polar orbit 234 miles above the surface. The MGS project scientist showed that the science loss would be severe. Lockheed Martin management pushed just as hard not to resume aerobraking. They didn't want to lose their spacecraft, or the whole mission.

Glenn was patient. Lockheed Martin did more analysis. What if MGS was aerobraked more slowly? More revolutions of the planet but less force on the solar panel per revolution? Would the spacecraft have a good chance of survival?

The mission designers were working feverishly to see if a slower aerobraking strategy could result in a good mission for science. As usual, they pulled off the miracle. There was a solution which could actually result in an even better, if longer, mission than had been planned. MGS could be edged into circular orbit gradually—over the course of a year rather than the planned four months—and cause that panel a lot less trauma.

At the end of the year, instead of sweeping down (north to south) the day side of the planet at 2 P.M., the MGS orbit would have moved around to where the downward pass would be at 2 A.M., with the south-to-north pass sweeping the sunlight side at 2 P.M. Lockheed Martin assessed that, although the spacecraft wasn't designed for this orientation, it could be made to work. It would essentially fly backward. The risky part was that to reach this orbit MGS had to swing very close to Mars for a long period of time. The damaged solar panel was vulnerable to too much stress if the atmosphere bloomed so that it was thicker than expected at the altitude MGS was traversing.

No one had ever tried to predict Mars's atmospheric behavior in such detail before. One thing we knew is that it's very volatile. As the spacecraft swung around every orbit it might have to traverse thicker parts of Mars atmosphere. The scientists needed to predict dust storms and temperature fluctuations to help the spacecraft survive, something no one had ever attempted before. At first the team had forty-five hours to make their calculations. As the orbits got smaller they had less and less time. By the time the team got a break while waiting for Mars to swing around the sun so that MGS could get into the 2 A.M. orbit, the predictions had to be made in about ten hours. Any time of the day or night that I dropped by MGS operations, I'd see Rich Zurek, the leader of the atmospheric advisory team, trying to figure out what the spacecraft would face next. Glenn and the rest of the small MGS ops team also seemed to be there at all hours. I was getting worried about exhaustion.

The Pathfinder team was getting pretty tired, too. The thirty-seven-minute difference between Earth's day and Mars's meant that their shifts rotated to match the Martian day. On

Earth that meant coming in later and later each day and they frequently had to work all night, especially when there were problems with the computer that interrupted communications.

Sojourner, meanwhile, was puttering happily from rock to rock. She tasted Shark and Half Dome and trampled Mermaid Dune—a long, grayish pile of what some scientists argued was sand while others said was just wind-swept dirt. As the weeks went by the rover team learned her eccentricities. The gyroscopes in her compass began to drift so that it was more reliable for her operators to just say "Turn the wheels twenty rotations" than to give her a compass heading. Her little cameras didn't have the color range of the lander camera, but she could get her nose practically on a rock, whereas the lander had to peer from a distance. It was Sojourner who imaged Prince Charming close up. Hank Moore, who named Prince Charming, believed that the Prince and a few other rocks had an uncanny resemblance to rocks, called conglomerates, found on Earth. These rocks are formed when running water rounds cobbles and pebbles and deposits them into a sand and clay matrix which, over time, gets compressed and makes a larger rock. On Earth water runs over these rocks for millennia to form them. That would imply liquid water was stable for a very long time on Mars a very long time ago.

Sojourner's APXS found that the soil chemistry was the same everywhere on Mars—the dust layer that the wind swept over the planet was ubiquitous. Within the first week Sojourner had achieved her contract: One Rock measurement, One Soil (chemistry and soil mechanics), and One Lander. Like a tiny child looking up at a parent she imaged the lander, draped in airbags that looked enormous from a rover's eye view—like putting your chin on the ground.

Despite the fairly frequent lander communications glitches and occasional miscalculations by the rover drivers that hung the rover's wheels up on rocks like Wedge, Sojourner had covered about 80 meters when her batteries died on sol 58.

The rover team was taken by surprise. To save weight the batteries were not rechargeable. Once they ran out the rover was totally dependent on sunlight. The batteries had actually lasted much longer than Ron Banes had predicted, and seemed to be still going strong. On the morning when they ran out the rover tried to wake up before full sunlight. Without batteries to prop up the limited solar array power the computer gasped and "browned out," and the rover "fainted."

The team scrambled to figure out how to revive her and after an anxious day got the formula right: Send commands only after the sun is well up and the rover is warm and fully awake. The rover's clever power design kept her alive and waking up periodically to see if anyone was talking to her. The team managed to get a command to Sojourner during one of the awake periods and on sol 60 she was back in action, working daylight hours only. She trundled into the near distance to peer over the edge of a little gully and saw dunes and ripples invisible to the lander.

Lander pictures kept pouring in: pink sky, blue clouds, buttermilk morning skies, and glowing sunsets. The whole panorama around the lander was imaged in each of the twelve camera colors, and the lander team started the "super-resolution" scan. In super-res each piece of the scene stood out with great clarity, but each piece contained lots of data and took a long time to trickle back over the direct radio link to Earth at a speed of about 8,000 bits per second—equivalent to a very low-tech computer modem.

Then on September 27, 1997—sol 83—the lander's rechargeable batteries failed, as we had known they would eventually do. Already they had lasted almost three times longer than the month the lander had been advertised to operate. While the rover could keep warm with the RHUs in her belly, the lander depended on nighttime heaters run by batteries which were charged by the solar arrays. The lander wasn't as lucky as the rover. When power was lost the lander also tried to wake up without power and fell unconscious. While it slept the radio got colder and colder and its frequency changed, meaning that the commands from Earth were probably not being received.

At this particular time the big antennas of the Deep Space Network were trained on Jupiter, receiving pictures from the Galileo orbiter. By the time the Pathfinder team declared a spacecraft emergency and captured the antennas, Pathfinder was below Mars's horizon.

Night after night the team struggled to communicate. A couple of times, on October 2 and 7, a signal came from the lander but never any data. I stopped by late every night to see what was happening and to bring cookies to the flight controllers who were clumped in the control room trying desperately to figure out what was wrong.

Ten unfruitful days into this process I dropped by flight controller Jennifer Harris's office. Jennifer, a twenty-seven-year-old MIT engineering graduate, had been left in charge of the project while the mission manager went on a long-overdue vacation. She and Dave Gruel, the former gremlin turned flight engineer, were slumped disconsolately, thumbing through sheaves of printout.

"Buck up, guys," I said. "You've had a great mission, even if you never get the spacecraft back."

Jennifer sighed. "The mission manager goes on vacation and I lose the spacecraft."

"Oh, nonsense," I shot back. "You guys are heroes." I thumped Dave on the shoulder. "Pathfinder was supposed to last a month. It went for three. So the batteries died. We knew they would. No one's going to blame you."

But the team kept trying to revive the spacecraft for another month, like the family of a terminally ill patient refusing to turn off life support. Finally, on November 4, 1997, they admitted defeat. At a final press conference Matt Golombek led a triumphant presentation of the science results and Brian Muirhead delivered a sort of eulogy for the mission.

People often asked: "What about the rover? Is it still alive?" We knew that the rover was still alive and well when communication with the lander was lost, but since Sojourner needed Sagan for a relay, there was no way to talk to her. The rover had just finished following a command we sent on Sol 80—sampling a rock named Chimp with the APXS on sols 81 and 82. Her onboard automation was programmed to wait for seven days for a command after the last sequence was sent up. On sol 87 it would have ordered her to start circling the lander, constantly checking, trying to hear a signal. We all had a sad image of the little rover rolling jerkily around the lander like a lost child, calling, "Hello? Hello? Is anyone listening?" Eventually, we knew, Sojourner would roll up onto a rock and her fault protection would stop her in her tracks, to wait endlessly for instructions to come.

The painter, Pat Rawlins, has portrayed the rover's possible future: A space-suited astronaut kneels by Sojourner, gently brushing dust off her solar panel. The astronaut's name, Truth, is stitched onto her chest, and her coffee-colored face shows affection for the rover, named for her ancestor, Sojourner Truth. Sometimes I fantasize that a grandchild of mine might pick Sojourner up from the dusty surface of Mars and bring her home.

We held a wake for Pathfinder and it really did feel like a wake. The team members stood around, swilling their beers, and talking in maudlin tones about our dear departed friend, and reminiscing about our adventures. We gloated over having pulled off both Pathfinder and the rover within our tiny budgets and tight schedule. We told stories about the early days of the mission and favorite moments on Mars, occasionally hoisting a glass to the deceased.

Between its landing on July 4 and the loss of communication at the end of September, Mars Pathfinder had returned 2.6 billion bits of information, including more than 16,000 images from the lander and 550 images from the rover, as well as more than fifteen chemical analyses of rocks and extensive data on winds and other weather factors. The Pathfinder scientists continued to work on the flood of information that Pathfinder and the rover had poured back to Earth. Altogether, Sojourner traveled over 100 meters on the surface of Mars, far more than the 10 meters we had hoped for.

Although the wake had been held and the November 4 press conference had mourned the lander and rover, the team made one last attempt at communication on March 10, 1998, when the Earth was high in Pathfinder's sky. Evidence of Pathfinder's impact on the public was clear—the mission operations room was packed with media people pointing cameras in every direction and buttonholing the team members who had reassembled for what everyone knew was probably a hopeless attempt to communicate with the lander, now mired in frigid Martian winter. No signal was received. At a tiny press conference Brian Muirhead declared Pathfinder officially dead and a misty-eyed Jennifer Harris thanked the world for its participation in the Pathfinder adventure.

The Pathfinder team, much in demand as the people with the Better, Faster, Cheaper know-how, had already largely scattered to other projects and I had to nag them to document their lessons learned before they disappeared. Thanks to the money we had gotten from the Headquarters Mission Assurance Office the rover history was already well documented. Not only had we used the money to reduce our risk, we had produced a complete report of all the analysis and test work we'd done, with its costs and results. We'd demonstrated that the risk of even a very tough job could be systematically managed, and we had written down, for the first time, how this had been done on a real flight project. When most projects were over the detailed lore of how they were done was usually only in people's heads, hence the emphasis on having delivered flight hardware as a key to promotion.

The MGS scientists were taking advantage of the longer aerobraking phase to do science, something they hadn't planned to do until they were in the circular mapping orbit. Although the lighting wasn't what they wanted, they were even closer to the planet (only about 75 miles high) just before and after aerobraking than they would be in circular orbit. This made for great pictures. The scientific goldmine of information we will be receiving from MGS when it reaches circular orbit in 1999 was hinted at by the first images we got from the camera. We saw pictures of canyons that obviously had had water in them at some point in their history. Lines of sand dunes marched down the bottom of many of the canyons and craters—probably places for future landers to avoid! The edges of the vast Valles Marineris seemed to have many layers, just like Earth's Grand Canyon. Maybe they were water-deposited sediments instead of layers of lava. Upon close examination we saw a geological artifact of a place where a meandering stream had rechanneled itself, leaving an oxbow. Even more tantalizing was a crater with what might be an ice lake frozen at its bottom.

The MGS magnetometer detected random magnetic fields that dot the surface. Mars has virtually no global magnetic field because of its dying molten core. These "bar magnets," probably lumps of frozen magma which welled up near the surface, show that at some point Mars must have had a magnetic field, something that is vital to nurturing life because it helps fend off damaging charged particles streaming in from the sun and cosmos. These random magnetic areas, theorized the magnetometer team, are artifacts of Mars's more lively past. The frozen magma "remembers" the magnetic field.

The laser altimeter found that the top part of Mars was flat, very flat north of the massive Tharsis bulge. The scientists were hard-pressed to explain why the northern terrain was so level. The only places that level on Earth are ocean bottoms. The altimeter revealed steep canyons and ridges in other parts of the planet. There is one volcanic summit crater that is large enough to contain all of greater Los Angeles.

The Thermal Emission Spectrometer (TES) tracked the waning south polar cap as it moved into southern summer and the dry ice sublimed into the atmosphere. The TES also began to see different minerals on the surface.

All of this data was what we needed to plan our future missions. We were now readying an orbiter and lander to fly in 1998 with the lander going near the south pole. MGS images revealed that the layered polar terrain—alternating bands of dark and light material—seemed more rugged than we had thought. The landing site would have to be even more carefully selected than Pathfinder's.

The 2001 missions were already getting started. Every twenty-six months we had to be launching something, but 2001 was getting overloaded. We had proved what few believed as recently as four years earlier: small rovers *can* do real science. Spacecraft *can* be built fast and cheap and still do the job. But the success of Pathfinder, Sojourner, and MGS had only increased the appetite of the government for more complex Mars missions. Somehow, though, the money never seemed to catch up with the desire for more science, more technology, an early sample return.

The people at the Johnson Space Center who are planning for eventual human missions to Mars needed data. What is the radiation environment on Mars? Would humans endure the three-year roundtrip only to be zapped with lethal doses of radiation on the surface? Viking had found no life, nor even any organic molecules in the soil. Did that mean it was toxic to humans? Some people talked blithely of making fuel on Mars so astronauts could travel light—not bringing fuel from Earth would save enormous amounts of money for launches. But would the schemes that functioned in the laboratory work in the harsh environment of Mars?

So 2001 was supposed to carry instruments to measure radiation, measure the toxicity of the Martian dust, and test making fuel. Scientifically, an instrument-laden rover that was much larger and more capable than Sojourner had been selected by the NASA Science Office to fly on the lander. Plus, they picked not two orbiter instruments, as Surveyor 98 was carrying, but three. Mars Surveyor 2001 had about 10 percent of the money that the Cassini mission to Saturn had, but was carrying just as many instruments.

After the 2001 mission, the plan for finding life that had been developed after the discovery of possible life-signs in a Martian meteorite called for another rover in 2003 and a sample return to be launched in 2005. A sample return would be very expensive. It would have to fly to Mars, leave an orbiter in space while a lander descended to the surface, and send a small rover to pick up the samples that either the 2001 or the 2003 rover had carefully collected and stored. Then a launch vehicle would have to propel itself—completely autonomously—from the surface and climb into orbit to rendezvous with the waiting orbiter. The ascent vehicle would hand the samples to the orbiter, and part of the orbiter would detach and began the two-year journey back to Earth. The return vehicle would eventually plunge into Earth's atmosphere, experiencing much more heat than any other vehicle had ever had to survive. The precious sample container, completely sealed so as not to contaminate Earth's environment—or to be contaminated by it—would parachute into the Utah desert. Finally, it would be picked up and rushed to a special sealed facility so that scientists could open it and ensure that no harmful organisms had made the ride to Earth—an unlikely event, indeed, but one that some people fear.

No matter how we looked at it, the sample return mission was going to cost hundreds of millions and take a lot of technology development.

I was spending a lot of time helping structure studies of how we could meet everyone's desires within our budget. The answer was, we couldn't. Money would have to be added to meet the raw demands. We'd already trimmed our program management to below minimums. For two years I was working a steady eighty hours a week to keep the overhead low and save the projects money. Finally, even I admitted I needed more help and even the project managers were urging me to beef up the staff. As the program grew I acquired a boss, whose major job is to interface with NASA headquarters and try to keep some control of the burgeoning desires for more Mars program performance that weren't supported by burgeoning money. He also has to help run JPL.

We already had a long-term relationship with our partner, Lockheed Martin Astronautics, to build our orbiters and landers, saving money by keeping up a quasi assembly line. This arrangement was so unusual that an interview with me talking about the cost effectiveness of this partnership was written up in *Businesslike Government*, a report from Vice President Gore to the president on the "reinventing government" initiative.

The Mars projects were busily inventing, perforce, better ways of doing business. Although the management style for each project was different, all were successful. The Pathfinder, Sojourner, MGS, and Mars Surveyor 98 teams all had quite different styles, but similar approaches. Lean staffs, minimal overhead, empowerment of people, and a willingness to do things in new ways.

My own management style was not to everyone's taste. The Mars Surveyor 2001 manager once said, half admiringly, half exasperated, "You treat everyone the same, bosses and workers alike!" For those who love hierarchy, command, and control, this is uncomfortable. I'm also willing to move ahead and then say "mea culpa" if I make a mistake. Bill Layman told me that was why I was his favorite manager. "You're not afraid to say 'I screwed up,' and then move on." A lot of people, especially in aging organizations, like to move more cautiously, or they like to impose requirements without being willing to take the blame for subsequent failures.

I was also doing a lot of administrative work: hiring people, worrying about the lab's salary structure, and selecting Martians of the Month. The Martian of the Month award was really an accident of the bureaucracy. When I was first promoted to head the Mars Exploration Program it created an unexpected crisis! Where was I to park? The highest-status parking area was completely filled by the lab's higher-echelon people. If I parked there someone would have to move out. To them, Tony Spear was the obvious candidate for expulsion, since he now worked for me. I knew Tony would be crushed if he lost his prestigious spot and I frankly didn't care where I parked.

So I proposed a deal. I would continue to park across the street if the parking people would let me have another on-lab parking pass to be used by whomever I decreed. They agreed gratefully. I established the Martian of the Month award, for which the prize is one month of on-lab parking.

But even more time consuming were the speaking engagements. While Pathfinder and MGS were bringing in the data, my job was to help get it out to the public. I felt as though I was turning into Carl Sagan. Everyone wanted me to speak. Hundreds of people wanted my autograph, and awards kept pouring in. Suddenly I was everyone's favorite female engineer, the person most frequently on women's groups' lists of who should receive their annual award. Women in Technology International inducted me into their Hall of Fame even before Pathfinder landed. I was among *Ms.* and *Glamour* magazines' Women of the Year and was featured in *Self* (I'm pictured jumping) and with the rover team in *Vanity Fair*.

While I cannot deny I was extremely flattered by all the accolades, it brought home something that saddens me. Our culture is so starved for female role models that a woman who simply shows up on television as an authority becomes a hero. At one banquet I was receiving an award with another woman, Sybil Brand, who pioneered safer prison conditions for women. A very elderly woman, she walked slowly to the podium to thank the audience for the award. She announced: "This is my three thousandth award." Good Lord! Could that happen to me? There should be millions of women in my position and a stronger competition for these prizes.

I could look around now, though, and see a lot more women who would be winning these accolades in a few years. Fifteen percent of the technical people at JPL were now women. A woman is leading the team to develop the small penetrators that will piggyback on the Mars Surveyor Lander and plunge 2 meters into the surface, measuring the subsurface water content. The woman who led Pathfinder's radio team is now the spacecraft manager for a comet mission. The woman who led the team which physically built and tested Pathfinder now supervised twenty people. Other women were trickling into the lower levels of line management and there were increasing numbers of female managers at all levels. There was even a woman on the Executive Council of JPL, though, of course, she was the director for human resources and not a technical manager.

Pathfinder was wildly popular. All the contractors who had had a hand (or even a toe) in the project brought out advertisements featuring their products. Maxon Motors, for instance, proudly advertised that their motors moved Sojourner. But even more companies who'd had nothing at all to do with the missions were basking in reflected glory: an oil company, a computer company, a car company—even a toothbrush company. It was all good publicity although it was a little irritating that they usually didn't bother to credit the real Pathfinder team. The image of Sojourner was copyrighted and was licensed to companies like the one making toy rovers, but other toy companies just made bootleg copies: get into the market, sell lots of toys, and get out before the lawsuits fly.

The images from Pathfinder and the mission itself were on every media's top ten stories list for 1997. A couple of magazines even received awards for the picture of the year—the one taken by Pathfinder's camera!

There were other rewards. A very sweet moment was a press conference in Washington to honor Valerie Ambroise for naming the rover Sojourner Truth. Now fifteen, she was poised as she stepped forward to read her essay to the press. Various NASA brass were there, driving a rover model for the photographers and making preliminary speeches. The man assigned to introduce Valerie and extol her creativity for naming the rover was none other than the fellow who had fought us so bitterly over having the contest at all! I felt avenged for the bad report card.

And finally, for the first time in years, I started to think about my future. I had achieved my passion. I'd landed (if virtually) on Mars. I'd helped open the door for humans to eventually live the events of *The Sands of Mars*. What now?

Your job will be to sell Mars. The opportunities are far greater now that we've really got something to put in our shop window. If we can get enough people clamouring to come here, then Earth will be forced to provide the shipping space. And the quicker that's done, the sooner we can promise Earth we'll be standing on our own feet. What do you say?

ARTHUR C. CLARKE, *The Sands of Mars*

Where Do You Go After You've Been To Mars?

A n old NASA buddy of mine, Frank Hoban, recently wrote a book about NASA's failed post–Apollo attempt to do low-cost missions. It is called *Where Do You Go After You've Been to the Moon?* I thought it was just a clever title, but after the Pathfinder landing and the successful orbiting and aerobraking of Mars Global Surveyor, I started to ask myself a similar question: Where do you go after you've been to Mars?

Where do you go after you've reached the pinnacle of what you imagined for yourself? As a child, I dreamed of a life just like the one I led while I was working on Pathfinder. Like the people in *The Sands of Mars* I worked with a team who explored Mars. Once that ended, what could I do to top it? Despite the fact that there were many more Mars missions up ahead, none of them would be quite the hands-on experience I had putting the rover team together, designing Sojourner, and watching her meander around Mars. Jake Matijevic is leading the 2001 rover team and has taken many of the Sojourner team with him. Henry Stone is again the Navigation and Control Manager and Bill Layman is helping with systems engineering and grooming, Tom Rivellini to take over after he retires in a year or so. Bill Dias is creating bigger and better scenarios for surface operations that will cover kilometers and collect samples. Many of the team are scattered, though. Howard Eisen is designing an orbiting radar mission. Lin Sukamto got married and moved to the Netherlands, and Ron Banes retired.

The Mars program has some intriguing missions planned for the rest of this century. We will launch our next missions in December 1998 and January 1999, which will orbit and land in late 1999. The Mars Climate Surveyor orbiter will document the atmosphere of Mars over a whole Mars year, and the Mars Polar Lander will explore the terrain near the south polar ice cap looking for water by scooping up fistfuls of soil with a 2-meter robotic arm and analyzing the soil with an instrument on top of the lander. The lander carries a camera very similar to Pathfinder's for surface scenery and another camera will take images that should provide spectacular views of the south polar area as the lander swings on the parachute and fires retro-rockets to make a soft landing.

Piggybacking on the lander are two tiny, 5-kilogram penetrators about a foot long, which will be tossed off the lander as it prepares to plunge into the atmosphere. The penetrators, surrounded by basketball-sized heat shields, will plummet to the surface without parachutes. The drag of the heat shields will slow the penetrators to about 120 miles per hour as they strike the surface with a force of 80,000 g's, driving them up to 2 meters into the ground. A tiny screw will be extruded from the side of the penetrator, scraping a little soil back into an experiment, which will measure the water content of the subsurface material. The back part of the penetrator will stay on the surface, connected to the section in the ground by a tether, and will relay the data from the science payload in the penetrator to MGS. Mars Surveyor 2001, 2003, 2005, and beyond are in the planning stages.

You can explore Mars with us by visiting our Web site: http://mars.jpl.nasa.gov.

What do you do after you've been to Mars? The same thing you've been doing for years and years it seems: try to get the bureaucracy to make realistic agreements with the engineers and plan sensible missions that will actually fly. More and more it has occurred to me that my ideas of how to manage complex, creative projects to a successful and cost-effective solution could have applications in other fields.

I spent a year after I was named to head the Mars program working on a book that would describe my theories about motivating and managing creative people. I've heard and read a lot of recent management gurus on reengineering, process-based management, fast-cycle time, and so on. These are all good concepts, but a lot of what the gurus say shows they've developed their theories in a classroom, not by getting their hands dirty trying to work with real people and their very real ticks, warts, and peculiarities. Much of what I believe about good management runs counter to currently popular wisdom. I think the whole downsizing, rightsizing, reengineering, fast-cycle time fads have largely ignored the fact that people have to implement them and that you should have some idea of why you're doing these things before you do them. Academicians in management schools appear to be severely ignorant of the consequences of implementing their theories, but industry and government—eager for quick-fix, instant gratification solutions—flock to their banners.

I finished my book, *Managing Creativity*, last year and published it on my Web site (http://www.managingcreativity.com). It's all based on experience, plus the management classes I've taken over the years, and while I firmly believe that what I wrote is right, I feel a need to back it up with academic research, so I've embarked on a Ph.D program and will receive my degree in the beginning of the new century.

Other people, though, are starting to agree with my principles. I'm speaking and consulting as well as teaching a class on Managing Creativity, and it usually strikes a chord. For creative teams to not only generate good ideas but bring them to reality requires a combination of near anarchy and discipline, a balancing act between stability and total chaos, often conducted in an environment not conducive to creativity. And that takes lots of skill in handling people, preferably people with a diversity of talents, attitudes, and ways of working.

I haven't yet decided what I want to do when I grow up, and I'm searching for a new passion. All the things I've learned about working in and managing creative teams are applicable to a much wider range of problems than space missions. I've already been asked to consult on a project to cure prostate cancer. At one level the problem is the same as flying a mission to Mars: technology has to get developed, plans have to be made, people have to be enrolled in the process, choices have to be made about how to spend money.

I'm worried about how my daughter and her children will live in the future. I'd like to help end the environmental disaster that humans are visiting on the Earth. I've seen the data on Venus, where lead would melt on the surface, and Mars, stuck in a permanent ice age, and I'd like to keep the Earth from going either way, thank you. It seems to me that there is money to be made from protecting the Earth instead of despoiling it, provided that technologies are creatively developed and sold.

Managing martians has been a career highlight. Martians, like other people, come in a wide variety of skills, personality types, levels of dedication, and willingness to work together. But, like JPL's Jovians, Saturnians, and comet chasers, they are all fiercely dedicated to excellence, innovation, and getting the job done. Working with them is a thrill, a roller-coaster ride. Getting project managers to work together for the good of the Mars Exploration Program instead of for just their own projects has been an especial challenge. Project managers are like alpha wolves, pack leaders—fiercely independent—and their devotion and that of their teams is to the single-minded pursuit of flying a mission. But the scarcity of money in today's better, faster, cheaper space exploration world has drawn even these alpha wolves into cooperation.

One of my proudest moments as a program manager occurred recently in a review of the 2001 project. It took me two years, but I had managed by persistence and by picking the right manager, Glenn Cunningham—who had to operate MGS anyway—to create a single program to operate all the Mars spacecraft. We just added the responsibility of developing operations systems for the future projects to Glenn's job description. Now the operations project is poised to operate the two Mars Surveyor 98 missions in addition to MGS, and 2001 is coming up fast.

During the 2001 review the operations development manager presented his concept for operating the 2001 mission. It spanned about twenty pages, detailing how the operations would be developed and would support the flight of the 2001 orbiter, rover, and lander. The 2001 spacecraft manager got up next. His concept was much less detailed.

He seemed bemused. "On all the other projects I've been on, the operations development would always be way behind the spacecraft. Here, the spacecraft has to adapt to the operations system."

I threw both fists into the air: "Yes!" I exulted. "That's exactly what was supposed to happen. Pathfinder proved that doing things that way could save enormous amounts of money."

If, when I sat in a sycamore tree in Oklahoma, I could have envisioned my life so far, even I would never have believed it. Persistence, determination, creativity, flexibility, and a willingness to grow psychologically have all played a role in my being able to play in my dreamworld of space exploration. I never became an astronaut, as I had dreamed about becoming—women were not welcome in NASA's astronaut corps when I was the age to attempt it. But I've virtually explored most of the planets: Mercury and Venus with Mariner 10, Jupiter and Saturn with Galileo and Cassini.

I haven't set foot on Mars, but in the 1960s I helped design the system that let us land there, and I've been part of the team that set the first wheel on the planet. I've worked and played with myriad creative, interesting—even if sometimes eccentric and contentious—people and have found the people to be the best part of the job. Some of the world's most interesting problems, at the forefront of innovation and exploration, have been mine to work on. My daughter is a wonderful human being and a joy to be with. I even have friends and recreation, and although the recreational opportunities have been less than I would like, in the past five years I've squeezed in a few fun things like playing a tavern wench in a recent Caltech student production of Shakespeare's *Henry V*.

I haven't yet decided what I want to do when I grow up, but there've been many lessons along the way to Mars. When you choose your goal, choose it from your passion. It's a lot more fun to pursue a passion than to slog along toward something you think you should chase, like money or fame, and a passion will help you through the inevitable frustrations. I've fought with people to the point of misery and lost sleep over things I can't control, tasted the bitterness of defeat and felt the joy of participating in a creative team and accomplishing near miracles—all to follow a dream.

Following a dream was my route from Wynnewood, Oklahoma, to Mars. It hasn't been a direct route by any means. I got sidetracked many times but each time I learned something.

These are some of the things I learned, expressed as Donna's laws:

The customer isn't always right, he may want something that can't be done for the money.
A really creative team will probably be as contentious as it is brilliant.
You may have to give up credit for an idea to see it happen.
There is never enough time and money—but you'll have to get the job done anyway.

> *Everything is a big hassle; if it isn't a big hassle you*
>   *probably don't understand the situation.*
> *Work should be done playfully as often as possible.*

I'd like to apply these hard-earned lessons to accomplish other things. I can't see the future but I can see what I'd like it to be: people learning to work together to solve their problems instead of killing each other in xenophobic frenzies; people going into space, accompanied by their trusty robots; people tending to the Earth with care.

The question is only: Which passion do I want to pursue? Stay tuned.

FURTHER READING

Books

Burrows, William E. *Exploring Space: Voyages in the Solar System and Beyond.* New York: Random House, 1990.

Dunne, J. A., and Burgess, E. *The Voyage of Mariner 10: Mission to Venus and Mercury.* NASA SP-424, U.S. Government Printing Office*, 1978.

Ezell, E. C. and L. N. *On Mars: Exploration of the Red Planet 1958–1978.* The NASA History Series, NASA SP-4212, U.S. Government Printing Office, 1984.

Goodstein, Judith R. *Millikan's School: A History of the California Institute of Technology.* New York: W. W. Norton & Company, 1991.

Gore, Al. *Businesslike Government: Lessons Learned from America's Best Companies.* National Performance Review, U.S. Government Printing Office, 1997.

Hall, R. Cargill. *Lunar Impact: A History of Project Ranger R. Cargill Hall.* Washington, D.C.: U.S. Government Printing Office, 1977.

Koppes, Clayton R. *JPL and the American Space Program: A History of the Jet Propulsion Laboratory.* New Haven, CT: Yale University Press, 1982.

Lee, Wayne. *To Rise from Earth: An Easy to Understand Guide to Spaceflight.* New York: Facts on File, Inc., 1995.

Magill, Frank N. (ed.). *Magill's Survey of Science: Space Exploration Series,* five volumes. Pasadena, CA: Salem Press, 1989.

Murray, Bruce. *Journey into Space: The First Thirty Years of Space Exploration.* New York: W. W. Norton & Company, 1989.

Web sites

Jet Propulsion Laboratory: http://www.jpl.nasa.gov
NASA: http://www.hq.nasa.gov

* U.S. Government Printing Office Documents may be ordered at
http://www.access.gpo.gov/su_docs/sale/abkst001.html